CRUISING IN
Seraffyn

CRUISING IN
Seraffyn

by
Lin and Larry Pardey

SHERIDAN HOUSE

This edition first published 1992 by
Sheridan House Inc.
145 Palisade Street
Dobbs Ferry, NY 10522

Portions of this book have appeared in
Boating, Yachting World and *Pacific Yachting*

Library of Congress Cataloging-in-Publication Data

Pardey, Lin.
  Cruising in Seraffyn / Lin and Larry Pardey
    p.   cm.
  Originally published: New York : Seven Seas Press, c1976.
  With new introd.
  ISBN 0-924486-36-8 : $14.95
  1. Seraffyn (Cutter)   2. Sailing.   I. Pardey, Larry.   II. Title.
  GV822.S39P37 1992
  797.1'24--dc20   92-31389
                                                          CIP

Printed in the United States of America

ISBN   0-924486-36-8

DEDICATION
To Lyle Hess, who designed our dream boat,
SERAFFYN OF VICTORIA
and
To the wonderful friends we've
met in many ports because of her.

Contents

FOREWORD

INTRODUCTION 15

1. *Seraffyn of Victoria* 19
2. Heading South 29
3. The Sea of Cortez Under Sail 38
4. More Sailing in the Sea of Cortez 46
5. Of Ships and Storms 55
6. Mexico 62
7. Central America, Gulfs and Currents 71
8. Panama and the Canal 82
9. Wind and Worms 88
10. Across the Spanish Main 92
11. Cartagena 102
12. Our Adversary and Our Ally, The Gulf Stream 113
13. Earning Freedom Chips 123
14. Virginia 131
15. Hurricane 140
16. The Long Leg 148
17. Horta or Peter's Blue-Water Sailor's Reception Center 157
18. The Other Side 165

AFTERWORD 170A

APPENDIX I: 1992 Update 170B

CRUISING COST SURVEY 171

APPENDIX II: After Seven Years, I'd Choose Her Again 180

APPENDIX III: It's the Details That Make Life Easier 183

APPENDIX IV: *Seraffyn of Victoria* 186

Foreword to the New Edition

Sixteen Years Later

TALEISIN, THE 29-FOOT CUTTER we now call home, lay at anchor in Bellerive Bay, Tasmania, when we received a letter asking us to write an update to the introduction to *Cruising in Seraffyn* for a paperback edition. Both of us found it hard to believe it had been 16 years since we'd written our first book.

The years had flown, leaving behind an amazing kaleidoscope of memories. After leaving Mallorca in 1976, we spent three-and-a-half years more cruising on lovely little *Seraffyn,* completing an 11-year eastabout circumnavigation. We returned to California and tried to keep *Seraffyn,* racing her weekends and cruising on her during holidays as we worked to build her bigger sister from materials we'd gathered as we cruised. But after a year of torn loyalties, we sold her and watched as she left for her eventual home base of Sausalito, then turned our full attention to the basket of frames that would gradually worm its way into the special place *Seraffyn* held in our hearts for so many years. It took three-and-a-half years to complete *Taleisin* and six months of sea trials before we finally sold our last power tools and spare wood to begin our cruising life again. After more than seven years of being "out there" — this time in the Southern Hemisphere, an area we never visited with *Seraffyn* — we were asked, "Do you still feel anyone can go cruising?"

Our answer is yes, anyone can go, and preparation is still the key, just as it was in 1976. In some ways, it is easier to get and outfit a cruising boat now than it was in 1965 when we started to build *Seraffyn.* Because of the fiberglass revolution, there are now many more pure cruising boats to choose from, boats of moderate displacement, with long keels and efficient cutter rigs. Sailors who don't have the skills or patience to build their own boat can buy one. For those who still wish to build or finish their own boats, either to save money or to get a more personal, more individualized cruising home, the increased interest in boatbuilding has made technology more accessible and materials easier to obtain.

Much of the equipment we had to build for ourselves when we were outfitting *Seraffyn* is now available right off the shelf. Dozens of different fiberglass dinghies are now available, as well as canvas goods, rigging gear, even bosun's chairs.

In 1965, only the affluent could finance a boat, and then bankers usually required other collateral. Some young couples today are choosing to finance a boat instead of a home for their first years together.

But these changes can be a subtle trap for those who aren't doggedly determined to save money so they can break free and go cruising. When you are buying a boat on credit, it is tempting to buy something larger, something with more equipment, than you would if you were shopping with cash. Instead of limiting themselves to boats at or slightly below their budget, people often say, "It's only a few dollars more a month." Or, they end up with a longer payment period. Often cruising is delayed, sometimes indefinitely. Some try to escape this system by saving enough to cover their boat payments for a year of cruising. But to legally leave the country they have to carry additional comprehensive cruising insurance coverage, which adds $200 or more a month to their cruising expenses. We have yet to meet a cruising sailor who could cover a boat mortgage and cruise long-term.

The gear now available off the shelf can make it harder to get going. If you add to the five-page-long list of vital equipment a radar at $3,000, satnav at $2,000, a $1,000 ham radio, a depth-sounder for $400, a $900 folding motor scooter, and a stainless steel propane barbecue at $150, you'll have spent in excess of $7,000 — more than a year's cruising funds (see Appendix I). All these items might be nice to have, but none are vital and none were easily available when we launched *Seraffyn*, so we weren't tempted and escaped without them to cruise enjoyably year after year.

The final danger in this array of tempting cruising gear is that by purchasing equipment to navigate and steer electronically, and to instantly furl sails, you may be tempted to set off before you have spent the necessary time learning to take sights, to handle your boat under sail, and to understand its balance and trim. It took Larry seven years before he felt confident enough to cross oceans on his own boat. This learning period gave him time to grow to love sailing and sailboats.

Rudy and Mary Kok, a young couple we met in French Polynesia in 1985, told us they spent three years sailing among the islands of Hawaii on their Cal 30 before they found their dreamboat, a Cape George 31. While they built the interior and rig for their boat, Rudy worked as a supervisor in an ink-making firm and Mary was a waitress and wine salesperson. Three years later they began sea trials, and 10 years from the day they bought their first sailboat as 22-year-old newlyweds, they were finally out cruising. They were well-prepared and confident, had enough money for a year and a half of cruising and were having a great time. The opposite happened to a couple of similar financial means from the U.S. Southwest. Three years after they first read about sailing and cruising, they bought a 42-foot gaff-rigged ketch. A year and a half later, after three months of sea trials and no sailing or navigation lessons, they set off cruising. That couple spent seven months getting to Tahiti, months during which they told us they were usually unhappy and often terrified because they didn't trust their navigation. They didn't have the experience to avoid or handle the next gear failure or sailing problem. Within a day of their arrival in Papeete, they began offering their boat for sale.

This leads to a problem our original introduction didn't cover. The ill-starred couple had told their friends they were setting off cruising "for the next ten years." Now they felt like failures, reluctant to face their friends and relatives and say cruising wasn't what they dreamed it would be. There exist just as many people who find a cruising life too uncomfortable and unstructured, too controlled by weather and too unsettling due to strange customs and unfamiliar places, as there are people who thrive on these same ever-changing circumstances. Some people become bored to tears after ten days at sea. Others dread landfalls and never feel comfortable about sailing into strange places. Still others miss their family and friends far more than they dreamed they would. Some people become desperate for an intellectual challenge that is different from the ones they find "out there." After nine years of cruising we did. That's one of the main reasons we sailed back to California to build *Taleisin*. We wanted to stop moving just for a while, to sleep free of thoughts of anchors and mooring lines, to shop where I knew the prices and language, to get mail easily and regularly. After four years, we were eager to be off again. But our experience reinforced this axiom. To give your cruise the best chance of being a complete success, leave yourself an escape clause. Twenty four years after we set off on *Seraffyn*, we use the same answer when people ask us how long we are going for. We still say, "As long as it's fun."

Lin and Larry Pardey
Tasmania
1992

Pho. I-1. Lin and Larry Pardey in the cockpit of their 24-foot cutter.

LIST OF ILLUSTRATIONS

1. *Seraffyn of Victoria* under sail..Title Page
2. *Pho. I-1.* Lin and Larry Pardey at *Seraffyn's* helm 15
3. *Pho. 1-1. Seraffyn's* backbone erected at the building site 20
4. *Pho. 1-2.* Larry laying out the rabbet in the keel 20
5. *Pho. 1-3.* A bow view of the "basket" of frames..........................21
6. *Pho. 1-4.* An early stage of the interior.............................21
7. *Pho. 1-5.* The teak deck goes on...................................22
8. *Pho. 1-6.* Bulwark stanchions cut and shaped 22
9. *Pho. 1-7.* Larry trying out the rudder for size 23
10. *Pho. 1-8.* Getting close to the "whisky" plank 23
11. *Pho. 1-9.* Lin had thousands of holes to plug......................24
12. *Pho. 1-10.* The transom waiting for its name 24
13. *Pho. 1-11.* The galley, partly built.........................25
14. *Pho. 1-12.* Looking aft into the port quarter berth..........................25
15. *Pho. 1-13.* A cheer went up as *Seraffyn* settled into the water 27
16. *Fig. 2-1.* Chart I: March 1969 to April 1970 30
17. *Pho. 2-2. Seraffyn of Victoria* under sail 32
18. *Fig. 2-3.* Area Chart: California to La Paz, Mexico........................35
19. *Fig. 3-1.* Area Chart: Cruising the Sea of Cortez 41
20. *Fig. 3-2.* Setting a permanent mooring without an engine.................42
21. *Fig. 3-3.* Swivel-and-shackle set-up for mooring...................43
22. *Pho. 4-1.* We explored Escondito by dinghy...................47
23. *Pho. 4-2.* Brisk sailing puts the rail under.....................48
24. *Fig. 4-3.* Area Chart: Cruising the Upper Sea of Cortez....................50
25. *Pho. 4-4.* Jésus Monobe and his 1930 Model A Ford.....................52
26. *Fig. 5-1.* Area Chart: Santa Rosalia to La Paz, Mexico 57
27. *Pho. 5-2.* Lin coiling down a halyard 59
28. *Pho. 5-3.* Our cutter is kept in top condition 59
29. *Pho. 6-1.* She sails so well we have never missed an engine.............63
30. *Pho. 6-2.* The steaks that evening were superb.............................65
31. *Pho. 6-3.* Our cruising companions, Gordon & Annabelle Yates 67
32. *Fig. 6-4.* Area Chart: Route down the Pacific coast of Mexico 68
33. *Fig. 7-1.* Area Chart: The arrival in Panama.........................72
34. *Fig. 7-2.* Chart II: May 1970 to January 1971..........................74-75
35. *Pho. 7-3.* The Coco Islands rock carvings.........................77
36. *Pho. 7-4.* Our view from the hotel in the Perlas Islands...................80
37. *Pho. 8-1.* Lin reading in the cockpit............................84
38. *Fig. 8-2.* Area Chart: Through the Panama Canal 86
39. *Fig. 9-1.* Area Chart: The route from Colon to Porto Bello..............90
40. *Pho. 9-2.* We walked out of the city to see the fortress 91
41. *Pho. 10-1.* The canoe was superb native craftsmanship...................93
42. *Pho. 10-2.* Made for a boys' club, it cost $40!......................93
43. *Fig. 10-3.* Area Chart: Porto Bello to the San Blas Islands 94
44. *Pho. 10-4.* Tom Moody and friends joined us for a sail..................99
45. *Pho. 10-5.* In the palm lodge a pot of food bubbled constantly..........100
46. *Fig. 11-1.* Area Chart Route from San Blas I. to Cartagena 103

47. *Pho. 11-2*. The fortified city of Cartagena....................................104
48. *Pho. 11-3*. We reached Cartagena after a 20-mile beat....................106
49. *Pho. 11-4*. A Cartagena fisherman repairs his net..........................107
50. *Pho. 11-5*. The dinghy serves well for lightering stores..................108
51. *Pho. 11-6*. The dinghy serves, too, for working on the topsides........111
52. *Pho. 12-1*. The forward bunk is cozy for cool weather in port..........114
53. *Fig. 12-2*. Area Chart: Windward route from Cartagena to Jamaica....115
54. *Pho. 12-3*. The blue mountains behind Kingston, Jamaica................117
55. *Fig. 12-4*. Chart III: February 1971 to August 1971.......................119
56. *Pho. 12-5*. Wrecks on the Cayman Island reefs.............................121
57. *Fig. 13-1*. Area Chart: The route from Florida to Virginia................124
58. *Pho. 13-2*. A meal in the cockpit...127
59. *Pho. 13-3*. We loved Virginia and the Chesapeake.........................130
60. *Fig. 14-1*. Area Chart: Leaving Virginia for the Atlantic.................132
61. *Fig. 14-2*. Our dining table does double-duty................................134
62. *Pho. 14-3*. Hauled out, *Seraffyn* shows her handsome profile...........137
63. *Pho. 14-4*. Rick and Susan Blagbourne.......................................138
64. *Fig. 15-1*. Area Chart: Bermuda...141
65. *Pho. 15-2*. Hurricane Agnes: Held beam-to-wind between the jetties...142
66. *Pho. 15-3*. Hurricane Agnes: The winds reached 85 knots...............142
67. *Pho. 15-4*. Hurricane Agnes: We rolled abominably.......................143
68. *Pho. 15-5*. Hurricane Agnes: ...as Ray Bashum shot photos of us......143
69. *Pho. 15-6*. The Gulf Stream kicked up an ugly sea........................145
70. *Pho. 15-7*. It rained so hard the seas were beaten flat....................145
71. Pho. 16-1. The galley is well set up for cooking at sea....................149
72. *Fig. 16-2*. Chart IV: September 1971 to September 1972.................150
73. *Fig. 16-3*. Area Chart: Bermuda to the Azores............................151
74. *Pho. 16-4*. Sailing the dinghy ashore from an anchorage.................152
75. *Pho. 16-5*. Last-minute jobs before leaving Bermuda.....................155
76. *Pho. 17-1*. Peter greeted us at his famous Café Sport.....................158
77. *Fig. 17-2*. Area Chart: Route through the Azores..........................159
78. *Pho. 17-3*. *Seraffyn* was surrounded by ocean racers.....................160
79. *Pho. 17-4*. We drank wine under a canopy of grape vines...............161
80. *Pho. 17-5*. Mt. Pico in the distance with its permanent cloud...........162
81. *Fig. 18-1*. Area Chart: The route from the Azores to England...........166
82. *Pho. 18-2*. We gradually overtook the schooner *Whilhelm*..............168
83. *Fig. AI-1*. Table 1: Price of a Cruising Boat................................172
84. *Fig. AI-2*. Table 2: Average Monthly Cruising Costs—All Boats.......175
85. *Fig. AI-3*. Table 3: Average Monthly Cruising Costs—Over 24 Months 176
86. *Fig. AIV-1*. *Seraffyn of Victoria*, Isometric Drawing.....................186
87. *Fig. AIV-2*. *Seraffyn of Victoria*, Sail Plan................................187
88. *Fig. AIV-3*. *Seraffyn of Victoria*, Inboard Profile.........................188
89. *Fig. AIV-4*. *Seraffyn of Victoria*, Accommodation Plan..................189
90. *Fig. AIV-5*. *Seraffyn of Victoria*, Construction Plan, Deck.............190
91. *Fig. AIV-6*. *Seraffyn of Victoria*, Construction Plan, Profile...........191
92. *Pho. AIV-7*. Lyle C. Hess, Designer of *Seraffyn of Victoria*.............192

Introduction

Anyone Can Go Cruising

SERAFFYN TUGGED GENTLY at her anchor in the last of the afternoon breeze. We lounged comfortably against the cabin side, watching Annabelle and Gordon Yates rowing across the stretch of water that separated their little ketch from our cutter. Annabelle climbed aboard *Seraffyn* and handed me a bucket of clams she had dug that morning, and I went below to sauté them in garlic, the perfect hors d'oeuvre for the iced rum punches Larry was making.

Gordon sighed contentedly, sipped his rum punch, and said, "Why didn't anyone tell me how easy it is to go cruising? I would have been sitting here twenty years ago if I'd known." Gordon was right: Anyone can go cruising. That is, anyone who really wants to, and does three things: First, decide that you are going, that nothing is going to stop you, and that from that moment on all your time and effort will be directed toward your goal. Second, accept the fact that it may take four or five — even 10 — years of preparation before you actually cast off your mooring lines and sail. And third, be prepared to evaluate what size boat you really need to live comfortably. You have to list necessities and make sure you don't include needless luxuries that only absorb cruising time and money.

The decision to go is the hardest part of the whole project. There seem to be so many reasons not to go: children, parents who are growing old, a business or job you've worked hard to develop, physical handicaps. But if you really want to go, you'll analyze each of these and probably discover each can be solved, or is just an excuse to hide your fear of heading into the unstructured pattern a cruising life seems to represent.

In her book, *Journey Into My Mind's Eye*, Leslie Blanch listens to her mother's tale of her romance with the charming Russian Traveler. Leslie asks her mother why she hadn't run off to Russia with the Traveler since "she was grown up and free to go anywhere she liked."

"One is never really free," was her mother's enigmatic reply. But this didn't satisfy Leslie, for, as she put it, "I had begun to discover that my mother rather enjoyed restrictions. They saved her the strain of making adventurous decisions. Ill health, lack of money, her duty to others — all these things gradually became her allies. She had opted for quiet."

We think children are the best reason to go cruising. We've met over a dozen families who cruise with their children, children from two years old to 20. The parents all agree, that children thrive on the life, and parents and children become a closer family unit. The children develop a fine sense of responsibility and the capacity to entertain themselves, and a shipboard education supplemented by correspondence courses puts them right at the top of their classes when they return to regular schools.

It is not easy or inexpensive to go cruising with children, but we met

Grace and Irwin Giroux, a couple with two young children on a 28-foot cutter, and they are thriving after three years afloat. When we met France and Christian Guillan in Gibraltar aboard their yacht *Le Tonnant* , they had sailed from France to Tahiti with two children, and were starting their second trans-Atlantic voyage while their newest baby was still an infant. Most people with more that one child find they need a boat about 35 feet long to be comfortable and carry enough supplies. But none of the families with children we met had any plans or desire to stop cruising.

If you wait too long to go cruising, family obligations will only increase. Parents aren't as likely to need your assistance at age 50-60 as they will when they are older. We know that if either of our parents needed help we would want to be with them.

The idea of waiting to go cruising until you retire sounds good but rarely works well. Sailing in strange waters requires physical strength and/or long practice. Sure, Humphrey Barton, now over 70, annually crosses the Atlantic with his wife, but he's had 40 years' experience. For an inexperienced person of any age, having to get up at three in the morning and fight off a lee shore to a safer anchorage in Force 8 winds, can be exhausting and unnerving; at 65, it's that much harder. There are nights like that, and other nights spent tending warps or clearing fouled anchors. Cruising requires physical and mental fitness. Some people of 70 are more fit than people 30 years younger, but it's rare to find a couple over 65 where both are in perfect health.

If a couple retire in good health and set off cruising on a pension, they should be prepared for inflation. A person 45 or younger might think nothing of finding a job for two or three months of the year to augment cruising funds. But when you are 65 you don't want to spend time that way, and might end up like some couples we've met who are limited to short cruises to inexpensive places because their pensions won't cover anything more.

Think about it: Why not go now while you're young? You can always go back to work later.

That's why we decided to go cruising. We had *Seraffyn* almost built and we also had a successful little business. As we were building our little dream ship, our boat-repair-yard/chandlery/accounting business developed rapidly. Some really good contracts came our way, and one day we stopped to analyze our situation. We discovered that if we remained in business for four more years we'd have *Seraffyn* to use for local sailing, and perhaps as much as $75,000 in the bank. The only problem we could foresee was the possible — although unlikely — collapse of the American boating industry.

We mulled this over, and a few days later Larry said to me, "Look, if we outfit *Seraffyn* , and sell the business now, how much money will we have?"

After some figuring I came up with a rough estimate of $4000 to $5000.

"Then let's sell out and go cruising. That much money will last us a year or two. If we like cruising, we'll find a way to earn more. If we want to stop, we can always come back and start another business."

We set off eight months later and though we lost half of our original cruising kitty through faulty investments, we've found it reasonably simple to earn enough to keep cruising — for eight years as of now. Almost every cruising couple we've met has had the same experience. Perhaps that's because people who can cope with offshore cruising can adapt to the jobs that are available as they cruise. Or perhaps, just because they are cruising people, they are more interesting to potential employers. Whatever the case, once you decide to go, get your boat and a year's funds, and *go*! You'll find it's easy to continue and not too hard to earn your way. If you decide to give up cruising you can always find a new place or situation.

Interestingly, it's easier for a couple of modest means to take off than for an affluent couple. People of modest means have less to give up. The idea of trying to retain business interests doesn't occur to anyone who merely earns a salary. Long-distance cruising and a business at home don't mix. That must be the reason why not one of the 10 or 12 couples we know who have cruised full time for five years or more, has a business back home. Two or three, such as the Hiscocks, Roths, or Guillans, live off royalties from writing, but most — like us — take short jobs as they cruise.

Physical handicaps make cruising seem difficult. Eric Hiscock is quite nearsighted, so his wife, Susan, has learned to handle their big ketch, *Wanderer IV*, whenever sharp vision is required: They manage as a team. The wife in another cruising couple has only one hand, but cruising is so satisfying to her that she and her husband have arranged their boat so she can handle it and their two children — with one hand.

Gordon and Annabelle Yates were about 45 when they decided to go cruising. They spent the next five years building a dinghy and learning to sail — as members of an inland sailing club. They built their first cruising boat in Las Vegas, Nevada, at the age of 50, when their fifth child left home. Then, within a month, Gordon made his decision — he quit his engineering job and had *Amobel I* trucked down to the sea. Today, eight years and two *Amobels* later, the Yateses are cruising the west coast of Central America.

Larry took longer to reach his goal. He decided in high school that if he wanted to see the world he needed a cruising boat. So he spent seven years in Canada buying used boats, fixing them up, sailing them, and selling them — all the while working at a regular job. In 1964 he headed south to California seeking his dream ship. He couldn't find her, so he spent the next three and a half years building her — *Seraffyn*.

That's 10 and a half years to get going, but he did it.

I was the lucky one. I met Larry when *Seraffyn* was just a bunch of lines on a loft floor, and a few large oak timbers. I had barely heard of cruising before the day I met Larry. For me, it took about an hour to fall for the dream, and only three and a half years to get under way.

Even people who can just write a check for a new boat find it takes more than a year to get started. First you have to locate the right boat. Then there are the many modifications to make it a "successful" cruising home. Finally and most important, there's the time spent learning navigation, sailing, seamanship, and how to live afloat. If, from the beginning, you accept this preparation time as necessary, you'll avoid frustration, enjoy your apprenticeship, and leave on your cruise well prepared.

Choose a modest, simple yacht, one you can afford (and still have money in the bank), a yacht you can handle easily, and you'll find real cruising comfort — mental and physical.

Many people think they need a 45-foot yacht for comfort, but what is real comfort? At sea in rough weather "comfort" is only relative — even on the largest yacht. Once you go cruising, you'll learn that "comfort" is a boat you can handle alone in the worst conditions; one you can comfortably maintain inperfect condition with less than a month of maintenance a year, and one you can truly afford.

Sure, it sounds wonderful to cruise on a 45-foot yacht with bathtub, hot and cold running water, your 500 favorite books, an electric sewing machine and two motorcycles. But, if you settle for a 30-footer, you'll leave sooner, you'll cruise longer per dollar, and you'll have the "comfort" of manageable boat maintenance.

The cruising survey at the end of this book will help you, but only experience will convince you. For example, Larry was a charter captain on a 53-foot ketch when I met him, and he worked full time, four days a week, maintaining that yacht! The owner spent about $1000 a month on her, not including Larry's salary. Larry knew what he was doing when he chose a 24-foot cutter for us.

As we said before, we've been at it eight years now, and the people we've met who keep cruising (without a private income) for three years or longer, own boats 30 feet or under! If you have a boat that's too big or complicated, it's only a matter of time before cost and maintenance get ahead of you, and you begin spending more of your time earning money and working on your cruising home trying to maintain your investment than you do cruising and discovering the world. Put comfort in its proper place and join those of us who have learned the secret: Go small, go simple, go now.

Richard J. MacCullaugh expressed our philosophy almost exactly when he wrote in *Viking's Wake* : "What if the spell of a place falls upon a youthful heart, and the bright horizon calls! Many a thing will keep till the world's work is done, and youth is only a memory. When the old enchanter came to my door, laden with dreams, I reached out with both hands. For I knew that he would not be lured with the gold that I might later offer, when age had come upon me."

Lin and Larry Pardey
Majorca, Spain
March 1976

1

SERAFFYN OF VICTORIA

Before the story of Seraffyn's *voyaging gets under way, it is worth mentioning that this book was written by the authors from three points of view: Lin alone; Larry alone: and both together. In various places, where the speaker changes, the reader should have no trouble determining who is talking. This chapter, about the search for a boat, starts out with Larry talking.*

—The Editor.

SINCE MY HIGH SCHOOL DAYS I had been looking for the ideal cruising yacht, one that would meet these requirements: First, she'd go well to weather. Second, she'd have natural teak decks. Third, she'd be able to carry a "hard" sailing dinghy in a safe place amidships, Fourth, she'd be small enough to be within my reach financially, yet roomy enough to be a home for me—and maybe a wife.

I was working as a skipper on a charter boat when I first saw *Renegade* in Newport, California. She was a gaff-rigged cutter, 24'7" on deck with a nine-foot beam. Under her first owner, Hale Field, she had been overall winner of the Ensenada race both in PHRF 1954, and CCA 1957—the smallest overall winner ever, and the only one to win in both classes. *Renegade* had made one voyage to La Paz in Baja California.

I called her new owner. "Not for sale," he said, just as I had expected. However, he did put me in touch with *Renegade's* first owner, Hale Field, and I drove to Hale's house to look at his plans and drawings. Hale explained that he had worked as co-designer of *Renegade*, drawing the gaff rig and scuttle cabin, specifying the wood-burning stove. Many of the workable and practical ideas for *Renegade* were Hale's, including the gravity water system and salt water tap in the galley. Hale arranged for me to buy a set of plans, and directed me to the man who had done the engineering and had drawn *Renegade's* lines and construction drawings, Lyle C. Hess.

Lyle encouraged me from the first. We spent long evenings together discussing *Renegade* and the many large and small changes that would eventually make her into my ideal pocket cruiser, *Seraffyn of Victoria*.

I preferred a lead keel to the iron one on *Renegade*. Lyle and I also discussed using a marconi rig with a permanent backstay to eliminate running backstays. Even details such as a double bunk forward in place of a pipe berth and head were talked over in our hours together.

I decided to build *Seraffyn* in Newport Beach, California, because the climate was great and the area was full of knowledgeable boat-building people. I found a shop with space large enough to build a boat and set to work.

As I lofted the full-size lines of *Seraffyn's* hull, I began to appreciate the many beautiful wooden curves I would have to shape in the months ahead. I drew her profile, sections, waterlines and buttocks, and faired them all with diagonals. My extra care on the loft floor allowed me to cut timbers and frames precisely, and there was no shimming or shaving to do later.

From the day I bought the heavy centerline timbers and began to shape them, wooden boat buffs constantly wandered in to the shop to offer encouragement, assistance, tools, advice and sea stories. I had just met Lin, and she watched as, very carefully, six men helped me lift the 16-foot-long piece of 6″x12″ clear white oak and put it through the thickness planer to prepare it for *Seraffyn's* backbone. The stern knee, stern post, and deadwood were cut next. For the stem, nine laminations of white oak were bent and bonded with resorcinol glue. Then, on our newly cleared construction site, all the timbers were blocked up and fastened together with half-inch bronze through-bolts.

"We're on our way," we shouted. But more knowledgeable friends said, "You've only just begun."

We put the backbone assembly on its side and started adzing, chiseling and planing until the cutwater and rabbet began to take shape. The keel timber was shaped down from 12″ amidships to only 2¼″ aft. Several friends came by to share a glass of wine and try their hand at swinging the adz. Box after box of chips was saved to be burned under the old bathtub that would serve as lead-melting kettle when we poured the keel.

It was a clear, windless day when we lit a fire under 3000 pounds of scrap lead, all collected by Lin, and her little pink car. Some hours later a beautiful stream of silvery molten lead spouted from our homemade crucible and filled the sodium silicate-painted plywood mold to overflowing. We shared a glass of wine with well-wishers as we watched our new keel cool.

Pho. 1-1 & 1-2. Left, Seraffyn's backbone erected at the building site. *Right,* Larry laying out the planking rabbet on the keel.

Howard Chapelle states that one of the most important pieces of equipment in any boatyard is a "thinking chair." I came to agree with him as I sat in mine, staring at the timber pile or loft floor while I planned each new move.

Futtocks for double-sawed frames were cut from mahogany, floor timbers from *apitong*. Finally, the stacks of pieces were assembled, bolted together and horned in, and the lead keel was attached with eight one-inch bronze bolts cut from used propeller shafts. Over a candlelight dinner that night, Lin and I drank a toast to what finally looked like, after nine months of hard work, the beginning of our dream ship.

A sawed-frame vessel such as *Seraffyn* saves time and materials during construction, since the frames serve as permanent molds. Next we bent on the ribbands, which fitted like a glove, rewarding us for the many hours I had spent on the loft floor carefully measuring and transfering the frame bevels. White oak, 1½" square, went into the steambox for about 90 minutes until it was pliable. Then, with the assistance of several friends who were well-primed with warm applejack, we bent the intermediate oak frames into place, nailed them to the ribbands and bolted them to the floors. We were ready to put in clamps, stringers and bulkheads.

Seraffyn became a local tourist attraction about this time. We enjoyed meeting the interesting people who came to see her. One evening we returned home to find Tommy Carswell, a boat connoisseur and builder, sitting with a jug of wine and a dreamy stare, inside the "basket" of the framework that would someday take us to faraway places.

A rainy day was brightened when Ed, the rigger who had worked as bosun on the 161-foot schooner *Goodwill,* made us a gift of his small rigging vise and wire prigger, then gave me lessons on wire splicing.

Ed had built his own Herreshoff 28 and he gave us one bit of advice I'll never forget: "Don't leave anything in the boat you aren't perfectly satisfied with. It's easier to take it out now than to worry about it later." When he left that evening, I

Pho. 1-3 & 1-4. Left, a bow view of the "basket" with ribbands on all frames in place. *Right,* an early stage of the interior, showing the robust construction, with the after bulkhead almost complete.

pulled out two steambent frames that had started to split and replaced them with new ones.

A 26-foot-long mahogany sheer clamp, 2¼″x4″, was scarfed together and varnished. With a Spanish windlass we slowly drew it into place. Just as we were about to fasten it in, we watched as the beautiful piece of mahogany shattered into four pieces. With a heavy sigh, we removed the wreckage and set to work laminating in a new one.

The bilge stringers went in next, along with a double-mortised, 4″x10″, five-foot-long white oak mast step. Building a boat sometimes seems an endless task. You work for days at a time without seeing any obvious progress. That's why I was glad Lin started a photo album of *Seraffyn's* construction. When I was feeling discouraged, I'd look through it and realize how much progress I'd made during the previous month. It sent me back to work with renewed vigor.

After spiling on five rounds of 1⅛″ mahogany planking with square-cut copper boat nails, we were stopped when we ran out of roves. Roves are cup-shaped copper washers—the female half of a complete boat rivet. Although we searched for them all over southern California, we had to accept the delay of ordering 12 pounds of them from England. To keep going while we waited for them, we began to deck the boat.

Teak strakes, 1¼″x1⅞″, flanked by covering boards of Honduras mahogany were fastened to the white oak deck beams. A full-length cockpit and cabin sill was cut from a two-inch-thick piece of teak. Tie rods to strengthen the side decks were made by using bronze clench rings and rod stock, and I was able to save both time and money by producing all my own bolts in exact lengths. By the time the decks were on, the roves had arrived from England.

Planking and riveting recommenced: Lin now became star of the show as she sanded and applied four coats of varnish to everything: keel, floors, planking, overhead, her hair and even the underside of the mast step.

Finally, after 2000 hours of work spread over two years, we were ready for

Pho. 1-5 & 1-6. Left, the deck on with teak planks nibbed into the covering board, and cabin sides going in. *Right,* bulwark stanchions cut and shaped, and getting a couple of coats of paint and varnish.

the "whisky plank" party.

Traditionally, a boat becomes a vessel only when the last plank is in place. This also signifies the halfway point in construction. Therefore, a bottle of whisky is shared around the boatyard as the "shutter plank" is fastened in place. Many well-wishers joined us for the ceremony. *Seraffyn's* designer, Lyle Hess, drove in one of the last three boat nails; Art Clark, a 72-year old boatbuilder and our constant technical adviser, drove in another; and, as I drove in the final one, the whisky bottle began its rounds. It was quite a party.

On Monday morning an interesting period of detail work began. I started carving patterns for bronze castings, and I chiseled out mortises for bulwark stanchions. Lin milled planking scraps into ½"x2" and ⅝"x2" stock to be run into tongue-and-groove stock for interior work. Then she started cutting and pounding in wood plugs. As I faired the hull with outboard joining planes great piles of wood shavings accumulated around the hull and were taken away in a wheelbarrow by Lin. Priming, caulking, priming again, and then paying the hull seams was a boring, tedious job that took three weeks. We planked the transom, cut in the waterline, and then on one long, hot day, we gave the hull a final hand-sanding, applied three coats of creosote to the bottom, let it dry thoroughly, and applied bottom paint. This nearly forgotten technique produces wonderful protection against teredo, because the creosote penetrates the wood for more than one-eighth inch. We have since gone for up to eight months in the tropics with bottom paint scraped off in spots, and never had any trouble. Eight years later, the creosote is still working well—no worry and no worms.

We were working on *Seraffyn* all day long by then—taking care of our repair/chandlery/accounting business in the evenings—so we enjoyed a break when George Elbin, our foundry man, called to tell us he was "pouring bronze" the next day. We took off the morning and drove over to the foundry, taking along another batch of patterns.

We watched, fascinated, as George pressed our wood patterns into the special sand used to make moulds, set up and poured the glowing metal, then trimmed and

Pho. 1-7 & 1-8. Left, Larry (before beard) trying the husky rudder for size. *Right,* the planking progressing—getting close to the "whiskey" or "shutter" plank.

"tumbled" the finished castings, after inspecting them for flaws—all in the same afternoon. We still remember George fondly—a bright smile in a soot-blackened face above the green-and-orange flame of his melting pot. Bronze casting makes good sense: If you make your own patterns, you get handsome, noncorroding hardware items that suit your boat exactly and cost less than galvanized iron fittings!

As we were finishing off the deck, my younger brother, Marsh, came from Canada for a visit. We stuck him with the dirty job of putting in the deck paying, while we installed the cockpit, built the rudder, and set up the bulwark stanchions. Then, we got another call we had been waiting for: Howard Beckman had great news for us. For a year he had been checking each load of mahogany he unloaded, watching for full-length clear pieces for our bulwarks. The day before, a load had arrived with two boards 24'7" long and 10" wide, and we needed 24'4" for each side. It made me believe in fate!

The interior went in quickly—it took less than two months. The tongue-and-groove made facings for all of the cabinetwork. Cedar bunkboards, a maple drain board and bare teak floors gave a rich-appearing interior as Lin came wood-plugging and varnishing along.

Meanwhile I built a hollow spruce mast, boom, bowsprit, boomkin and spinnaker pole. Hand-splicing the rigging was one of my favorite jobs.

Fittings began to arrive. Seven bags of sails from England, a clock and barometer from Germany, cushions from Newport, California, castings from the foundry, and wonderful small gifts from our friends. One would bring a cleat, another a snap-shackle. Each new item added to our growing excitement.

Day by day we grew more anxious to start sailing. We set our launching date, then sent out an "open" invitation to anyone who wanted to come. Lin ordered two cases of champagne and called a boat-moving firm. We through-bolted the cabin sides to the deck carlins, laid on the tongue-and-groove cabin top and canvased it, assembled the skylight, forehatch and companionway hatch. Then, a

Pho. 1-9 & 1-10. Left, Lin had thousands of fastening holes to plug. *Right,* the transom just waiting for the name to be carved into it.

week before the launching date, realized we couldn't possibly be ready in time.

Unbidden, Jim and Barbara Moore, professional boat painters and wonderful friends, came to our rescue, along with Jay Greer, a wood-carving genius, and Pete Watts, a carpenter. As Jim and Barbara prepared the topsides and applied two coats of paint, Jay carved and gold-leafed *Seraffyn's* name in the transom. Pete helped me install winches, portlights, deadlights, the mast boot band and cleats. Lin kept all of us fed and supplied with parts as she tried to varnish around us. Inside the boat, Jim Harmon, another carver, cut our registration numbers and tonnage into a deck beam. The joyful but frantic hustle and bustle of that final week is difficult to imagine.

When the boat-movers arrived we tried not to act like expectant parents as they jacked the boat and shoved her around. We were dragged off to dinner by Jim and Barbara while the movers did their work. When we returned our yacht was sitting on the truck bed, ready for her early morning ride to the water.

The next morning we moved the boat and mast to the waterfront shipyard where she was lifted off the truck and placed in a cradle. We stepped the mast and started splicing the lower ends of the rigging, gave her transom a final coat of varnish, and the bottom its last coat of antifouling paint.

Launching day dawned a perfect, cool, misty Newport Beach winter special. Our champagne was put on ice, and *Seraffyn* was the star in an old-fashioned launching. Now fully rigged and ready to sail, she was dressed with signal flags, and her sails were bent on and covered with sail covers. The guests began to arrive: My parents arrived from Canada with three friends; people drove in from as far away as Santa Barbara and San Diego. In all, over 250 people, along with six fully dressed yachts, came to help us celebrate. *Renegade of Newport* was there.

At noon, Lin, as intoxicated on excitement as on champagne, grabbed *Seraffyn's* christening bottle, prepared to swing, and totally forgot her lines. I heard her shout, "Here we go, *Seraffyn!*"

Glass shattered and champagne sprayed. A cheer went up as the lift settled slowly and *Seraffyn* floated exactly on her marks. As is traditional, the builder was

Pho. 1-11 & 1-12. Left, the galley partly built, with sink in place, just forward of the port quarter berth and settee. *Right,* looking aft into the port quarter berth. Note husky knees and vent opening into the lazerette.

launched next. His assistant, who was caught wasting the last bottle of champagne in a bubbly spray shower over the whole crowd, followed. Festivities lasted deep into the night.

APPROXIMATE COSTS FOR THE CONSTRUCTION OF SERAFFYN OF VICTORIA—1965 TO 1968

Plans	$ 200
Timbers	250
Framing and planking mahogany	740
Steaming oak for bent frames	77
3000 pounds of lead (scrounged)	no cost
Bronze rod for bolts	200
Bronze screws	120
Copper square-cut boat nails	70
Roves	25
Teak for decks	340
3 gallons resorcinol glue	48
Deadlights and port lights	150
Spruce for spars	120
Anchor winch	150
2—No. 3 bottom-action sheet winches	200
Wire for rigging	120
Dacron line	200
Bronze castings	210
Sails	1400
Cushions	150
Sextant, Zenith transoceanic radio and other navigation equipment	400
Anchor rode, anchor chain, two anchors	300
Through-hull fittings	200
Stainless steel tanks (water, kerosene)	120
Interior equipment (stove, ice chest, etc.)	300
Paint, bedding compounds, varnish, etc.	200
Launching and trucking charges	250
150 gallons of red mountain wine (approx.)	225
Miscellaneous (rent, tools, etc.)	1000
Approximate Materials Costs	$7765

Total construction time: 4200 hours over 3½ years

At the launching, Raleigh Kalaygean, a well-known wood boatbuilder from the area, estimated that it would have cost $28,000 to build *Seraffyn* as she stood ready to launch.

We officially moved on board sometime during that night. Next morning we had our first sail as we proudly took *Seraffyn* to her new slip.

Now we really began to appreciate having a yacht designed by a man who was not only a shipwright and designer, but also a fine sailor. Three years before, Lyle had told us that since a boat designed purely for cruising isn't bound by any racing rules, "There isn't any reason a cruising boat shouldn't be fast." On our first sea trials we were delighted to discover he was right. *Seraffyn* showed a wonderful turn of speed, particularly in the lightest breezes. With her large rudder and modest

Pho. 1-13. A cheer went up as *Seraffyn* settled into the water—right on her marks.

forefoot, she also proved so maneuverable in close quarters that we discarded our idea of fitting an outboard engine.

For the next four months we sailed in every spare hour as we prepared for our cruise. Between shakedown cruises we installed a windvane, a gravity-feed water system, a three-burner stove with oven, butane tank and stored 3000 pounds of supplies and gear aboard. We wrote list after list, trying to be sure we had every bit of work done before the great moment arrived—Departure Day.

2

Heading South

"Where are you headed?"
"South!"
"How long are you going for?"
"As long as its fun!"
"Going around the world?"
"Not planning to . . ."

Larry and I never got tired of chatting with dockside voyagers: They made our approaching departure seem more real. Three and a half years of building, saving, and planning were behind us—the whole world lay ahead.

Our destination was uncertain, so we bought charts for every port between California and the Panama Canal. These, along with general charts, took up all the spare space we had. *Sailing Directions, Pilot Charts, Bowditch,* three volumes of *H.O. 214* tables, and *Ocean Passages for the World* filled our navigation locker.

Fifty gallons of water, eight gallons of kerosene, a full tank of butane, and $200 worth of canned and fresh food put our 24-foot floating home right down to her designed waterline. Bon voyage gifts and our slightly overfed bodies submerged the waterline one-half inch. We wanted to keep *Seraffyn's* light air sailing performance, so we soon learned to watch her "cargo."

My parents joined the fleet of friends who escorted us under sail down Newport Bay. A light breeze filled our sails as we waved goodbye to our hometown of five years. Lyle Hess, who designed *Seraffyn,* was aboard, and he took the helm as we reached out on a smooth sea. One by one the escort boats turned back, and we headed south for San Diego.

I went below to stow the last-minute gifts—liquor and wine, cakes, cookies, fruit, books, and one large green can labeled: EMERGENCY SUPPLIES: OPEN ONLY IN CASE OF DIRE NECESSITY.

A light northwesterly breeze pushed us gently down the coast under spinnaker. We celebrated our first evening at sea with a New England boiled dinner: corned beef, cabbage, and potatoes— accompanied by freshly baked bread.

After a night of easy sailing under star-filled skies, with porpoises gamboling around us, we spotted Point Loma. At noon we reached into San Diego harbor on a brisk wind and rounded up at the San Diego Yacht Club.

Over dinner that evening we said goodbye to Lyle and his wife, Jeannie, who had driven down to pick him up; then we were on our own.

We spent the rest of the evening stowing gear. That big green can just wouldn't fit anywhere! Or maybe I was just too curious to make a place for it;

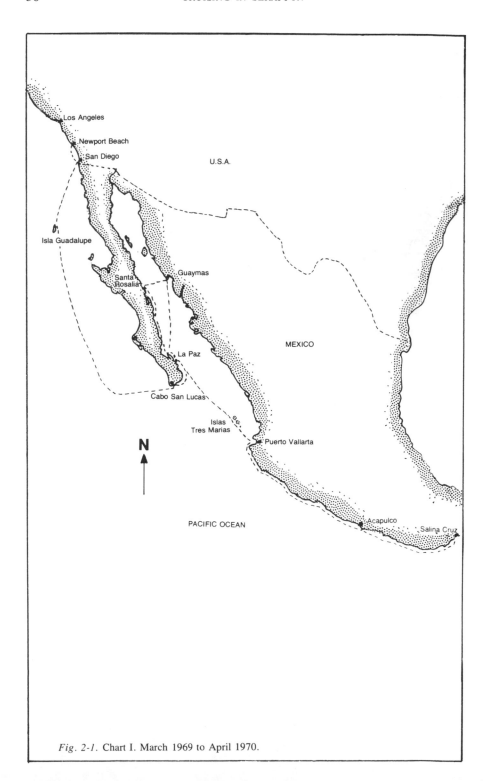

Fig. 2-1. Chart I. March 1969 to April 1970.

anyway, I convinced Larry that we should open it. A well-wrapped bottle of scotch emerged; we immediately declared an "emergency" and saved ourselves from a desperate thirst.

Next morning we discovered one of the greatest joys of cruising. We awoke, looked at our "work" list, realized we were "retired" that we didn't have to rush, and that shopping could wait a day. It was time we started practicing to be tourists.

Previously, we had visited San Diego only on business. Now, as we walked and bused our way around, we discovered a new city. For a week we looked at boats, visited museums, poked around boatyards. At the yacht club, we lounged by the pool and met new friends. In the afternoons we explored the harbor under sail.

We spent the next week getting the boat in shape for our final departure, and buying all the spares we had heard weren't available in Mexico—things such as sail needles, sail twine, stainless steel shackles, books, wine, canned butter. One afternoon we sailed over to the Silver Gate Yacht Club to watch a slide presentation of a round-the-world cruise given by some Canadian friends and their 13-year-old son, who had just arrived in San Diego after three years at sea. Leiv and Charley Kennedy had built their successful 36-foot sloop, *Kalea*, and were now headed home to build a new one. Eight years later the Kennedys are nearing completion of their 50-foot ketch. For a larger boat they sacrificed eight years of potential cruising!

After last minute purchases, we treated ourselves to a real American farewell dinner of prime roast beef, and then turned in early for a good night's sleep.

In the calm of morning we slipped our docking lines and Larry set our 14-foot oar to row out the narrow slip entrance. Our plan was thwarted as a headwind sprang up and determinedly held us back. A dockside audience was gathering, and we were preparing to warp our way out when a handsome rowing punt approached and towed us—ignominiously—out to open water.

We were soon reaching along smartly on an early morning breeze, and overtook a harbor tour boat as it headed down San Diego Bay. We eavesdropped on the tour guide's commentary and observed the sights while the tourists stared at our little cutter. When our companion turned back at Point Loma, we fell off on a reach for Isla Guadalupe, 200 miles to the south. A 20-knot breeze hurried us along with the main and lapper set wing-and-wing. A grey mist turned the ocean dark green, the confused sea turned me a shade of pale green.

While we were in the shipping lanes we stood watches, two on and two off, as Larry tried to reach an agreement with "Helmer" our self-steering vane. I spent my off-watch time lying miserably on the cabin sole, wondering why I'd ever got involved with a sailor.

The next evening, clear of shipping lanes and still 50 miles north of Isla Guadalupe, we hove-to. The easier motion and a good night's sleep cured my seasickness, and I decided I was glad I'd met Larry.

We got underway early the next morning and Larry, with much patience, discovered some of the tricks of the steering vane.

Our morning LOP, figured from the *H.O. 214* tables, indicated Guadalupe lay 30 miles ahead, and an hour later, under clearing skies, we watched the island grow steadily larger on the horizon.

In the excitement of our first foreign landfall, we set the staysail along with the lapper and full main. With 555 square feet of canvas set, *Seraffyn* broad-reached along at six knots in the 15-knot northwester.

A wide-open, crescent-shaped bay with all hazards clearly visible seemed to

Pho. 2-2. Seraffyn of Victoria.

present no obvious problems, but nevertheless, since we lacked a detailed chart, we sketched the northeastern anchorage from details given in *Sailing Directions*. Isla Guadalupe's cliffs leap straight out of the ocean to over 3000 feet. As we drew nearer, we looked for the landmarks mentioned in *Sailing Directions*.

"Larry, there are whitecaps in the anchorage," I said.

"Probably just a tide rip," he told me.

As we passed the northernmost cliffs, a fierce gust of wind laid us over on our beam ends, and before we could react, we took a knockdown that put the cabin sides awash. Water rushed into the cockpit and surged down the companionway.

"Baby, please come up," Larry whispered as he shoved the helm down. Like a lady, *Seraffyn* rounded smartly into the wind.

Larry dashed forward, cast off the jib and main halyards, pulled down the jib with its downhaul, and let the main tumble into the lazyjacks. In the powerful williwaws we eased away under just the 104-square-foot staysail, dipping our lee rail in each fierce downdraft. A look below showed that the after floorboards were slightly awash but not covered, so we held off pumping for a few minutes.

Seraffyn beat in toward shallower water, and came about smartly. As we approached the recommended anchorage, we saw a small flotilla of lobster-holding pens. A black-bearded man ashore saw us and signaled us to wait, then shoved his 20-foot dory into the three-foot surf, rowed out fisherman-style (facing forward), and led us to a spot clear of the pens.

Our anchor went down in seven fathoms, and we tried our high school Spanish on our new friend, Arturo. I handed him a large California orange. He took it, his face splitting into a smile, waved the orange over his head to show his friends ashore, and immediately bit into it skin and all. We arranged to trade for some lobster, and Arturo rowed off toward his traps. We set to work on the mess below decks.

"What did you think when that gust hit us?" I asked Larry as I pumped the bilge.

"When I pushed the helm down and watched the water lapping against the cabin sides, it flashed through my mind that this just might be the shortest cruise in history," he said.

Our mopping-up was interrupted by a scratching sound on deck. We rushed up to stop Arturo just as he brought our "herd" of lobsters up to six. We had to protest strongly to stop him at that. How many lobsters can two people eat?

The williwaws abated as the sun set and, sated with lobster (with three left for the next day), we turned in.

A glorious calm in the morning lured us into staying another day to explore the cliffs and watch the island's elephant seals. After breakfast Larry left me to my puttering, and rowed ashore to look around. He rowed back furiously when the first williwaws hit.

"Let's leave," I suggested as soon as he was aboard.

"Can't—promised to have breakfast with the fishermen tomorrow," he said. "Besides, the wind's directly offshore. Worst that can happen to us here is that we'd be blown out to sea."

I watched the anchor as the williwaws hit us. The boat surged back, but barely straightened out half of the 150 feet of 5/16″ BBB chain attached to our 22-pound Danforth. Satisfied, I joined Larry below to dig through our collection of books.

Next morning we gathered up all the fresh fruit and vegetables we could spare and rowed ashore to meet the fishermen. First, we were taken on a guided tour of the elephant seal colony—several hundred large-snouted mammals, graceful as otters in the water, but slow and awkward on land. They were completely unperturbed by our close inspection as they sunbathed on the dark beach, shooing away flies with well-aimed tosses of sand from their flippers.

We were then taken to the hut of the head fisherman, Juan. His wife prepared coffee and tortillas and we spliced together enough Spanish and English to learn

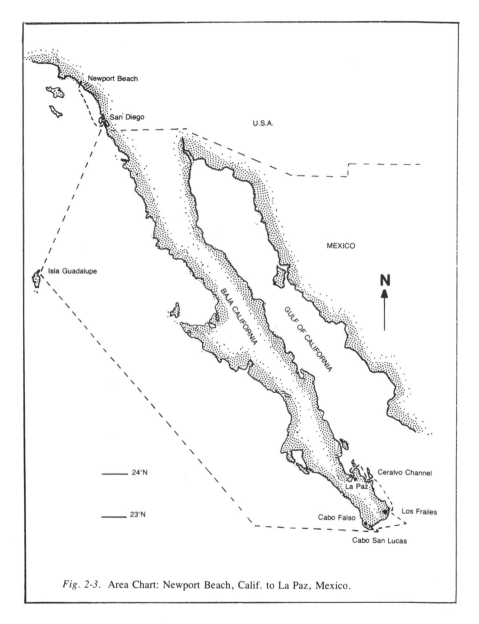

Fig. 2-3. Area Chart: Newport Beach, Calif. to La Paz, Mexico.

that the island's 10 men and one woman lived and lobstered alone on Isla Guadalupe for six months at a time. Twice a month a pickup boat brought fresh food and water from the mainland, and took away lobsters. The boat was now a week overdue, the camp was low on food, and the lobster pens were full. Every six months the lobstermen returned to Ensenada to be paid. After two weeks of living it up in town, most of the men were broke and headed back to the island.

The first williwaw of the day cut short our visit, and we quickly departed, with a letter of introduction and four bottles of pickled abalone to be delivered to Juan's uncle in Cabo San Lucas.

Juan picked up our 6'8" dinghy and instead of launching it, tossed it into the stern of his fishing dory. Then he and Larry shoved the dory into the surf, and we headed for our boat. On the way Juan insisted on picking out another lobster from his holding trap for our dinner. We refused an eight-pounder and settled for two 1½-pounders.

Back on *Seraffyn* we re-stowed the dinghy in its chocks, hauled up the anchor, and ran out to sea under the staysail. We waved goodbye to Juan, and anticipated the fun that must lie ahead if other Mexicans were half as interesting and generous as the lobstermen of Isla Guadalupe.

Three miles offshore the williwaws died. We set our full main and lapper and edged slowly away from the lee of the island. Just before sunset, the afternoon

Pho. 2-4. The pleasures of cruising: Lunch in the cockpit.

northwesterly caught us and we began an exhilarating sleigh ride that continued for the next three days.

Larry adjusted the windvane, reefed the main and adjusted the lapper on the pole. With Helmer completely in control, we settled down for cocktails, steak, lobster, baked potatoes and a tossed salad while we watched a fiery sunset over the fast-disappearing island.

That night we both slept soundly, far from the shipping lanes, running along at over five knots. Morning found us far enough south to discard our winter clothes and start sunbathing. I spent my time hanging over the taffrail watching the little trim-tab on the rudder that kept us on course, and reading, writing, cooking the food still fresh in our icechest, and playing a rousing cribbage series with Larry. As three days passed, Larry's noon sights showed runs of 125, 151 and 130 miles. The easy motion of our seaworthy little home and the sunny skies made us want to sail on forever.

Only one incident marred our days. Early the second morning, while running under just the genoa, our spinnaker pole worked free of its chocks and fell overboard. By chance, I saw it go. "Larry," I yelled, the pole just went over the side!"

He dashed up on deck, quickly released Helmer, and headed up, hard on the port tack. I soon lost sight of the pole in seas that seemed much higher as we beat back into them. After five minutes we came about and reached along the trough of the waves. Just as we were about to give up and accept that the pole was lost, two seagulls settled on something; it had to be our pole! I took the helm while Larry guided me to leeward of our "object."

We eased up to it, and I let out a cheer as Larry bent down and heaved the 16-foot pole aboard. The sea takes unkindly to being robbed of its prey and it smacked us broadside with a wave that sprayed the boat from stem to stern and threw a great dollop of salt water down the open hatch.

We fell off on our course again, and this time secured the pole with extra lashings. The difficulty of seeing the pole in the water gave us a sobering appreciation of the problem of spotting a man overboard.

On the third evening we reached the latitude of Cabo San Lucas, and changed course to beam-reach onshore. We still made over five knots under main and lapper. We stood alternate watches while crossing the shipping lanes, counting five ships per watch. Morning showed Cabo Falso 20 miles ahead. We rounded Cabo San Lucas right after noon and, as if the sea was reluctant to give us a perfect voyage, we suddenly ran out of wind.

An hour later we beat into the bay, and even before our anchor was down, we were invited to dine and shower aboard an old friend's sportfisherman. We spent a week at Cabo San Lucas, visiting with friends from Newport Beach, meeting Juan's uncle, and savoring fresh seafood from both the sportfishing boats and the Mexican shrimpers.

There, also, we encountered a really unique sailing yacht, *Clara,* a 35-foot Nathaniel Herreshoff designed yawl, built by the "wizard" himself in 1887, for his own honeymoon. *Clara* still had a perfect sheer at the age of 82, a tribute to her scientific construction which included metal knees connecting the deck beams and frames, and a double-planked bottom.

Cabo San Lucas was primarily a sportfishing resort when we were there in April 1969, with only a small village whose citizens were employed by either the local cannery or the hotel. Most supplies for the boats were flown in by private plane, but beautiful fresh vegetables were grown locally by a Japanese farmer. We filled a gunny sack with his produce for a dollar!

After a week we hoisted sail one morning and started the beat to La Paz. Light airs plagued us at first as we tried to gain an offing. The next morning, clear of the tip of Baja, we encountered a nasty, short chop caused by a 30-knot northwesterly. With double-reefed mainsail and yankee, we eased sheets and lay in the trough of the chop for the whole morning until we could reach into Los Frailes.

At Los Frailes we met a couple aboard a Newport 30 returning to the U.S. after a six-month cruise. Unfortunately, our breakfast on board *Princess* was interrupted by a light southerly which we couldn't ignore. We said goodbye, got under way, cleared the point, and set our spinnaker.

Helmer loved steering with the spinnaker and main in the six-knot breeze. Accordingly, we set the boom vang, put up our sun cover, and got out our favorite book of poetry. Larry read the *Rime of the Ancient Mariner* to me. How different the Mariner's sailing ship was from ours! With our light-air sails we could make two or three knots in a breeze that wouldn't have even rippled his heavy canvas. We passed close by a Mexican fishing boat anchored on an offshore bank. "Who's steering?" the crew shouted. We pointed to Helmer.

By nightfall we were becalmed off Buena Vista amidst the largest school of porpoises we'd ever seen. Morning began a day of frustration. Twice we tried to beat into Cerralvo Channel. As soon as we reached a point abeam of the island, the wind would die; then the current would flush us out to sea. A third attempt was successful, however, as we beat in close to the mainland, then came about and reached in to anchor just off a small fishing camp. *Sailing Directions* had said that Cerralvo Channel was difficult for a sailing ship to beat into, and it was right.

The next morning we had a light southerly breeze again, so up went the spinnaker—only to have the wind shift 90 degrees before the chute was fully set. Fourteen sail changes and 16 hours later, we finally sailed between the San Lorenzo Channel markers—exactly at midnight. A stiff southerly breeze in La Paz Bay gave us a good beat to the harbor channel.

An incoming tide helped us as we short-tacked into La Paz with Larry at the helm and me on the foredeck helping the staysail across. Halfway up the five-mile channel we shook out the reef in the main. We made 100-foot tacks to starboard, then slightly longer ones to port; I stayed on the foredeck, watching for the whites of the crabs' eyes. At 0900 we dropped anchor in front of Don José's shipyard, and the wind died, only to be followed by a nice northerly breeze a few minutes later. The man on the yacht next to us rowed over. "Pretty little ship," he said. "First one we ever saw beat up La Paz Channel. Welcome to paradise."

3

The Sea of Cortez Under Sail

LA PAZ IS A DELIGHTFUL BASE for exploring the Sea of Cortez—once you learn the tricks of anchoring and getting ashore with the tides. Three or four knots of tidal current in the harbor, changing direction three or four times daily, and prevailing winds that blow across the flow, mean that most vessels get a real test of their ground tackle— and their crew's anchoring skills.

Although we never learned why, all the boats chose to swing to only one anchor, and since they did, we had to as well. A long-time resident taught us this trick: Anchor as you would in any two-fathom anchorage, paying out 50-feet of chain as you drift down current, then quickly drop 100 feet of chain in a pile. As the tide changes, your boat swings around the pile of chain and never gets near enough to the anchor to foul it. It's an unusual trick, and it works.

From the day we arrived at La Paz, we began to meet other cruising people, some of whom had been cruising the Gulf annually for 10 years or more. We exchanged visits and meals with people on such varied yachts as *Mai Tai*, a luxurious 60-foot motorsailor; *Sea Princess*, a 55-foot cruiser; *Dorado*, an 85-foot motor vessel; *Naif*, a modified Herreshoff 28 ketch, and *Amobel*, a 32-foot gaff-rigged, home-built, home-designed trimaran. Between visits, we explored the land.

Don José, the 75-year-old patriarch of a family of seven sons, and owner of the largest shipyard in La Paz, greeted us on our first day ashore. He gave us a tour of his yard and introduced his sons, Tito, Toto, and three others, each son working for his father on a contract basis. One runs the woodworking shop, another the fuel dock, a third the engine repair shop. Don José runs the books.

Leaving Don José's, we took a cab to town to face our most dreaded task —clearing our papers. The somber, uniformed gentleman behind the port captain's desk cracked a smile as Larry and I tried out our faulty Spanish. When we had finished our prepared speech, he spoke up in perfect English: "Welcome to La Paz. Keep practicing our language and I'm sure you will enjoy your stay." He stamped our papers, and directed us to the post office. Throughout our one-year visit in Mexico, every official gave us the same courteous assistance. I think our attempted Spanish was the main factor, but Larry claims my being a woman helped.

I decided to attack the marketing myself in the *Mercado Central,* and went at it armed with some pesos, a shopping bag, and a Spanish-English dictionary. I toured the crowded stalls, trying to identify the strange foods I saw and summon enough nerve to make a purchase. At a stand with a smiling woman behind it (and no crowd in front of it), I pointed to a bin of oranges. *"Dos, por favor,"* I said.

The woman gave a great laugh, picked up two oranges and said, *"Naranja."*

My puzzlement must have showed. *"Na-ran-ha,"* she repeated slowly.

I caught it and repeated, *"Na-ran-ha"*

"I que bueno (very good)!" she shouted. She dropped the oranges, grabbed a head of lettuce, and said, *"Lechuga."*

For 20 minutes the lesson continued, my teacher being joined by several other stand-keepers and a housewife with two small children. When my basket was full, I paid my seven pesos ($.56) and promised to return. I shook hands all around and left, waving goodbye, my head whirling with new Spanish words.

After a week of socializing, eating Mexican food and shopping, Larry found the ice plant and filled the water tanks, and we weighed anchor, using the last of the southerly breeze with the ebbing tide to sail out of the harbor.

La Paz's wind pattern was seemingly designed for sailing vessels. From sunset to mid-morning the *coromuel* blows at 15 to 25 knots from the south. Before noon the northerly breezes fill in. With only a little planning you can run or broad reach anywhere you want, north or south, from La Paz to Isla San Francisquito.

We sailed to Pichilinque ("peachy-linky") Bay to dig some of its famous clams. On our arrival, Gordon and Annabelle Yates greeted us with lunch on their yacht *Amobel*—fried mackerel caught two hours earlier.

Two Mexican families live on San Napaloma, the island that forms Pichilinque Bay. A member of one of the families, Victor, introduced himself as the naval watchkeeper. "The what?" we asked.

As Gordon Yates translated, Victor explained. "In 1894, the United States signed a 100-year lease with Mexico for the right to use San Napaloma Island as a coaling station. The Mexican government agreed to supply a full-time watchkeeper for the duration of the lease. So, I stay on this island with my family and get paid to watch you sail in and sail out."

José, living on the other side of the point, is a shark fisherman, as was his father before him. He proudly showed us his 30-foot sailing dugout canoe, which had a six-foot beam and a cargo capacity of one ton and was equipped with a 20-horsepower outboard. José also gathered salt from the large evaporation ponds on the southwest end of the island.

The clams of Pichilinque were as good as they were said to be, and as easy to find as a stroll down the beach. I had never before eaten a clam, let alone dug one, and visions of snapped fingers passed through my mind as we waded in the mud until we felt our toes bump something hard, then simply reached down into the mud to pick up two or three clams. We soon learned the trick of keeping a bucket of clams hanging overboard just below the surface, so that the live clams cleaned themselves. They were then always ready on short notice for cocktails, dinner, or snacks.

We spent six weeks exploring the three islands closest to La Paz. A two- or three-hour sail gave us a new anchorage any time we wanted a change. Detailed charts, drawn by Alan Douglas, a local sportfishing captain, proved to be very helpful. Every eight or 10 days we'd sail back to La Paz for ice, water, and a little socializing, plus a good Mexican dinner at 10 or 15 pesos ($.80 or 1.20) per meal.

Candelero Cove became our favorite retreat. One time we anchored in its crystal water for a week of luxurious solitude. A well on the hillside provided a cool evening bath after mornings spent sprucing up our varnish work, sorting stores, or making a wind scoop (or galley sail), and afternoons of swimming and exploring. By the seventh day, we had abandoned clothing altogether. On the eighth, a small plane circling into the cove sent me scurrying for cover. It circled twice more, and dropped a note in a plastic bag, "See you later?" the note said, and was signed by two good friends from California.

"Our cove's getting crowded," Larry said, so we moved to the next one, two miles north.

Our days of perfection were interrupted when we got a contract to deliver a power vessel to California. We still had sufficient funds to keep cruising, but took the contract because we felt that chances to earn cash might be rare. We spoke to Victor at Pichilinque, and he agreed to watch *Seraffyn* while we were gone.

We'd be away for several weeks, and we wanted to be certain our boat would be secure. To begin with, we set our 22-pound Danforth anchor and lowered half of our 300 feet of chain. At the mid-point we shackled on a swivel to which we led a long line. Then we drifted downwind, paying out the rest of the chain until we reached the bitter end. Here we attached our 33-pound kedge and dropped it overboard with a long trip line. Then we hauled the boat back to the swivel, attached two five-eighths-inch nylon lines to it with shackles, and secured each shackle with a wire seizing. We lowered the swivel into the water until it was below our keel and cleated the two five-eighths-inch lines on deck with good chafing gear on them.

Driving a power boat about 1200 miles up the coast was a boring job and we were happy to complete it and get back to *Seraffyn,* which we did a month later. We returned with a cassette recorder, dozens of new books, and a gift for Victor. We found *Seraffyn* riding happily at anchor just as we had left her. Victor had lit her anchor light nightly and washed the decks and varnish daily. He hadn't been able to do anything about the pelican that had taken up residence on our white-speckled mast, but we vowed to get rid of it. A set of well-pointed bronze spikes, braised to the heads of two wood screws and set into the masthead fitting, discouraged the big bird, and he left.

Seraffyn had been in the water six months now, so we decided to haul and paint her at *Don Jose's* yard.

"As soon as the yachtsmen run away from the *chubascos,*" Don José said, "then I will have lots of time for you."

Tales of *chubascos,* small but violent Mexican hurricanes, usually drive most yachtsmen north to California for the summer months. However we had read *Sailing Directions* carefully and studied *Pilot Charts,* and concluded that an average of only three storms a year reach hurricane force. Further, the Gulf has excellent anchorages no more than 50 miles apart, and warnings of all major storms are broadcast daily; finally, southerly winds prevail all summer. So, what better time to sail north and explore the gulf?

Just before our haulout we had a hurricane warning. The whole town buzzed about the *mal tiempo* coming the next day. We sailed back to Pichilinque, set two anchors, and waited. We had a deluge of rain that evening, but no wind.

At haulout time, we surprised *Don José* by sailing right onto the ways car. Running downwind under just the staysail, we dropped a stern hook over as we approached, and snubbed it to slow us down. We left it set and used it to pull ourselves off the car when we were launched again.

With *Seraffyn* all shiny and bright three days later, we prepared to go back in the water. Don José, with a nasty gleam in his eye, said in Spanish, "Come into my office for the reckoning. "You remember I said it would cost you five or six

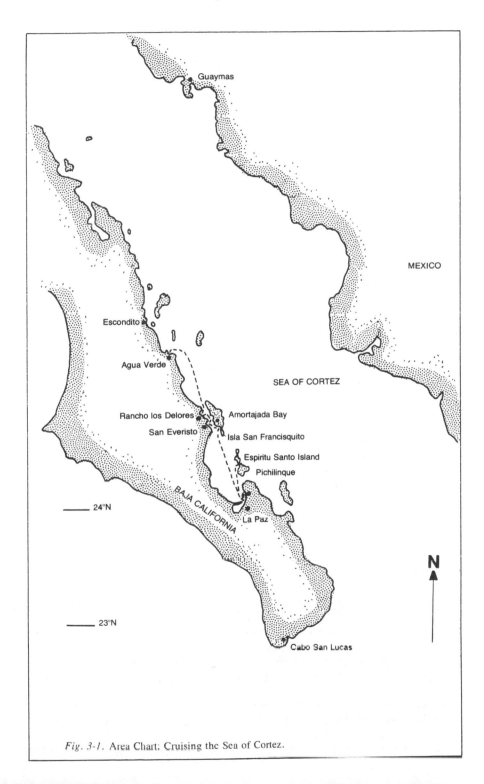

Fig. 3-1. Area Chart: Cruising the Sea of Cortez.

hundred pesos? Well, you used my yard for three days, and my man for two, and my son's machine shop, too. Therefore, your bill must be five hundred pesos.''

For $40.00 we had no complaints and later brought Don José two boxes of .22 shells for the rifle that hung on his office wall.

A new store had gone up in La Paz, a large American-style market, complete with frozen foods and canned goods at low American prices. We loaded *Seraffyn* to her waterline, said *hasta luego* to our friends, and, on the next morning's tide, set sail.

A morning's run carried us to the barren, horseshoe-shaped island of San Francisquito. We anchored and turned in for a *siesta*. The sound of an engine woke us.

"What is it?" asked Larry.

I peered out the forehatch. "An apartment house with two German shepherds, thirty people—two of them playing guitars, two palm trees, two speedboats, and towing a landing barge, has just dropped anchor to leeward of us,"' I announced.

"You sure have a great imagination, Lin," Larry said.

"Look for yourself," I told him.

We watched the converted buoy tender *Marisala,* with her three-story-high accommodations, while the skipper gave water skiing lessons to one group of his charterers, a second group went skin diving off the landing barge, and a third—with the German shepherds—explored the beach. At sunset this triple-decked carnival powered away. We later learned that this $200-per-week-per-person

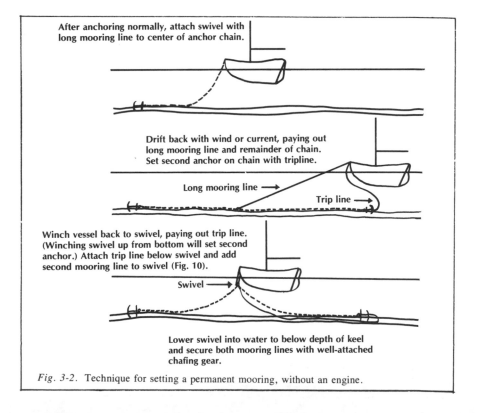

Fig. 3-2. Technique for setting a permanent mooring, without an engine.

operation is a great success, most of the bookings for *Marisala* coming from repeat customers season after season.

One of our next stops, Amortajada Bay, proved to be a real mistake. No wonder no one lives or stops there. Beautiful as the anchorage is, it is home to millions of miniature mosquitoes. We christened them "flying teeth," after a night of frantic slapping, and moved on to San Everisto at daybreak.

We worked our way northward in the Gulf, stopping each evening at a new village or bay. Gentle breezes from the south and southwest let us use our balloon drifter or largest genoa to advantage.

Rancho Los Dolores is located on an open roadstead, but we had been advised to stop there. Since the barometer was high and skies were clear, we anchored and went ashore at this bright green oasis in the desert of Baja. A rowboat landed just as we did, and we followed the two young Mexican boys up the path. The chubbier of the two carried a huge red snapper balanced on his head, like a dripping, scaly, 30-pound sombrero.

Ernesto, the owner of the rancho, greeted us, saying, "Have a seat, it is too hot to be out walking now. Have some cow's milk from this morning." We sat on the patio of his tile-roofed home and his wife served us fresh cold milk from the ice cellar. At dusk, when it was cooler, Ernesto patiently helped us with our Spanish as he took us for a tour of Rancho Los Dolores. Figs, grapes, mangos and papayas were his main crops. Even with no roads to the rancho, marketing his produce presented no problems. Passing Mexican fishing boats stopped to pick up the fruit. A week later, at a restaurant in Loreto we tasted the rancho's most famous product—fig brandy, sold only on a supply-your-own-bottle basis.

Irrigation water for the lush vegetation came from two artesian wells three miles inland, and a gravity-feed system carried it to the groves. We took 10 gallons of the pure water, plus several pounds of fruit when we left, and promised to tell

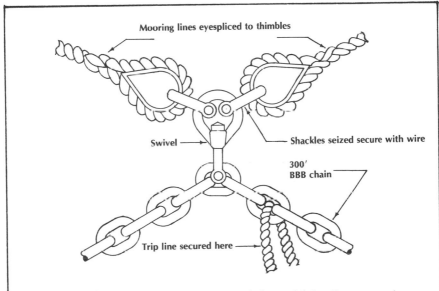

Fig. 3-3 The swivel-and-shackle arrangement used when we left *Seraffyn* on two anchors at Pichilinque while we delivered a yacht north.

our friends to visit Ernesto and his wife who had little contact with the outside except by ham radio.

Storm warnings in lower Mexico prompted us to sail to Agua Verde for a safe anchorage. By evening, though, the warnings were canceled. In fact, the wind started to die even before we reached the anchorage. We rounded the shoals two miles off Agua Verde, took a bearing on Solitaria—the huge thumblike rock that guards the entrance —and were suddenly becalmed. We had to use our ash wind to get into the bay.

With the night moonless and blacker than the inside of a cow, the white beach glowed at us out of the surrounding darkness. "Looks like we're close enough now. I'll go drop the anchor," Larry said. The chain rattled out and after 200 feet still found no bottom.

"This can't be right, we're right next to the beach," I said. Yet the lead line showed over 20 fathoms, so Larry began the miserable job of bringing up the anchor. Even with the windlass, getting in 200 feet of 5/16 inch chain with a 22-pound anchor on the end is not Larry's idea of an evening's entertainment.

We slowly worked in closer to shore, casting the lead, found eight fathoms, and set the anchor. The beach looked as though it was 50 feet away. The morning light revealed that we were, in fact, still a quarter mile off the beach.

The next afternoon we moved to a new, breezier anchorage about a mile from the town, to escape the 100-degree heat of the landlocked bay. On our second day there, an old man paddled over in a canoe, with a small boy wrapped in a blanket.

"My grandson is very ill. You are *Norteamericanos,* so you must know about medicine. Will you help him?"

Lupe, a six-year-old goatherd, had stepped on a thorn, and the wound had become infected. By the time we saw him, eight days had passed and his heel was swollen to the size and appearance of a grapefruit. Angry red streaks ran up his ankle, and he was running a high fever.

We got out our medical manual, *Being Your Own Wilderness Doctor,* (Stackpole Books, Harrisburg, Pa.), and dug into our excellent medical kit which we had assembled with the book's guidance. The problem was quite clearly blood poisoning, and we felt we had to take some action at once. We used heated salt water to clean Lupe's foot, and he sat perfectly still while Larry lanced the wound. For an hour we kept his foot in the water as the infection drained. Then we gave Lupe a general antibiotic, told his grandfather how to care for him, and sent them off with some of the fruit from Rancho Los Dolores and a promise to visit them the next day.

That visit revealed to us poverty such as we had never imagined could exist in the supersonic world of 1969. Some of the village's 90 people lived in caves with only mats for doors. The rest occupied grass huts. The community water supply and laundry were one stagnant pool. Goats and dogs wandered uncontrolled in and out of the houses. There was no electricity, and cooking fuel was driftwood or scrub.

Lupe's house was no different—just a shelter of matting shared by him and 11 brothers and sisters. But Lupe's fever was gone when we got there, and he was smiling. His mother offered us coffee and fruit. We bathed his foot again and showed his mother how to care for his wound.

Other village children were brought to us with similar problems, mostly simple infections. We were given the cotton that was the town's only medical supply, and tried our best to teach them some techniques for fighting infections, but our Spanish was not really adequate.

As we were leaving, the leader of the village told us proudly, "Next month we get a schoolteacher and our village will no longer be poor."

Several months later we learned of the miraculous results of the Mexican government's educational program. Any university student who donates his first year after college to the country is not only reimbursed for all his educational expenses, but is also paid a salary. He is sent to an underdeveloped village with nothing except his knowledge. The teacher who came to Agua Verde gained the respect of the villagers by helping them dig a new well in a better location on the hillside, and organized the villagers to build animal pens, and plant crops. When a cruising yacht asked the teacher what the village could use, he gave them a list headed by canned or powdered milk, pencils, paper, and books. A collection of these articles was taken up among the cruising fleet and delivered to the village by the yacht *Dorado*. We learned then that Lupe had recovered and was going to school with the rest of the village children.

Before we left Agua Verde, however, one more child was brought to us, a three-week-old girl, the 13th child of Lupe's aunt. She had been born in the heat of the summer—100 degrees in the day, 90 degrees at night. The baby couldn't eat or drink, and was slowly dying. We had no cure for her and left for the boat saddened by our inability to help.

With Lupe definitely on the mend we left for Escondito, the most hurricane-proof anchorage in the Sea of Cortez.

4

More Sailing in the Sea of Cortez

OUR 1000-SQUARE FOOT blue-and white chute pulled us along at six knots as we ran through the Danzante Channel, heading for *Escondito*. Now it was time for me to get a new sailing lesson. I had helped gybe a spinnaker before, but always in a crew of four or five. Usually I had handled a sheet or guy, but now, with only two of us, the job looked frightening even in a 15-knot breeze.

Larry explained the gybing procedure step by step: First, I had to ease the sheet until the spinnaker was dead ahead, with the sheet and guy the same length. Then, while I held *Seraffyn* dead before the wind, Larry would go forward, unclip the 16-foot pole and, end-for-ending it, tell me to bring the mainsail across. I'd release the boom vang, pull the main in, and head slightly onto the other tack, letting the mainsail out as the boat gybed. Larry would put the pole in place, and come aft, adjust the sheet and guy, and reset the boom vang. Sound simple?

To my amazement, when we actually did it, the gybe came off perfectly. Twice more we gybed, and each time that big balloon kept pulling. I wished for a bigger audience than just the man-o-war birds that soared overhead. On the other hand, had we been sailing past our yacht club, we would probably have wrapped the spinnaker around the headstay.

Two hours later, we had just dropped the spinnaker in the lee of the mainsail and rounded up when Larry's favorite straw hat flew overboard. Rescue stations! Minutes later, the soggy hat firmly on again, protecting Larry's sunburned nose, we reached into the bay at Escondito.

Escondito is a three-quarter-mile-long lagoon with a 40-foot-wide deepwater entrance, connected to the beautifully protected bay called locally *La Infirmaria*, or "waiting room." At the first sign of a hurricane, fishing boats from all over the area rush to its perfect safety. As there were no hurricanes reported, we didn't need its protection, and used a more open anchorage under the towering cliffs of the bay. We explored Escondito by dinghy, climbed the nearby cliffs at dawn, and filled several days reading, swimming, and doing maintenance work.

Then one day Larry said, "It's time to go sailing again," and we left. Cruising north, we were headed by variable breezes and selected an isolated anchorage on Carman Island when we couldn't lay Loreto. A Mexican fishing boat entered shortly after us and gave us some ice. Throughout the summer we managed to get ice whenever we needed it, either in ports or from fishing boats. Our well-insulated ice chest holds 100 pounds of ice which lasts for eight to 10 days.

This same fisherman gave us a useful weather-forecasting system for the summer months in the Gulf. "Watch your barometer," he said. "If it stays above

Pho. 4-1. We explored Escondito by dinghy, climbed the neighboring cliffs at dawn, and spent several days reading, swimming, and doing maintenance work.

thirty, you will probably get northerly winds. If it goes to twenty-nine point five, expect winds from the south. When it drops to twenty-nine, start looking for a safe, *chubasco*-proof anchorage. And if it goes to twenty-eight point eight, get into that anchorage quick, and put down an extra anchor.'' I became an active barometer watcher from that moment on.

By chance, one evening, we turned on our shortwave receiver just as one yacht in La Paz said to another, ''*Tehani* has headed toward Loreto to take Lin and Larry, on the *Seraffyn,* a pile of mail.'' At dawn we set sail to meet *Tehani.*

The mail delivery was a windfall, even including a box of my favorite U.S.-made semisweet chocolate bars. After two months of learning Spanish by necessity, the company of English-speaking people with news from La Paz called for a celebration and, as the barometer was falling, both boats sailed north to the Coronados Islands for a joint clam dig and barbecue on the beach.

Since we were content with the safety of the anchorage at Isla Coronado, and since our barometer read 29.50 (winds from the south), we put our cushions in the cockpit to sleep in the open. (Larry had built our cockpit so that the cushions from our quarter berths exactly fit it, and it converts easily to a 4'0" x 6'2" honeymoon bunk.)

Just after midnight we both awoke as an unusually cool breeze whispered by. By the time we had tossed our bedding below, 60 knots of wind slashing down off the island hit us, breaking the battens in our awning, and laying the boat over, with the rail awash. In an instant, we had lightning, thunder, and driving rain. *Seraffyn* lay beam-to the wind, so we struggled to get the furled jib off the bowsprit—to reduce windage. Larry crawled forward and I dashed below to open the forehatch. As Larry unclipped each hank, I slowly dragged the drenched and whipping sail below decks. The waves threw spray that felt like buckshot. With the sail below, Larry put out 150 feet of extra chain.

Seraffyn's head came up into the wind and she rode the chop easily. A sudden flash of lightning showed we had dragged nearly a half-mile. Astern, we caught a quick glimpse of rocks on a lee shore. Thank God our anchor had finally caught! But why hadn't it held in the first place?

At dawn when we raised the anchor to sail closer to the weather shore, we discovered why. For the third time, our Danforth anchor had fouled. The first time had been in Pichilinque, when a piece of brain coral had jammed between the flukes and stock. The next time, in Loreto, the anchor came up backward with the chain wrapped around the rectangular plate that joins the flukes and stock. This time, an abandoned fish net had jammed between the flukes and stock, making the anchor as effective as a ball of marlin. Only the weight of the extra 150 feet of 5/16-inch chain we had put out had been holding us. We renewed our determination to buy a CQR as soon as possible. Whenever possible, after that incident, we would dive down to check visually the set of our anchor.

Pleasant sailing filled our days as we worked our way up the Gulf to Concepcion Bay. A hurricane warning sent us north into Santispac, where we anchored snugly behind one of the eight islands of the bay. We rode to two anchors while the wind gusted to 50 knots. For two days the normally deserted anchorage was filled with fishing boats. La Paz, 150 miles to the south, was deluged with rain and hit by winds up to 75 knots.

When the stormy weather ended, we launched and rigged *Rinky Dink,* our 6'8" lapstrake fiberglass pram, for a day of exploring. Larry and I (and a good picnic lunch) drifted along under the dink's 38-square-foot blue-and-white sail. After lunch, we went ashore, got a bucketful of clams near a spring, took a swim, and started back to the boat. About a mile from *Seraffyn* we sailed behind an island

Pho.4-2. Sailing with the rail under in a brisk breeze. Note reefed jib.

and in its lee spotted an anchored dugout canoe. In the canoe sat a long-legged, long-haired blond girl and a man—also non-Mexican—hunched over something they were holding on their knees. Curious about this sight, I asked, "What are you two doing?"

"Playing dominoes," was the reply.

Thus we met Barbara and Whit Whitcomb, two Californians who spent part of each summer exploring the Sea of Cortez in a rented native canoe. They filled their days with skin diving; and their domino game of the moment had been caused by an invasion of red ants that had chased them from their campsite. We invited them for cocktails and sailed on. They arrived near dusk and cocktails ran right into dinner. After being away from towns for nearly a month, a dinner for "company" presented a bit of a problem, but the clams saved the day. I made Cruiser's Chowder and fresh-baked bread, and there wasn't a drop or a crumb left. Here's the recipe for the chowder:

Cruiser's Chowder

4 medium potatoes peeled and diced
1 medium onion diced
3 tablespoons butter, margarine or bacon fat
½ cup or more of clams and their juice (canned will do)
1 can evaporated or condensed milk
½ teaspoons parsley flakes
  Salt, garlic and pepper to taste

Boil potatoes in enough sea water to cover until soft to touch. In a small frying pan, sauté onions in butter. Add onions, clams and butter to potatoes in their seawater. Slowly add milk over a low flame. Season with pepper, garlic and clam juice. Be careful not to boil. Top with parsley. Serves four.
Preparation time: 20 minutes.

Instead of letting Barbara and Whit go ashore to set up a new camp, we took the forward bunk cushions onto the foredeck, and the quarterberth cushions into the cockpit, and made two double bunks. Our cassette player produced the strains of Beethoven and the only other sounds in the starry night came from our dinghy gurgling astern, with the 20-foot dugout canoe trailing astern of it.

In the morning Whit suggested he and Larry go skindiving for breakfast. Larry had never used a spear-gun before and beamed as he held up the first fish he had ever shot. "Got him on my first shot, but of course he looked bigger through my mask," he said as he climbed back aboard.

Barbara and I covered our giggles as Larry filleted his six-inch prize.

Thus started a 12-day skindiving cruise. We sailed into Mulege where Whit returned the canoe, bought fresh stores, three cases of beer, and 100 pound of ice. Then the four of us set off, the great white lobster hunters seeking the mythical eight-pound lobsters of Isla San Carlos.

Barbara proved to be a natural at the helm as she steered a sailboat for the first time, and a fresh beam wind quickly took us the 20 miles to the gypsum pier at San Carlos. White marble blocks formed a partial breakwater, and we anchored behind it for the night. In the morning we moved north to the cove described by one of the

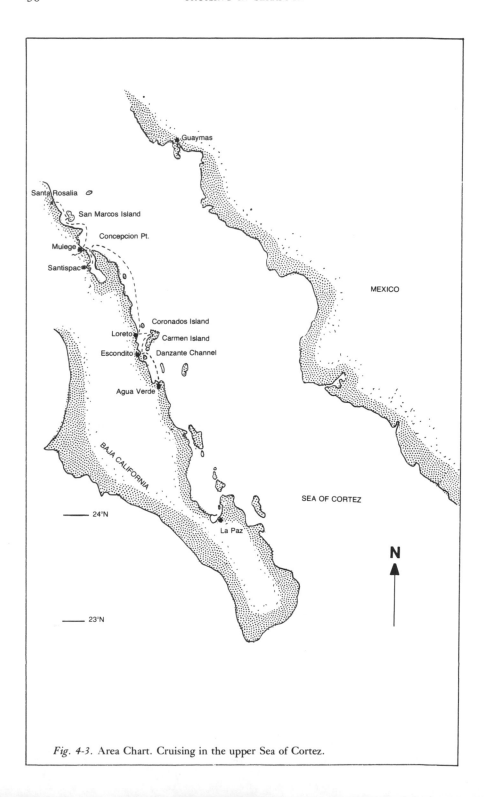

Fig. 4-3. Area Chart. Cruising in the upper Sea of Cortez.

villagers at Mulege, anchored, and spent two wonderful days.

The first day's diving provided some jellyfish stings, four half-pound lobsters, and some good fun. The second day was just as successful.

Then we sailed north to the copper mining town of Santa Rosalia. We had heard bad reports about this town from cruising people.

"It's dirty and ugly, the harbor's small and crowded, there's no place to eat a decent meal, and the people aren't friendly."

As we sailed along the black obsidian beach, and then between the blackstone breakwaters, we studied the rusty wreckage of copper-mining machinery left over from 200 years of mining. We anchored in the small, well-protected (and deserted) harbor and went ashore.

Exploring the waterfront ruins we found a complete steam-driven, narrowgauge railway and all its gear rusting in a big shed, all of it of French manufacture. We later learned that during Maximilian's reign as emperor of Mexico, the French had acquired the land, and sent sailing ships there to load the high-grade copper, as many as 20 ships a year beating their way up the Gulf. Early in the 20th century the Americans ran the mines for a time, and now a Mexican company had taken over.

As the heat of the afternoon set in, we wandered toward town. The streets seemed deserted. The first store we passed was an ice cream stand. Down the street, a strolling man spotted us and ran over to us.

"Do you speak English?" he asked us haltingly.

"Yes," Larry answered.

"I was once in Vancouver," he said. "Welcome to Santa Rosalia. You are the first tourists we've seen in years. May I buy you ice cream?"

His halting English and our Spanish were adequate to guide us to the only open restaurant in town. We sat in the center of the wide open but deserted Tokio Café. Soon a little round Japanese gentleman came over, smiling and bowing.

"I am Jésus Monobe," he said. "Can I help you?"

We asked for a menu.

"No, I have none," he said, "but I will cook a good meal for you."

"Can we order some cold beer?" we asked.

"No, but I will get you a drink," he said.

He returned in five minutes and placed a tumbler of scotch and ice in front of each of us.

Dinner was delicious: salad, beef in sweet sauce, rice, and refried beans. As we sat drinking coffee, a 1930 Model A Ford drove up outside. We scrambled out to look at this wonder, its original paint job peeling, its top in tatters, its radiator capless and patched with concrete.

Jésus said with pride, "It is mine. Would you like a ride?"

In we tumbled. The engine clattered to life. Jésus roared, "*Agua!*"

One of his seven sons came running out with a bucket of water, poured it in the radiator, and we were off—radiator spraying, children, dogs and chickens flying out of our path. As we toured the town every child in sight waved and shouted.

"Is there anything you need for your boat?" Jésus asked us when we reached the harbor.

"Ice!" we shouted over the noise of the ancient engine.

Without a word, Jésus drove along the docks and around a deserted wooden shed. He pulled up to a chute in the wall, opened the back door, banged on the building with his foot, and yelled, "*Dos barras de hielo.*"

Pho. 4-4. Jésus Monobe, our wonderful friend, and his 1930 Model A Ford.

Two 50-pound blocks of ice came rattling down the chute. The first slammed into the backseat and the second landed on top of the first, kept going, hit the opposite door, shoved it open, and bounced on the dirt road.

After we had reloaded it, the Laurel and Hardy act continued. When we reached the pier, our dinghy lay 15 feet below. How were we to get the ice down the ladder?

Suddenly Larry climbed down to the dinghy, rowed off a few yards and yelled, "Shove the ice off the dock."

The first block hit the water a bit too close to the dinghy and drenched Larry. The second block made a less spectacular descent, but still drew applause from the dockside spectators.

Barbara and I left the men to row the ice out to the boat and drove back to town with Jésus to get our purses and packages at the Tokio Café. Jésus figured the bill: 12 pesos ($.96) each for the dinner, and 10 pesos for the ice.

"The whisky is from my home, a gift to you," Jésus said as he drove us back to the docks.

Two lays later we joined the oldest and youngest sons of Jésus (both of them also named Jésus) and several of their friends for a day of skindiving. We loaded our dinghy in the back of the pickup truck and, after driving 20 miles, parked under the only tree on a deserted stretch of beach.

We spent an energetic and splashy morning, catching several lobsters (Barbara scoring for the female contingent by getting the largest, a three-pounder), plus some conch, clams, scallops, and red snapper.

At noon we returned to our rendezvous to find that Jésus Sr. had arrived with four youngsters from town who were tending a fire. A wrought-iron spit, made 100 years ago by Jésus' great grandfather, was wrapped with marinated tenderloin of beef which was slowly roasting next to the fire.

As each of us handed our day's catch, Jésus used his skill to transform it. The conch he pounded and chopped and covered with lemon juice. For toothpicks, he reached over his head and took the thorns of the tree. A gallon of refried beans still hot from home, a six-inch stack of tortillas, and a salad of onions, tomatoes and cucumbers drenched in lemon juice, oregano, chili, and salt, made a superb lunch.

Afterward, we loafed on the sand and searched for arrowheads until dusk. Then we began our homeward trek in silence, watching the beauty of the Sea of Cortez on one side and the sun settling into the desert on the other.

Three days later as we sailed toward Santispac, *Rinky Dink* trailed behind us holding Whit and Barbara's diving gear and our four pairs of shoes, still sandy from the beach. The wind picked up and *Seraffyn* clicked off the miles until we were abeam of Mulege. Then someone looked astern and yelled "Hey! The dinghy's upside down."

We hove to and righted the dinghy. One oar was still tucked inside and luckily the other was floating nearby, but the diving gear and four pair of shoes were gone. Since then we have never towed the dinghy more than 10 miles.

We sailed into Concepcion Bay after dark, with Whit at the helm and Larry up in the chains, sounding.

"Fifteen fathoms, 15 fathoms, 14 fathoms," he shouted as we reached in under mainsail in a five-knot breeze.

"Excuse me while I go to the head." Larry said in the midst of his job. Then, "Okay, I'm at it again," he said a few minutes later, preparing to cast the lead again.

Abruptly, his startled shout of, "Eight feet, ready about!" saved us from grounding in the soft sand. We ran back to a three-fathom spot and anchored for the night.

We set two anchors in Santispac Bay, then rowed ashore where we all hitched a ride 12 miles to Mulege. At Whit and Barbara's hotel, the manager invited us to be his guests for the night and we were happy to accept because the *Fiesta de Santa Rosalia de Mulege* was starting the next day. It was an event full of music, color noise, and happy confusion.

Two *mariachi* groups, a brass band and two guitarists competed for attention against a greased pig chase and a horse race, all in Mulege's one-acre town square. Tubs of ice brought in from Santa Rosalia cooled the many cases of beer donated by two Mexican breweries. Vendors hawking their products added to the clamor. Shortly after we arrived we were joined by Jésus Monobe. "I thought you would be here," he said. "I wanted to make sure you had a good time."

The five of us danced to the Benny Goodman sound of the brass band, intrigued by a definite Mexican tempo in each tune. Suddenly the music stopped and the crowd surged pell-mell toward the end of the square. We followed running until we reached the big dramatic event of the day.

The mayor and the captain of the port faced each other toe-to-toe with fists raised, flushed and glaring angrily. Several punches were thrown as they slowly circled each other, few connecting and none doing much damage. After a 10-minute melee, during which the crowd cheered them on, the two inebriated men looked at each other, laughed, embraced, and the fiesta started again.

Since we had missed the end of the horserace, we found Philipe, the bartender from the hotel who had ridden a small white mustang, and asked "Who won the race?"

He modestly replied, "My horse came in first."

After a fine dinner at the Hotel Mulege, we said goodbye to Whit and Barbara, and hitched a ride back to Santispac on a gasoline truck. *Seraffyn* seemed slightly empty when we returned to her.

We got up the anchor and sailed north again, back to Isla San Marcos to pursue our new passion, chasing the elusive eight-pound lobster.

Soon after we had anchored behind the gypsum pier, a local fisherman rowed out to see us. "I hear you want to dive for lobster on the other side of the island," he said. "It would be dangerous to take your boat out there in this wind, so why not come with me while I go fishing."

We took our diving gear and joined Carlos in his 18-foot dugout canoe. After buying five gallons of gas for his outboard, we set off. Our trolling line snapped taut the instant we cleared the pier. A two-pound mackerel was our first prize, and then Larry and I were kept busy pulling in our hand-lines while Carlos steered.

We anchored at the northwest end of the island where the two of us donned our flippers and masks. I snorkled along one side of a lava ridge, glancing at the darting spots of color made by the tropical fish, while carefully keeping tabs on the canoe. As often as I have dived. I still get frightened when I can't see the boat, which represents safety should an emergency occur. Larry disappeared around the other side of the ledge where it fell off from about 20 feet into the dark blue of a deep underwater canyon. As I swam lazily back to join Carlos, Larry came swimming full speed toward the canoe.

"What's wrong?" I asked.

"I was diving quite peacefully till I got near a school of huge grouper," he said. "First time I was ever in the middle of a school of fish where I was the smallest one there! It made me feel so damned insignificant."

During our five-hour circumnavigation of the island, Carlos had much more success with his fishing than we did with our diving. Just before reaching *Seraffyn* we landed on a small beach, and the two men cleaned the catch. While they worked an invasion party of pelicans edged closer and closer and scrambled raucously for each piece of scrap thrown to them. When a bunch of seagulls joined the crowd, one cavalier pelican rushed in, snapped up the carcass of a 4-pound grouper Larry had just filleted, and waddled down the beach, pursued by angry seagulls. With the fish head in its pouch and the tail dangling from its bill, the pelican tried to take off, only to find it was completely off balance. We roared with laughter as it hopped awkwardly down the beach harried by the crowd of gulls. We finally rescued it by throwing more scraps to the gulls.

Carlos left us after sharing a rum punch and offering us the choice of his catch. We took two nice fillets for dinner, and Carlos took the remainder to the mainland to sell.

5

Of Ships and Storms

THE NEXT DAY we were disappointed by a grey sky and showers. We puttered around the boat, missing the sun we had come to expect as "guaranteed" each day. About noon the wind backed suddenly, and increased. Instead of lying safely in the lee of the land we were now directly to weather of a rocky shore in seas that were starting to build quickly.

"Lets's see how fast we can get out of here," Larry said.

I checked the clock and began stowing things below, preparing for the beat to windward, while Larry rolled up the awning. We hoisted the dinghy aboard, double-reefed the mainsail, winched in 150 feet of chain, and were beating out under reefed main and staysail in 14 minutes. That still stands as our record for a high-speed departure from any anchorage.

We beat to Santa Rosalia, and westerly gale winds blew for two days. We had planned only a few days but ended by remaining there for a month. Jésus Monobe was our guide and Spanish teacher and each time we prepared to leave he would find a new reason why we could not go:

"You can't go now. It is the birthday fiesta of my son." Or,

"Oh, no, not tomorrow—we are having a baseball game!" Or,

"Impossible! There is a picnic tomorrow."

And so the days sped by delightfully, until we felt we really could tarry no longer. We announced our departure for the third or fourth time. But again Jésus objected. "Wait two more days," he said, "A large freighter comes then, and I have many friends in the crew."

Two days later the harbor pilot approached us. "Please move your boat to the north end of the harbor," he said. "I must bring a ship into this pier. It is the *Bannervale.*"

In the quiet of the late evening we watched the lights of the freighter as it approached our anchorage, moving at what seemed a very high speed. Just inside the narrow entrance, the crew released two huge bow anchors, setting off a shower of sparks as the chain roared out through the hawse pipes. The two dragging anchors slowed the ship as she began her entry into the 700-foot-long harbor. Lines were made fast from her bow to the outer sea wall, and then suddenly the stern started to swing toward us!

There were shouts on the decks above us, then a great thumping from the engine: Full throttle aft, full forward, the prop partially above water and throwing geysers of spray for yards to either side. To our horror, the stern of the 315-foot ship grew larger and closer with each passing second.

Larry decided to lift the anchor and let the *Bannervale's* prop wash shove us aft a few yards, giving the ship more clearance. We put the anchor down again 100 feet from the sea wall, and still the huge stern edged toward us in the darkness, closer and closer. Finally, the huge prop cleared us by less than 30 feet. Then, the wash started pushing *Seraffyn* first to one side, then to the other, as the ship's engine went from forward to reverse and back again. *Seraffyn* surged as far as she could to port, away from her anchor, came up short, then swung the other way. As she came up short on the starboard lunge, the anchor chain rode up under the bobstay, bending the wire and tugging the end of the bowsprit downward and bending the masthead forward by a good six inches. If anything went wrong now we were only a few feet away from losing our boat.

As we prayed for our anchor and chain to hold, someone on the *Bannervale* turned a spotlight on us. After another nightmarish five minutes the ship was turned at last and laid alongside the southern pier—while we were laid out along the cabin sides shaking from the nervous stress of our nightmare ride. It took us a couple of hours to get over that fright.

This traumatic experience convinced us that good ground tackle is the best yacht and life insurance there is. With a good nonfouling anchor, well-weighted with nonchafing, strong chain, you get a peaceful night's sleep or a worry-free day ashore. Dragging is almost always a case of poor choice of anchor for the type of bottom, insufficient weight to hold the anchor down in a position to do its job, or too little scope. And, our husky anchor windlass means that either of us can haul up the anchor under almost any weather conditions.

Next morning we walked over to the *Bannervale* and were greeted by the chief engineer. "I turned a spot on you to let you know we knew you were there," he said. "Nasty ride we gave you. We've got a bottle of scotch here by way of apology. Come aboard for lunch, will you?"

We joined Mac, as the engineer was called, and the captain for lunch, and afterward Mac gave us lessons in the art of checker playing by trouncing both of us. The *Bannervale* was bound for Guaymas the next day, and we invited Mac to join us there for a day of skindiving.

At last it was time really to say goodbye to Jésus and Santa Rosalia. Final farewells are always sad. One of the drawbacks of cruising is leaving the nice people you meet in each port. The parting words spoken by the Santa Rosalians—"You can't leave, you are our *gringos*,"—brought tears to our eyes.

Under sunny skies, with a light southerly breeze, we set our main and genoa for a reach of 100 miles due east across the Gulf to Guaymas. The morning weather report spoke of a tropical disturbance near Acapulco, more than 600 miles south of us, moving northwest at nine knots, but it didn't worry us because the barometer was steady. But as we cleared Isla San Marcos the wind started to increase and to veer slowly, and the barometer started to drop. With the dependable protection of Santa Rosalia so close astern, we decided to run back.

We were broad-reaching under just the staysail, making nearly six knots, and the lights of the breakwater were showing closer and closer when, with only five miles to go, the wind died abruptly.

Then almost instantly, the wind changed out of the northwest, taking us by surprise. Rather than beat into Santa Rosalia, we turned and once again ran toward Guaymas. Soon the barometer started rising. Six hours later the wind dropped as suddenly as it had come up, and we lay becalmed in open water with plenty of sea room to drift in—watching the barometer fall again!

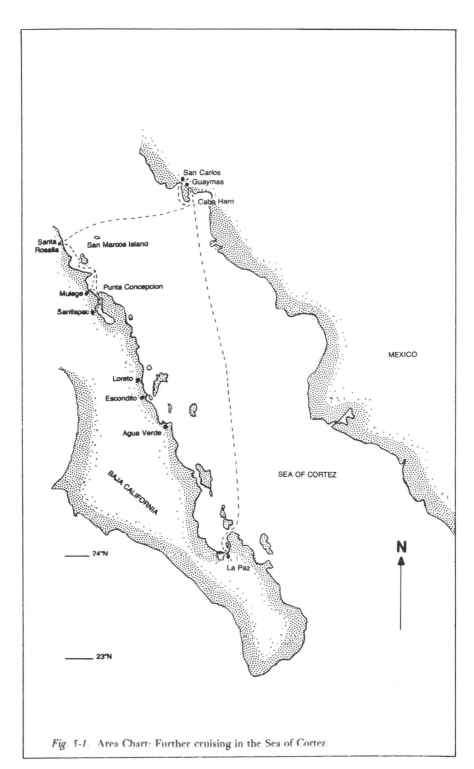

Fig. 5-1. Area Chart: Further cruising in the Sea of Cortez.

Just after dawn, we saw wind approaching from the south. Larry suggested we wait five minutes to check its strength before we set sail. A few minutes later we were again close reaching under staysail and double-reefed main—moving at nearly six knots. The seas didn't build into large rollers as one would have expected; instead, due to currents and somewhat shallow water, the chop just kept getting steeper. Once, as we lifted over a wave, another one struck us under the windward bilge, jerking the hull in just the right way to dislodge our Zenith Transoceanic radio from its seemingly secure spot on the starboard side of the cabin. The radio jumped five feet across the cabin, caromed off the stove, and landed in the sink. We rushed below to inspect it and found no damage except a cracked plastic handle. Seven years later, that radio is still working perfectly.

The welcome sight of the distinctive Tetras de Cabras, north of Cabo Haro, confirmed our position about 40 miles offshore, and at dusk the big light of Cabo Haro loomed as a clear guide to the harbor of Guaymas.

The wind seemed to abate slightly as we approached under a full moon. Larry pointed out a nasty-looking squall to the south of us. Just as we rounded Cabo Haro and fell off to run north on the range lights, the squall covered the beautiful moon. Then came blinding rain and lightning and 45 knots of wind, driving us at an unbelievable speed toward the multiple-range lights of the entry. Rarely do you get such conditions—beam reaching with a following sea. We roared down the waves on a foaming bow wave 30 feet wide!

"Drop some sail so I can figure our course before we have to change it," I yelled to Larry as I dripped over the harbor chart.

Larry laughed and said, "I hate to, the boat has never moved so fast. She's trying to surf."

Before we lowered the main, we took bearings that indicated we were making over seven knots—a glorious sail for a five-ton, 24-footer.

The excellent lights led us in to a cozy spot in the inner harbor, and we anchored in two fathoms. We rinsed ourselves off in the rain and, after sipping a hot rum, climbed into the cozy double bunk forward, ignoring the shambles left by wet charts and clothes in the main cabin. We slept well that night.

The first item on our Guaymas agenda was to pick up the two months' mail waiting for us at the port captain's office. When we introduced ourselves and presented our crew list, the port captain exclaimed. "I'm so glad you are here! Your mail is melting all over my desk drawer!"

We had to put several of our letters on ice before we could open them to read the news—and eat the chocolate bars sent by friends as a joke about my sweet tooth.

Next day we sailed out into the big ship anchorage and dropped our hook astern of the *Bannervale*. We joined the chief and captain to compare notes on our passages. Theoretically, October 1 ends the Mexican hurricane season. Our storm was on October 1. The captain said that no radio report had mentioned the disturbance that hit us, which he had recorded as gusting over 65 knots. Local reports of 28 fishing boats destroyed on the sea wall at Mazatlan, 200 miles south of us, were confirmed in the newspaper later that day.

Mac joined us for an afternoon of sailing and diving in Catalina Cove. Our catch was not too good but a passing fishing boat supplemented it with local crabs.

Guaymas was the first mainland Mexican port we had entered. The bustling, wealthy city is a mecca for American tourists who can reach it by a direct high-speed highway. A modern yacht marina is located at San Carlos, six miles from the city, and we were ready to do a few days' work that could only be done at dockside. We set our spinnaker and ran north into San Carlos.

Tied to a floating dock, with fresh water available 10 feet away, we did our standard job of "spring cleaning." We removed every movable item from the boat—cans, cushions, dishes, bunkboards, floorboards—everything! The night watchman assured us that everything was "safe" on the dock as long as the *chiquito banditos* didn't find anything edible.

The next morning our Spanish showed its weakness when we finally understood the meaning of *chiquito banditos*: racoons! Their footprints were everywhere. Bags of noodles, boxes of cornflakes, even a package of rice were torn to shreds and the contents eaten. Our losses were slight but the mess was considerable.

As we prepared to take a hose below to begin the "grand wash out," two Americans approached us and inquired about our cruise. We cut them short by asking if they would be around for a few days. When they said they would, I said, "Come for dinner on Saturday at dusk. We're too busy to stop right now."

Then with hose and a bucket of soapy water, we scrubbed *Seraffyn* from chain locker to stern post, flushing down the soap and dirt as we went along, and pumping the bilges as she filled. We inspected every inch of the boat as we dried it with a chamois. Then we returned everything to its place, checking each item before putting it back on board. Things such as paint cans with only a half-inch of old paint were chucked out; our rubbish heap was staggering. We polished our oil lamps and trimmed the wicks. Larry inspected the rigging from mast truck to deck. Then, after three days of varnishing the exterior brightwork, we had a new boat.

Seraffyn's absolute simplicity and small size, with no vulnerable mechanical toys, and no sensitive electronic gear or wiring, have allowed us to repeat this operation once or twice a year, resulting in a sweet freshness below, sparkling

Pho. 5-2 & 5-3. Left, Lin coiling down a halyard at the mast. *Right,* with our cutter serving as our calling card for repair and modification jobs, we keep her in top condition.

bilges, reliable sailing gear, and a proper waterline level as our reward.

Few cruising people—even experienced ones—realize how much salt is carried below decks by sodden foul-weather gear, wet feet, and bathing suits, or how it accumulates, causing constant dampness which leads to mildew. By eliminating the salt, canned foods with no protection remain in our food lockers right up against the planking for as much as a year without any serious rusting.

Friday afternoon, in response to our phone call from Guaymas, Bill Farber arrived from the States, bringing several requested items: Books, new tape recordings, and a spear-gun. Saturday morning, Bill and Larry tested the gun by spearing enough fish for the dinner party we had planned.

Just at nightfall the Americans arrived with two more people.

"We've come to take you to dinner," they said.

"Dinner is already in the oven," we replied. Larry, Bill, and our four guests—Haro, Joan, Roger and Lisa— relaxed in the cockpit with drinks while I covered the fish fillets with a tomato and onion sauce. I boiled up the bucket full of shrimp we had bought for $1.00, tossed a salad, and made mashed potatoes. Just as we were attacking the bowl full of shrimp, a large power yacht backed into the space between us and the next boat.

We recognized the owner of the marina who said, "Come on out to dinner with us." After helping them secure their 40-foot yacht to *Seraffyn,* we insisted they join us for dinner. Our bowsprit seemed to point toward the sky, but nine people ate dinner in the cockpit comfortably.

The next day, with Bill we wandered through the streets of Guaymas, enjoying the music of the *mariaches* as they wandered from café to *cantina.* We found the best meal yet in Mexico in a back-alley café recommended by Mexican friends. Tony, the owner, served us two tamalis, refried beans, tortillas, and drinks for six pesos ($.48) each, while his family sat watching television at a table next to us.

When Bill went back to the States, we sailed south toward La Paz, planning to be at the finish line to meet the ocean racers who would be arriving from Long Beach, California, in a couple of days.

After a day and half of drifting south, we picked up a northerly breeze and ran toward La Paz wing-and-wing. We had heard that Annabelle and Gordon Yates were in La Paz, so, on my last night watch, I carefully wedged a cake into the oven and baked it. Larry and I changed watches, and I climbed into my bunk without thinking any more about the cake.

When Larry woke me as we entered the harbor he said, "Thanks for the lovely cake. It made my watch go really fast."

"That wasn't only for you, it was for Annabelle and Gordon, too," I said, feeling sure he was teasing me. Larry's face fell and he showed me the pan—with only a two-inch square of golden cake left. (There are moments when boat wives gnash their teeth.) We anchored near *Amobel* and were soon opening the pile of mail the Yateses had collected for us.

Three days later, we powered out to the Long Beach-La Paz Race finish line aboard *Black Douglas,* the committee boat. Six hours later *Blackfin* and *Windward Passage,* both 72-foot ketches, came easing up the San Lorenzo Channel in a hot tacking duel—after 1000 miles of ocean racing!

We were disappointed at the number of gear failures reported by the racing fleet: four masts and one rudder; several boats finished without running lights, two without water. Cruising boats sure have to be more reliable!

Once again we left *Seraffyn* with Victor in Pichilinque, while we did another yacht delivery job, taking a Cal 40 to California. Even with a Mexican crewman aboard we soon were longing for the freedom from the tiller which we had aboard *Seraffyn* with her self-steering vane.

We returned to La Paz by jet, carrying the CQR anchor we had sworn to buy, just in time for Christmas. Then we had a haulout scheduled for *Serraffyn*. Heavy northerly winds blew for a week, but we hauled anyway, because although the Sea of Cortez still offered many months of exploring, the sunny south was beckoning. We said goodbye to our friends and, fully laden with stores again, we sailed for Puerto Vallarta.

We ran down the Cerralvo channel guided by the lights of Punta Arenas. By morning we felt the first of the long Pacific swells after eight wonderful months in the protected waters of the Sea of Cortez.

6

Mexico

LARRY WOKE ME suddenly on our second night at sea with a startled shout: "Look how close that ship is!"

We had gone to sleep feeling secure, certain we were outside the shipping lanes. Larry had awakened—as usual—every two or three hours to take a look around. I was shaken as I stared at the huge cruise liner that loomed over us and seemed within touching distance as it crossed our bow. Could it have seen our little 24-foot cutter? Our navigation lights seemed large to us, but from aboard the glowing ship they might have been almost invisible. The ship was actually about a mile off as it passed us, and we were in no real danger, but it felt like a close call.

Afterward we discussed the incident and agreed that henceforth neither of us would rest well unless the other was on watch, in or out of the shipping lanes. We decided to adopt a new routine of standing watches at all times, three hours on, three hours off. With Helmer steering, standing watch meant reading a book, writing letters, puttering in the galley or star-gazing—there was no "work" except a careful look around every 10 minutes. We've continued this practice ever since, and it makes for greater safety and a sound sleep for the person off watch.

We sailed past the Tres Marias Islands the next evening, looked at the lignum vitae-covered slopes, but kept going. The Tres Marias are prison islands, and special permission to land is required. At daybreak *Seraffyn* reached into Banderas Bay and approached Puerto Vallarta. We stood on deck snapping photos of the dense tropical greenery as land grew closer. After eight months of the desert landscapes of Baja California, the lush jungle surrounding Puerto Vallarta was an explosion of green.

A three-foot swell was running through the roadstead, and as soon as the anchor went down we found ourselves lying in the troughs, rolling. Larry laid out the stern anchor and got into the dinghy. He looked at me. "Lin, haul in the anchor line." "Lin, stop laying down on the job." "Lin, you can't be seasick, we're anchored."

His words didn't seem to make much impression on my stomach.

As soon as the stern hook pulled us head-to the swell, I felt better and packed our bag, ready to go ashore for a shower and a look around.

Puerto Vallarta has been "discovered." The sleepy old town is dominated by five huge beach hotels. Crowds of sunbathers cover the sand. Daredevils in parachutes fly high above the beach, towed by speed boats. Large groups gather around bonfires on the sand to roast delicious red snapper on skewers. We saw two couples running along the beach toward the pier as we rowed ashore in our pram

Pho. 6-1. Seraffyn sails so well we have never really missed the engine we did not install, and either of us can sail her alone.

and a sunburned, red-haired girl led the way. This very un-Latin activity caught our attention.

"Hi! Hand me your bag and we'll take you to our hotel for showers and a drink," one of the men said as we stepped ashore.

I looked at Larry and he looked at me. Neither of us recognized him. "Do we know you?" I asked, trying to hide my embarrassment.

"Nope, I'm Bill Smith," he said. "We're Canadians and saw your flag as you sailed in. We're building a cruising yacht at home in British Columbia, and we know the first thing a cruising sailor wants after a few days at sea is a shower and a cold drink."

After introductions all around, they took us to their hotel for luxurious hot showers and cold drinks. We made plans for a morning horseback ride through the jungle.

Behind its big, gaudy hotels, Puerto Vallarta is still a sleepy, charming Mexican town. Unfortunately, the swell in the anchorage made us feel insecure, and so did the scattered wreckage of a large power yacht that lay in pieces on shore not far away; a month earlier, that boat's anchor had dragged in the marginal holding ground. Rather than worry about giving a repeat performance, we said goodbye to our Canadian friends and sailed onward. We've since learned that a new marina has been built at Puerto Vallarta. It is safely upriver, just to the north of the town.

Cabo Corrientes, renowned for its strong currents and williwaws, had us becalmed in the same spot all night. Then, on a morning breeze we sailed into Ipala, a tiny cove that was filled by *Seraffyn* and a few turtle hunters' canoes. Ipala is so small it is only a name on the chart. But *Sailing Directions* describes it well, including the statement: "Beware of a set of rocks almost exactly in the middle of the horseshoe-shaped bay."

We reached in slowly under mainsail, each landmark coming into view as described. Suddenly, 50 yards dead ahead, we spotted what appeared to be a huge rock, just awash. As we prepared to come about, the black "rock" lifted its silver wing tips and a 12-foot manta ray glided slowly beneath the surface. We spotted the real rocks some distance off our bow and anchored safely away from them.

A few minutes after we had put a harbor furl in our mainsail, two men paddled out to us in canoes and came alongside. One of them asked if we had any sugar for sale. They were camping in Ipala for the turtle season and their supply truck was not due from Mexico City for three days.

As I went below to get some sugar, I heard one of them whispering in Spanish, "Is the propeller on that side?"

"No, nothing on this side," the other answered.

In the clear water, our deep keel and rudder were clearly visible.

"Do you have a motor?" one of them asked.

"No, only sails" Larry replied.

"Pobrecitos. (poor little ones)" they exclaimed, pointing to their brand-new Volvo-Penta diesels.

"Why don't you have an engine?" is a question we are often asked, and these men asked it too.

Our standard response, "We can't afford one," was immediately understandable to two Mexican turtle fishermen, but many yachtsmen think that cruising without a motor is both frightening and dangerous. Perhaps the reasons behind our decision are worth explaining.

To install a small diesel engine properly with tanks, hull fittings, shaft, prop and controls would cost us at least $2500—the same amount we spent for all living and cruising expenses during the 12 months we spent in Mexico! A year's freedom for the price of an engine. Also, the space under the cockpit usually occupied by an engine is used by us to carry seven bags of sails, freeing the forepeak for our cozy double berth and, quite literally, doubling the storage space and water-carrying capacity of our 24-footer. Without an engine, we are forced to be doubly careful with navigation and planning, but we are rewarded by the satisfaction of working our way into harbors under sail, thus sharing the experiences of the great explorers who first discovered many of the places we have visited. Sparkling clean bilges is a final reward, and a 14-foot oar allows us to scull *Seraffyn* at one knot on windless days. But we know that if we had to be "back to work" every Monday morning, *Seraffyn* would probably be fitted with an outboard motor.

The turtle fishermen insisted we come ashore for a dove hunt, so we unpacked our .22 rifle and joined them for a very noisy, futile hunt—but a pleasant trek through the woods. I stopped the show that afternoon by hitting a beer can at 100 yards, the men being not so much impressed by my accuracy as by the way I held the rifle—which showed I had never used one before.

As we passed the shed where the day's turtle catch was being butchered, the head of the village asked if we would take turtle meat in exchange for five pounds of sugar. We accepted gladly: the steaks were superb. Later, stew and turtle soup used up the last of the fine meat.

After leaving Ipala we started daysailing down the coast, finding good anchorages every 30 to 40 miles. Most of them had no villages or people, and we were told later that the area of Mexico bounded by Mazatlan in the north and Manzanillo in the south is considered Mexico's Wild West. Bandits still roam the

Pho. 6-2. The steaks that evening were superb.

area and we heard a first-hand account of a yachtsman who was shot—although not mortally—in a melee with bandits ashore.

Sunny days and clear water made our daily runs a joy, but we were just getting a bit interested in seeing people again when, approaching Tenacatita, we saw a yacht we knew. *Hunakai,* a 34-foot Block Island ketch, lay anchored beside a 42-foot sportfisherman, *Andiamo Now.* Joe and Nancy Hill rowed over from *Hunakai* for dinner, during which each of us boasted about our boat's speed, and soon a friendly wager developed: We would race, anchor-up-to-anchor-down, over a 12-mile course south to Navidad, any sails allowed except spinnakers, *Andiamo Now* to serve as starting and finishing line (by powering ahead of us)—the winner "privileged" to make cocktails at the finish.

At 1230 the next day we hoisted our genoa and mainsail, lifted our anchor and reached out, *Hunakai* right abeam under genoa, main and mizzen. We both worked to windward, *Hunakai,* with her 10-foot longer waterline, gaining just a bit. Four miles later we set the whisker pole for our genoa. Wing-and-wing we slowly caught and passed Joe and Nancy as their mizzen blanketed their mainsail on the dead-downwind course. We were anchored just off Navidad 12 minutes before *Hunakai,* and *Andiamo Now* gave us a loud victory toot. Then everyone boarded *Seraffyn* for the promised prize of iced drinks.

Navidad, a resort for Mexicans has an open market. We visited it and, as usual, sides of beef were hanging on stall fronts—swarming with flies, except at one butcher's stand.

"How do you keep the flies away?" Larry asked the butcher.

"I use fly spray," he answered, giving the carcass another shot of Raid. We ate fish during the rest of our stay.

When we sailed into Manzanillo, our next port south, we saw another familiar yacht. Gordon and Annabelle greeted us once again with freshly caught fish and invited us us to dinner aboard *Amobel.* The harbor was filled with cruising friends from the Sea of Cortez and, after agreeing to rendezvous with them at Acapulco, we sailed onward in pleasant Pacific breezes.

We decided to stop at Isla Grande, an island famous for its parrots. Larry sighted the island at dusk on the third day, and headed in. The 20-mile light wasn't visible. With no light we couldn't enter the bay, so we sailed 12 miles farther south, and beat into the well-lit anchorage of Zihuatanejo.

At dawn a boarding party of customs officials came alongside. "Are you carrying any marijuana?" they asked, without boarding us.

"No," we replied. "Would you like to look below?"

"No, thanks," one official said.

"Why is there no light at Isla Grande?" Larry asked.

"The big ships all have radar so they don't need a light to go in there," the official said, "and the little yachts only stop there for marijuana; if the light isn't on, it stops the traffic in drugs."

Our stay in Zihuatanejo was delightful. We met a young German writer, Rainer Rauhaut, who fell in love with *Serrafyn.* He had to go to Acapulco to see a dentist and Larry said,"Why not sail with us and save yourself the six-hour bus ride?" Rainer accepted eagerly.

Three days and 120 miles later, Rainer had decided that sailing was for him, although we had spent 25 hours completely becalmed, during which a huge hammerhead shark circled us ominously for several hours.

We expected Acapulco to be a tourist town and we weren't dissappointed.

Pho. 6-3. Our good friends and frequent cruising companions, Annabelle and Gordon Yates.

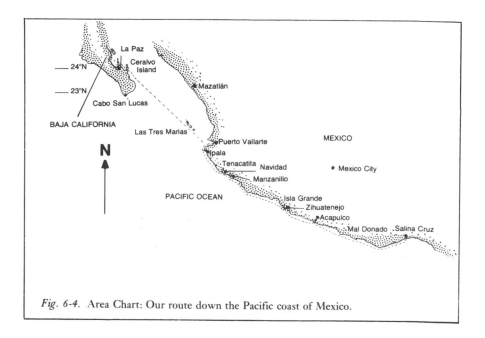

Fig. 6-4. Area Chart: Our route down the Pacific coast of Mexico.

But, we would never be closer to Mexico City, and we wanted to visit there, so we stayed at the resort. We got permission to use a fishboat mooring for *Seraffyn* during our absence in Mexico City. Just before we left Acapulco, Larry decided to borrow a SCUBA tank from a neighboring yacht and check the mooring—and it was a good thing he did!

The robust, heavy-link chain was connected securely to a huge block of concrete on the bottom. A short, lighter length of of chain connected *Seraffyn* to the heavy chain. But the shackle connecting these two lengths of chain had lost its pin and they were only hooked together by the open shackle! The first strong wind would have straightened out the pinless shackle and let the boat drive ashore. We put on a new half-inch galvanized shackle and "moused" it securely with wire.

When we had finished this job, Larry swam around the bottom unfouling other boats' anchors. When he came up, he said, "Bottom looks like a trash dump."

Cruising friends agreed to keep an eye on *Seraffyn,* so we were able to enjoy a week of hotel living, museum visiting, and pyramid climbing on the 8000-foot-high plateau of Mexico City. We returned in time to serve on the Long Beach-to-Acapulco Race greeting committee. The weeks slipped pleasantly by as yachts and people came and went. One day *Clara* arrived. She was the 82-year-old Herreshoff yawl we had first met at Cabo San Lucas. Ken, her owner, came over and asked Larry if he would inspect her to discover why she leaked whenever she was sailed hard on the wind.

Larry's survey revealed that someone had removed five floor timbers that directly supported the lead ballast keel, and had installed a copper water tank in their place. With these vital structural members removed, of course she leaked. A less well-constructed yacht might have really opened up under the stresses of sailing. Ken and Mary sailed *Clara* back to California soon afterward to have her repaired properly. We later heard that *Clara* made the 1400-mile beat easily with only regular pumping needed to keep her dry.

Each yacht that arrived from the south warned us of horrible gales in the Gulf of Tehuantepec, an area stretching from Acapulco south to the Guatamala border. Broken spreaders, tattered sails, and tired crews substantiated these stories. The lowlands of Tehuantepec funnel the northerly winds that sweep down from Canada into the Gulf of Mexico during the winter months into this area, and they blast it. Since the wind blows directly off the sandy shore, the safest route across the gulf is to hug this weather shore for the 400-mile run. We prepared for the trip by laying in all the food and liquor *Seraffyn* could hold; we had been told that food prices in Costa Rica were high (and they were).

The minute we left Acapulco, we felt currents tugging us southward. The first stretch along the coast was easy until we were 40 miles from Salina Cruz, the southernmost port in Mexico. We had just decided to by-pass the port and make a dash 'across the Gulf of Tehuantepec when the barometer started falling and the wind backed to north. So, we beat into Salina Cruz harbor and anchored in the only available spot—the middle of a fleet of shrimpers. By morning a southwesterly storm was blowing hard, but we were snug.

When the storm blew itself out, four more shrimpers entered the already crowded harbor. We recognized *Punta Banda,* a much-dented steel trawler, which we had passed three days earlier, so we rowed over with our gallon bucket to buy shrimp. We were invited aboard, and I bombarded the captain with questions. "How do you set your nets? Why do they have chains on them? What comes up besides shrimp?"

"Wait, wait, go slow," the captain protested. "It's easier to show you. Come shrimping with us tonight."

We accepted the invitation eagerly.

The captain got on his radio and asked which trawler would be remaining in the harbor that night. When he found one, he said, "Watch the little sailboat, and don't let anyone go near it."

That evening Larry and I put on warm jackets and rowed over to *Punta Banda.* Two crewmen lifted our dinghy onto the cabin top, the trawler's slow-speed diesel started to purr, and the anchor came up. We rumbled slowly out onto a flat sea reddened by the sunset.

Soon after clearing the breakwater, the men started easing massive sets of chain, net, buoys, boards, and wire cable into the water, one to port and one to starboard, each set hanging from the end of a 20-foot outrigger boom. We watched the nets sink from view and 15 fathoms of cable run out from the winch drums. As soon as the winch brakes were set, we could feel the immense drag of the nets scraping across the bottom. This done, the captain invited us into the cabin for a dinner of turtle stew, while he explained how the gear worked.

Large wooden boards (called "doors"), are used as carefully balanced paravanes and are attached to each side of the mouth of the net in such a way as to hold it down and open. The lower lip of the net is held down by a chain which is laced to it, and the upper lip is kept afloat by buoys.

The shrimp are scared up off the sea bottom by a length of chain that rattles in front of the mouth of the bag and the jumping shrimp are scooped into the net.

One hour later the captain ordered the small "try" net to be lifted. As it swung dripping over the rail he removed a handful of medium-size shrimp, and a sea shell. He explained that the small net was exactly one-tenth the size of the big one, so he just multiplied by 10 to determine how much shrimp they were getting, and if they were over good shrimping ground.

We sat chatting with the crew until the clang of the big winches told us that the two large nets were on the way up.

As the narrow end of the net was unlaced, a shiny, mass of wiggling sea life cascaded onto the afterdeck. When both nets were emptied and reset, all six crewmen, including the captain, set to work sorting the two-foot-deep pile of wiggles that covered the 10′ x 12′ area.

First a seven-foot moray eel was thrown overboard, snapping as he went. Hundreds of small flat fish, more eels, rock fish, and twigs were shoveled out through the scuppers. Sea shells were thrown to me. Then the six men sat on stools, snapping the heads off shrimp, throwing them into baskets according to size, and tossing the trash overboard. The powerful glow of the deck lights illuminating the scene revealed sea birds flying in our wake, noisily diving for the edible trash. Then, as the last shrimp head went overboard, the captain ordered the nets up again.

By midnight, Larry and I were sleeping in a spare bunk. At daybreak the nets came in for the last time. As we headed back to Salina Cruz the cook cleaned my sea shells.

We anchored near *Seraffyn* and rowed home laden with a gallon of shrimp, and a smaller bucket of shining shells. Later in the day we rowed over to *Punta Banda* with a bottle of scotch as a thank-you, and then set to work eating a two-pound shrimp cocktail.

7

Central America, Gulfs and Currents

WE HAD ENJOYED cruising Mexican waters for nearly a year, but now, we felt that it was time to move on. In six days, our cruising permit and visas would expire. Winds were mild and fair, so we bought ice and fresh food, and prepared to leave Salina Cruz.

At departure time, Larry started to winch in the anchor chain; it wouldn't budge. The chain went straight down into the murky water and out of sight. Larry winched until *Seraffyn's* wide boottop was almost under water. Then we jumped up and down on the taffrail, but still the anchor didn't move. As we sat there wondering what to do next, a man rowed out from shore in a dugout canoe. *"Senor,* you have fouled your anchor on the wreck of a two-hundred-foot dredger that sank here ten years ago," he said. "I can retrieve it for you for one hundred pesos ($8.00 U.S.), or you can cut your chain and leave, and I will retrieve your anchor later and sell it to the next yachtsman who stops here."

Larry looked at me and muttered, "He's obviously done this before." We told him we would think over his proposal for an hour, and he paddled away.

After donning mask and fins, Larry swam down the anchor chain. One foot under water he disappeared into the murk. A short time later he surfaced, frustrated. "I don't dare work around that jagged rusty steel when I can't see anything. I'm beginning to think a hundred pesos is a bargain to save a twenty-five-pound CQR anchor and two hundred feet of good chain."

Our Mexican diver returned later and went to work for two hours with no gear except his canoe, which was handled by his son. "Your anchor is right down in the hold of the dredger, and the chain is wrapped all around the ship's rigging," he told us, as he surfaced after his first dive. A few minutes later he brought up our anchor, and then slowly untangled the chain.

When we were free at last we moved to a clear spot in the harbor and re-anchored. We added a bottle of scotch to the diver's pay; he had done a good job in tough conditions, and had suffered several nasty cuts and scratches in the process.

Heading south again, we kept a close watch on the barometer and a careful eye to the northeast—where the mountains lay. A light northerly breeze gave us about 75 miles a day. The high clouds that announce the fierce gales of Tehuantepec never crowned the mountains. For five days we had a magic carpet sail: days, sunny, nights, clear and starlit, a phosphorescent trail bubbling astern. Helmer steered, and our largest genoa and mainsail pulled us along wing-and-wing. The seas were as calm as a pond. We lived luxuriously, eating Salina Cruz shrimp,

71

drinking chilled Mexican beer, reading, chatting and lounging in the sun. On the sixth day, we crossed into Guatamalan waters—just one year and 3612.5 nautical miles since entering Mexico.

We knew from Mexican news reports that "two Central American countries" were shooting at each other over an umpire's decision at a soccer game, and a third was threatening a fourth about territorial rights. To avoid these "politically disturbed" areas, we continued south directly for Costa Rica.

But we had celebrated our escape from heavy weather in the Gulf of Tehuantepec too soon. As we crossed the Gulf of Papagayo, strong winds hit us dead on the nose. We were sailing along when we saw a squall approaching. Before we had the genoa completely down, it was blowing a gale. We reefed the main and waited for the squall to end; it didn't. Under staysail and double-reefed main, we beat toward Punta Giones, 300 miles ahead. The first night, we decided to heave-to —mainsail double-reefed and tiller lashed slightly alee. Looming seas roared toward us, but *Seraffyn's* bowsprit lifted bravely to each one, and in the morning the foredeck was dry.

At dawn on the second day, the wind moderated and we set our staysail again. After Larry shot the sun, we found our noon-to-noon run was a poor 36 miles. A strong northwesterly current was working against us. During the afternoon, a large grey booby circled us, trying awkwardly and unsuccessfully to land on our arcing spreader. He circled again; this time he tried the boom gallows but again with no luck. His third attempt was successful as he settled on our bowsprit; since we had no jib up, he seemed perfectly happy and sat there staring at us and preening his feathers.

As night fell, the wind picked up again. We decided to try our sea anchor. *Seraffyn* would heave-to happily without it, but someday, we felt, we might have to use the sea anchor in an extreme storm, or when we had limited sea room, and this was a good time to test it.

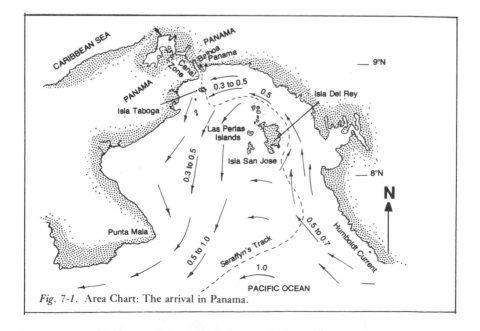

Fig. 7-1. Area Chart: The arrival in Panama.

With the main double-reefed, as soon as the eight-foot-diameter parachute filled with water it pulled *Seraffyn's* head directly into the wind with a jerk, but within a few minutes we felt the sea anchor becoming less and less effective. We winched it in to find it had wound itself around the trip line, collapsing the chute. We removed the trip line and set the anchor again; this time it worked fine. The parachute tried to hold us head to wind, but allowed our bow to fall off on either tack about 40 degrees. During the night the motion became irritating because the main slatted furiously through the eye of the wind every 10 minutes or so. Still, we seemed secure. In the morning the wind had moderated, and we hauled in the sea anchor. As we crested each wave, the sea anchor line would slacken a bit and we could winch in about six feet. When the sea anchor was finally under the bow, Larry grabbed the lines on one side of it and spilled out the water. Then he heaved it on deck and stowed it. Without the trip line, the swivel had worked well, the rope hadn't kinked and the lines didn't scramble.

We set sail again, our log showing a noon-to-noon run of 60 miles, while our noon sight put us one mile astern of our previous noon's fix! What a disappointment. When our regular nightly wind-increase arrived we decided to heave-to under reefed mainsail. This produced a much easier motion than the night before when we were riding to the sea anchor. Our booby was still perched on our jumping bowsprit. "Next time we use the sea anchor," Larry said, "I'd like to try leading the warp from a point about halfway between the chainplates and the stemhead. That way I think she will lay-to on one tack instead of changing over, and causing all that annoying motion down below. Besides that, lying about forty-five degrees to the wind should take some of the strain off the rudder fittings, the rudder, and the sea-anchor cable."

Our third day's run in the stormy weather was only eight miles, so that evening when the winds did not increase, we raised the jib. We hated to disturb our friend the booby, but Larry had to go out on the bowsprit to set the yankee. As he slid out on the sprit, the booby refused to move and Larry actually had to push him off. He squawked raucously, flew off, circled once and landed on the boom gallows. A few minutes later he flew off for good. By morning we were reaching through smoother seas.

Fourteen days out of Salina Cruz, we spotted Punta Giones, and a grey whale spotted us. The 30-foot giant circled us several times, and we wondered if he had amorous feelings toward *Seraffyn's* hull. If so, he was fickle, for he soon continued his southern migration. By nightfall we were approaching the entrance to the Gulf of Nicoya, but the Cabo Blanco light didn't come on. We were furious as we had entertained visions of a night at anchor, and a breakfast of fresh fruit. With no safe alternative, we hove-to till dawn, when we had a fine reach up the Gulf under full sail. We anchored at dusk in the big ship's anchorage, raised our "Q" flag, and waited for the customs men to come out and inspect us.

We waited. We sent a message ashore with a local fish boat. We waited some more. No message came back. The southerly wind began to make the anchorage uncomfortable. After 20 hours of waiting, we lifted our anchor and, while I swung the lead in the bow, Larry took us carefully into the estuary behind Puntarenas. No chart is available for this anchorage because of its shifting nature, but we had a recent drawing done by a fellow yachtsman. We half expected to run aground, so we headed in on the first of a 12-foot rising tide. Once inside, we stayed close to the large mooring buoys, since the shrimpers on them obviously drew more water than we did. Under just staysail and main, we sounded our way four miles up the estuary

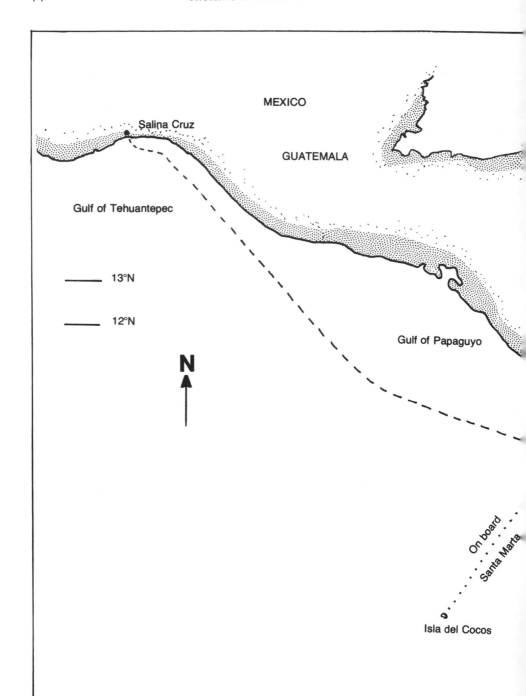

Fig. 7-2. Chart II: May 1970 to January 1971.

toward the yacht club. One mile short of it, and far beyond the last trawler mooring, we nuzzled our way quietly into the mud on the windward side on the channel. Unperturbed, we ate a leisurely lunch, and then floated free, sailed to a yacht club mooring, launched the dinghy and rowed ashore. The club gave us every assistance, even lending us enough local currency to take a taxi to town to get cleared by customs.

"How many tons is your yacht?" the head of the health office asked.

"Five tons," Larry said.

"That's too small to carry many germs. You may consider yourself cleared," the official said.

Officially entered in Costa Rica, we found a corner café, and enjoyed our first ice cream in 16 days.

The islands of the Gulf of Nicoya offered wonderful cruising, with Puntarenas as our mail and supply depot. Four movie theaters, a dozen inexpensive restaurants, and four discotheques within walking distance of our boat kept us amused during the warm tropical evenings. We met the American managers of the two competing shrimp-packing plants. They were the best of friends, and we spent many delightful evenings sharing shrimp and laughter. Frigerificos, one of the two companies, was looking into the possibility of starting a lobster industry on Coco Island, 300 miles offshore. They had only one problem—none of their crews knew celestial navigation; they asked Larry to navigate an exploratory trip.

"I'd love to go, but I wouldn't like to leave Lin alone for a month," Larry said.

The manager thought a moment. "If Lin is willing to replace the cook, we'll give him his vacation, and she can go in his place," he said.

Shopping for a crew of six for a 24-day voyage (using someone else's funds) was pure pleasure. We got 12 cases of soft drinks and 300 pounds of fresh food and fruit, took on 20 tons of ice and 125 lobster pots—and all were loaded aboard *Santa Marta,* our 54-foot trawler. Our expedition—a Costa Rican captain, engineer and diver, two diesel launches, a Canadian navigator, and two Americans—left at 0200 on the tide. The Caterpillar diesel purred as we crossed the quiet surging seas with the outriggers set out to dampen the rolling.

Johnson, our captain, didn't really trust this newfangled business of staring at the sun through a sextant, and watching the compass instead of steering by a headland or the depth-sounder. He kept staring wistfully back toward the now invisible land until noon of the second day, when Cocos Island popped up dead on our bow—under a wreath of clouds.

Lying 600 miles north of the Galapagos, at the northern end of the same underwater mountain range, Isla del Coco marks the point where the Humboldt Current spreads out and becomes just a drift. Strong currents and rapidly changing weather patterns have been the basis for the many strange tales about the island. Abundant sea life, dominated by sharks, flourishes along its four-by-eight-mile circumference. Costa Rican ports are full of stories about buried treasure on the isle, and the holes and excavations of unsuccessful treasure hunters have left raw scars on the beaches. An almost impenetrable jungle reaches right down to the shore, broken at intervals by narrow waterfalls. It was on Coco that Robert Louis Stevenson was inspired to write *Treasure Island.* Voss sailed here, too, searching for Peruvian gold.

During the afternoons, Larry and I explored the beaches and streams near our anchorage, and found rocks carved with the names of seamen and ships dating as

Pho. 7-3. Carving on the rocks revealed that the Coco Islands had been one of the favorite watering spots for whalers of the 18th Century.

far back as 1615. Some of the names and dates showed that Coco Island had been a favorite watering spot for the whalers of the 18th century.

Captain Johnson was a master cook, and we ate the bountiful seafood we found—crabs, conch, fish and lobster—prepared Costa Rican and American style in an impromptu cooking competition that got started between the captain and myself. Everyone won.

It quickly appeared that lobstering would not be commercially successful on Coco because there was too little shallow water in which to set pots; the shore dropped off to several hundred fathoms within a quarter-mile of the beach. So, after 14 days we left, laden with three wild pigs the crew had shot, but with only 100 lobster tails.

We were glad we had seen Coco, but Larry felt the holding ground was too poor and the anchorages too exposed to warrant beating 300 miles to windward in *Seraffyn* to see it again.

As *Santa Marta* approached Puntarenas, the shrimp trawling nets were put over and we caught 300 pounds of large prawns, just so we wouldn't return with a poor catch.

Larry worked hard for four months in Costa Rica to replenish our cruising funds. He rebuilt a 48-foot sportfishing boat that was suffering from dry rot, and trained a young Costa Rican to skipper and maintain the vessel.

I worked on *Seraffyn,* meanwhile. I put three coats of varnish on everything, painted the bulwarks, cove stripe, and bowsprit. Then, on the day I was putting the final coat of paint on the waterways, a pelican flew low overhead, and his droppings splattered right on the fresh paint, two feet from my brush! I shrieked like a banshee, and Larry came running. When he discovered what was wrong, he calmed me down and wiped the paint off with thinner. I repainted the area —glaring angrily skyward until the job was finished.

On weekends we cruised to nearby islands or traveled inland by train, bus and motorcycle. Costa Rica enchanted us. Rushing rivers cut deep gorges down the mountainsides, and orchids climb up through the lush tropical trees. We ate tropical fruits we had never seen and rarely heard of before, *mamonees,* breadfruit, paw-paw, *plantanos*. Costa Rica was beautiful, peaceful, and prosperous. With no armed forces to drain the economy, a large portion of the national budget could be spent on health and education. The climate was ghastly hot and humid near the coast, but we needed sweaters in San José, the charming capital city lying 7000 feet above the sea, which we visited three times.

We watched a constant parade of boats on the narrow estuary of Puntarenas —canoes, small freighters, shrimp trawlers, and, occasionally yachts. But when a 100-foot, three-masted Baltic trader sailed around the point, following a local trawler, we stopped working to stare, wondering where it could possibly moor. The Baltic trader came to rest in the middle of the estuary and put one anchor down. "I wonder if he noticed that everyone else is putting out two anchors?" Larry asked me.

The tide changed while the customs officers were still on board the trader. In less than a minute she turned with the outgoing flow and hit a small steel coaster. Her bowsprit hung up on the coaster's rigging and snapped off. For two hours, men worked to free the two boats, with more screaming and accusations than physical labor. The trader limped out of the estuary before dusk with a tangle of rigging where her bowsprit had been.

For two months, we heard rumors about the trader. Then one of the owners of the shrimp plant told us her whole sad story. The trader had been bought in Europe by an American who had searched for the "biggest boat for the least money." Obviously he had no idea of the cost of running a large sailing vessel. He persuaded several friends to come along with him for the voyage from Europe to California. By the time the trader reached Puntarenas, everything had gone wrong: The boat was leaking badly, the crew had jumped ship, and the owner had no money. After the anchoring trouble we had seen, he had powered over to Jesusita Island, 12 miles away, and anchored again. Because the local rum cost so much, he rigged up a still on board and started making bootleg whisky.

One day the Costa Rican who was acting as his salesman ashore went aboard the trader and the two men got into a fistfight over money. The fight became so fierce that in the heat of rage, the Costa Rican bit the sailor's thumb right off! In equal rage, the owner threw the Costa Rican overboard and went below to nurse his now thumbless hand.

The Costa Rican swam ashore and went home for his rifle. He returned with it and sat on shore, less than a 100 yards from the ship, shooting at her waterline. The trader was already leaking badly. The bilge pump was on deck, and every time the owner came up to pump, the Costa Rican shot at him, and he had to duck below. He couldn't start the pump, he couldn't lift his anchor, so within 24 hours the Baltic trader sank, and the owner swam to the opposite shore. At low tide one could still see the trader's three masts sticking up between Jesusita and Little Jesusita Islands.

When we had completed our jobs, hauled and painted *Seraffyn,* and restocked the food lockers, we got ready to leave again. Amazingly, six months had slipped by since the day we had arrived.

We sailed for Panama early in November 1970. By nightfall of the first day out, we had cleared the Gulf of Nicoya. We arranged our watches, Larry taking the first one. I came on deck, when Larry called me near midnight, and found a lovely night. It was warm; I wore only a light sweater and a pair of shorts. The velvet black sky twinkled with stars. A light breeze kept us murmuring along at about three knots, close-hauled. Cabo Blanco, six miles off and abaft our starboard beam, flashed its light twice every 10 seconds. I leaned back against the boom gallows and contentedly listened to the sounds Larry made below as he climbed into his bunk.

About an hour later I heard a strange sound. At first I thought it was a lone porpoise coming alongside to look us over. At regular intervals I heard it blow, coming closer and closer from astern.

Suddenly the moonlight glistened on an enormous black whale, just 20 feet from our quarter. *Seraffyn* is 24 feet long and the whale looked at least twice that. I ran to the companionway. "Larry, come up quickly," I whispered urgently. He came up seconds later, rubbing his eyes. "My watch already?" he muttered.

"No, Larry, there's a whale, and he's awfully close."

"Why did you wake me up for something as silly as—Oh, my God!" Larry stared in awe as the vast expanse of black flesh arched out of the water not 10 feet from our cockpit, and then slid below the surface again.

"Lin, turn on the radio, real loud," Larry whispered. "Maybe the noise will drive him away."

I turned on the radio; we stamped on the deck and shouted; we blew the fog horn. But regularly, every two minutes, the whale surfaced beside us and saluted us with the overwhelming odor of his foul breath.

"Let's come about," Larry said, disconnecting the windvane. "Maybe he'll just keep going."

We put *Seraffyn* on the other tack. I steered as Larry watched. The sound of the whale's blowing slowly receded, and we sighed with relief. He had merely been headed south and wasn't interested in us at all. Larry put *Seraffyn* back on course, engaged Helmer again, turned to me and said, "I'm for a stiff drink, and then, if you don't mind, I'll take the rest of my off-watch."

By the next morning, a northwesterly gale had developed that shoved us on our way for three days. We followed the sailing directions in *Ocean Passages for the World* and kept well off Cabo Mala ("Cape Bad"). The Humboldt Current sweeps north along the eastern side of the Gulf of Panama and shoots out seaward on the western side. We laid our course directly for Colombia, to take advantage of the current as it runs between the Perlas Islands and the mainland, toward Balboa.

One evening fifty miles off Punta Mala we were just finishing dinner and Helmer was steering when we hit something, hard. We rushed on deck just in time to see a huge sea turtle shaking its head in our wake. Then, during our late-night watch, we hit something else. It wasn't a turtle. A huge log rolled under the length of our keel, sending showers of phosphorescence in our wake. At such moments we really appreciated *Seraffyn's* 1⅛" planking and long keel. Spring tides had scoured the shores, and whole trees were floating in the storm-tossed waters. We kept a careful watch for three hours, until we cleared the edge of this tidal-flotsam line.

We sighted the Perlas Islands in clearing weather on our fifth day out, and the tall light of San José Island, (maintained by the Canal Zone authorities) greeted us as we reached in at dusk. That was the last navigation light we saw that night. Five others, maintained by Panama, were shown on the recently issued, large-scale chart, but were either not there or not lighted. Larry fixed our position from the San José light as we reached past it, confident that we would soon pick up the next light. He calculated the current and allowed for the spring tides with their 18-foot rise and fall.

Within an hour we realized that the other lights just weren't working. To leeward lay a sloping muddy shore, to windward, low rocky islands. Larry worked out our speed as best he could from our limited information and steered slightly to the leeward side of the channel. The seas were fairly smooth, since islands lay less than three miles to windward of us. We set our full mainsail during the pitch-black night, longing to spot just one light to guide us, as we listened anxiously for sounds of surf. It was tense sailing.

Six hours after we had entered this frightening channel, we felt the ocean swell as we passed beyond the tip of the Perlas Islands. We beat into clear water, exhausted from the tension, and hove-to. A steady parade of ships' lights marched past us toward the Panama Canal, and we stood watches until dawn. When the sun rose Taboga Island appeared dead downwind. Finally knowing our position, Larry calculated that our speed must have been nine knots over the ground (in the darkness!) as we were shoved through the Perlas channel by current, tide and wind.

We raised sail to run the six miles to Taboga. With main and staysail wing-and-wing, our log recorded six knots. But the island just didn't get any closer! Then two hours later the tide changed, and the island shot toward us. In less than an hour we were anchored off the pier of the peaceful resort. Six miles away lay the hustle and bustle of Panama City and the Canal.

Pho. 7-4. This lovely view was off the porch of the deserted hotel in the Perlas Islands, where we had a shower and lunch.

When no customs launch approached us, we packed our shower kits and clean clothes, and rowed ashore.

A man lounging near the pier said, "There are no Police, no customs, and no excitement on this island."

We paid for a shower at the deserted hotel, and ate lunch in its deserted dining room. Then we phoned the Balboa Yacht Club in the Canal Zone, and were assured a mooring would be available for us the next day.

We relaxed on board that evening, watching with interest the American schooner, *Heritage,* sail in. The husband and wife and their four daughters had left Puntarenas four months before, saying casually, "We'll see you in the Canal." They had cruised the Costa Rican coast and through the islands and there they were, as if it had been planned to the minute. Yet we were not really surprised by this as we were constantly meeting old friends in new ports. It's almost a "floating community," with just as much gossip and even more willingness to lend a helping hand as you'd find in any small town back home.

In the morning both boats raised anchors at the same time and sailed together to the outer buoy of the Canal Zone, where we had been told to wait for our clearance. Two hours later the customs boat arrived. We signed a two-inch pile of papers and got rid of the customs and health officials just in time to catch the last of the flood tide. *Heritage* powered up the Canal, and we short-tacked the two miles, reaching the anchorage just at dusk.

The yacht club launch came out as we approached. and the launch man pointed out our mooring. The tide had started to ebb, so we made one pass to see how much way we'd have on as we approached the buoy. On our second pass, Larry let the jib sheet fly, walked forward, and leaned over the lifelines to grab the mooring pennant as it trailed in the water.

Suddenly, where Larry had been, I saw a pair of feet, wrong way up. Then four fingers grasped the bulwarks and a drenched, sputtering Larry reached over the rail and handed me the mooring line.

"Slim," the fat club launchman, roared with delight as Larry climbed back aboard. "Welcome to the Balboa Yacht Club!" Slim shouted."I'll bet you're ready to come ashore for a shower."

Twenty cruising friends waiting on the yacht club veranda gave Larry a round of applause as we stepped out of Slim's launch.

8

Panama and the Canal

CRUISING IN FOREIGN WATERS introduces you to all sorts of unusual foods. We had grown to love the "fruits" of the sea—lobster, clams, shrimp, fish. Costa Rican rice dishes and Mexican beans had become favorites in our menus. But when we reached the Panama Canal Zone, after 20 months away from home, we happened to stroll past the American commissary, and the sight of full-breasted turkeys lying in rows made us drool. Only employees of the Canal Zone are allowed to shop at the commissary, but a yacht club member asked us if there was anything we especially wanted. I gave him a complete Thanksgiving shipping list, which he bought for us. On November 24, 1970, we set sail for the Perlas Islands. As soon as we'd fallen off on a beam reach, I put our eight-pound stuffed bird in the oven to roast.

We anchored behind Contadora Island six hours after leaving Balboa, and then sat in the cockpit gorging ourselves on turkey, dressing, gravy, cranberry sauce, candied yams, fresh salad, and mince pie and reminiscing about our cruise and planning future voyages. No Thanksgiving dinner ever had a more apprecia- tive pair of diners.

I wish we had spent a month in the Perlas islands instead of a week. These gemlike islands are only sparsely settled; the inhabitants are descendants of slaves who escaped from Panama when the famous pirate Morgan destroyed the city. One of their more profitable occupations is growing marijuana, and the fine quality of Panama Red has won it an international reputation. But what unwary buyers do not know is that the natives of the islands make more money by informing authorities in Panama of each purchase than they do by selling the stuff. As a result, the Panamanian government confiscates several vessels each year, and levies heavy fines. We were told that's how the president of Panama became the proud owner of an 85-foot luxury yacht named the *Alice D.*

An average tidal range of 14 feet makes beachcombing in the Perlas espe- cially productive. Some friends from the Canal Zone arrived one evening after we had finished our dinner and showed us where we could fill a bucket with Peru- vian conch by snorkeling in only three feet of water.

When we returned to Panama, we arranged to have our radio and chronometer overhauled, and then set off with John Gough, an engineer, and his girlfriend, Cindy, a teacher, both from the Canal. The four of us sailed over to Taboga Island and had just anchored when it started to rain—the standard weather event at 1430 every day. But the rain didn't stop at 1500 as it was supposed to. Cindy and I got tired of listening to the men's sea stories, so we dressed in foul-weather gear, got into the dinghy, and rowed over to a refrigerated freighter at anchor nearby, with a tuna clipper cuddled on each side.

"Do you give tours?" we shouted, trying to make ourselves heard over the roaring generators and the driving rain.

"For two young ladies, any time!" the answer came back from the deck. We tied up the dinghy and climbed aboard, and a crewman escorted us to the captain's quarters.

"We've almost finished off-loading the last two months' catch," the captain told us, "so we'll be leaving soon, but the clipper on the other side is staying. I'll call and have one of her men take you on a tour of both ships. We'll move your dinghy for you."

A crewman arrived from the other ship and took us on a tour that led from the galley to the engine room, past the six 2000-gallon brine vats that freeze the tuna solid, and piles of 100-pound frozen tuna, and then through the laundries and libraries. Then we were led to the captain's quarters to meet Captain Duda.

"I've just opened a bottle of Russian champagne. Come in, join me," said Duda, the young, tanned and bearded captain.

"We'd love to, but John and Larry will be starting to worry about us," we said

"Yes, we thought so, and I sent one of my crewmen to bring them over in our launch," Duda told us.

We had quite a party that evening. Duda, a Yugoslav, was both captain and part-owner of the Chilean tuna clipper. He invited his mate and engineer to join us. The seven of us sipped the captain's supply of wines and liquors and demolished a five-course dinner, washed down with four bottles of champagne.

We were interrupted when a crewman entered to tell the captain that no one had thought to look overboard before they hosed down the desks. As a consequence, both our dinghy and the clipper's launch, tied directly under the scuppers, had been sunk! This news was a little startling, but soon both boats were lifted on deck, bailed dry, and scrubbed. We thanked the captain for everything, said goodnight and rowed off with a bottle of Chilean vodka, and a five-liter wicker-covered bottle of Chilean red wine. *Rinky* radiated a distinct odor of tuna as we rowed home.

We sailed back to the Panama Canal Yacht Club the next day. On our mooring, the four of us lay watching ships from many countries pass in transit only 100 yards away. Suddenly we saw a vessel swing out of the marked channel—a big blue Chilean tuna clipper heading right through the yacht anchorage. It was Captain Duda. "Have a good voyage!" he yelled to us, with a wave.

The Canal pilot was gesticulating furiously at Duda, but we couldn't catch his words. Just as well, perhaps.

The longer we were at the Canal, the more long-distance cruisers we met, and almost all of them agreed that most of the articles in yachting magazines about the "perfect cruising boat" seemed to be written by people who had never gone cruising.

"If we conduct a survey of all the long-distance cruisers we meet from now on, maybe we could tell people the real facts," I said to Larry. The next day we worked out a two-page questionnaire, and before we began our Canal transit, we had interviewed 15 cruising couples who had been cruising from six months to 21 years.

How do you get a 24-foot sailboat without an engine through the Panama

Canal? Not easily, we discovered.

We had made several friends at the yacht club, and one of them offered us the use of an outboard motor. Another loaned us an extra fuel tank. Larry built a temporary bracket of 2x4's and plywood, padded with carpet, to mount across our boomkin. Then we went confidently to the Canal offices to arrange our transit.

"Can you do a minimun of five knots?" asked the official.

"We think we can," we replied.

"Can you provide meals for the pilot?" he asked.

"Easily!" we said.

So we paid our $4.83 fee (based on our tonnage) for transit and pilot, and then signed seven more papers including a release that said the Canal Company was "not responsible for any cleats damaged by less than 15 tons pressure."

Two days later Larry went to fetch Wade Swaboda and Jim Coberly, the two friends who had offered to come along and handle lines for us. I baked fresh

Pho. 8-1. Lin reading in the "honeymoon" bunk set up in the cockpit.

doughnuts, then lay on deck sunbathing. At 0900, I watched as a pilot boat stopped alongside a 60-foot yacht at the far end of the mooring area. A minute later it approached a 45-foot ketch—a bit closer to us. Then it hailed a 35-foot yawl to windward of us.

"No, we're not the *Seraffyn,* she's the tiny cutter with the bowsprit, moored over there," said the owner of the yawl, pointing at us.

The pilot gave a sad nod and said, "I would draw the smallest yacht in the fleet."

He didn't realize his voice would carry to us, and I was glad I'd bought a prime rib roast to make his journey with us a bit less painful.

As soon as George, our pilot, boarded he did the same thing Larry had seen each pilot do on his four previous transits of the Canal. George went forward and checked our ground tackle, asking how much chain we had and how quickly we could release it. Our crew was soon on board, so we started the outboard and cast off the mooring.

George radioed to the canal control: "*Seraffyn* now approaching locks."

The outboard coughed, sputtered and quit.

"Hoist the mainsail," said Larry.

"*Seraffyn,* engineless. Have approaching ships keep clear," George radioed.

"Let me at it," growled Wade, an M.I.T. graduate with a doctorate in mechanical engineering. Within five minutes Wade had solved the problem. Who would have guessed that a 9.8 HP outboard motor would have its own fuel pump? We had pressurized the fuel tank and caused an air lock.

Underway again we entered the first lock. Four men tossed us monkey fists with light messenger lines attached. We sent up our 100-foot lines, and positioned *Seraffyn* snugly in the center of the lock, under the towering stern of a grey freighter.

Since each of our lines was led through a closed fairlead or snatch block and on to a winch, we had no trouble taking in the slack and keeping *Seraffyn* in position as the first of 50 million gallons of water rushed into the lock. We rose 28 feet in 15 minutes.

As we reached the level of the Pedro Miguel Yacht Club, Larry pulled the outboard starter and "it" roared into life. We started moving. I served the doughnuts and coffee. We watched a salvage tug approach, shoving a white creamy wake before it. As we cut across the tug's wake, a coffee mug toppled over as the bowsprit dipped. "It" was drowned out when the boomkin dipped under.

"Hoist the mainsail," Larry said.

"*Seraffyn* engineless. Approaching ships keep clear," radioed George.

"Let me at it," said Wade again.

With spark plugs dried, "it" roared to life again and we moved into the second lock which took us up to the level of Gatun Lake.

Just beyond our last upward lock, sunk in 42 feet of water, lay a Chinese-owned Victory ship that had caused monumental headaches. A week earlier, an error on the ship's bridge had caused it to sheer off and hit the Canal side where rocks had ripped a 200-foot-long slash in its side. The ship sank immediately. Its watersoaked cargo of rice and cotton had rotted, creating a revolting stench. Ship movement was restricted to one-way traffic while two salvage vessels tried to control the oil leakage from the freighter.

We later learned that all of the salvage efforts had failed to raise the ship, so a huge hole was dredged in the shore alongside it and the ship was rolled into the hole and buried. Cost: eight million dollars!

We powered past wonderful waterfalls, and George kept us amused with stories about the Canal, ships and piloting. He described the simple working of the locks and their maintenance. We were amazed to find that all of the Canal machinery is operated by hydraulic power. Valves are opened and closed by water pressure. The only motors used are the 25 HP electric ones that open and close the lock gates. No reinforcing steel was used in the construction, only solid concrete, poured in one massive year-long pour for each set of locks.

Once clear of the Gaillard Cut, we had a headwind to contend with and even with "it" doing its best, our speed dropped to 2½ knots. It became obvious we wouldn't get through by dark so I started dinner, and Larry and George decided to take a short cut.

Gatun Lake was created by building a huge dam to contain the Chagres River. Tropical valleys full of lush foliage were flooded. After 55 years, the mahogany trees not only haven't drowned and rotted away, but are still growing, so navigation is restricted to "swept" channels. The main channel is cleared to a depth of 42 feet. The Banana Cut is the shorter route, used by workboats and local vessels and

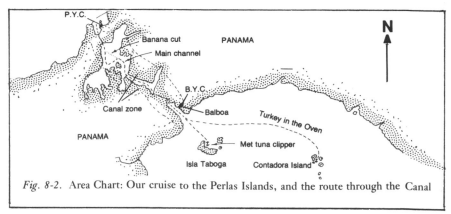

Fig. 8-2. Area Chart: Our cruise to the Perlas Islands, and the route through the Canal

provides a 10-foot depth.

It saves two miles and is marked by buoys. Larry had been through the Banana Cut three times on yachts during daylight, but George had never tried it because this was his first transit on a yacht. Larry takes complete blame for what happened when George agreed to try the short cut, and George only agreed because we were already tied for the record of the slowest canal transit—over ten hours to reach the halfway point.

We headed into the cut at dusk. The unlit buoys went sweeping by us every five minutes or so—exactly as the as the chart showed. Then we noticed a gap.

"Would someone go on the foredeck with a light and watch for the next buoy?" George asked. We slowed the outboard and crept along, peering intently into the total blackness. (It was only later we learned the buoys had been removed a week before for maintenance.)

"Is that our buoy?" George asked as the light picked up a bit of white.

"George, it's not a buoy, it's a stump!" Larry said.

George immediately turned us on to a reciprocal compass course. Then after a few minutes of studying his Canal chart intently, he said. "A course of forty-eight degrees should take us between two small islands and into the big-ship channel. We'll go slowly and the Canal Company will accept responsibility for repairing any damage if we should hit a stump."

We crept along and soon spotted three islands. As we passed between the two smaller ones, George said, "Someone go up on the foredeck. There should be a white buoy just ahead of us."

Four of us went forward; George remained at the helm. The combined weight of three men and myself lifted the stern of the boat until the outboard prop came out of the water. There being no water resistance "it" revved up with a great roar as it leaped out of the water. We heard a ripping sound as it twisted the plywood and 2x4 bracket. (Fortunately, we had been extra careful as it was a borrowed outboard, and had attached a safety line to the taffrail.) Larry discovered the bracket wasn't broken completely when he inspected the damage. So he used a piece of bronze plate and two C-clamps to reinforce the bracket. We got under way again, George intently studying his chart, one man on the foredeck as lookout, and me below making more hot coffee.

We passed two more small islands and suddenly we could see the flashing lights marking the large-ship anchorage at the head of the Gatun locks. George looked wonderfully relieved and said, "Just head for the second white flasher."

We revved up the outboard and relaxed, relieved that we had escaped the mortification of running a sailboat into the top of a tree. "What's the number of that light?" George asked as we glided by.

"Number eighteen," Wade answered.

"By God, it's the wrong one!" our white-faced pilot exclaimed. "We just went between the wrong islands and across the stump patch. We're lucky the water level is high today."

As we finally locked down, George explained that in his two years as a Canal pilot he had never before been on a ship smaller than 200 tons. He'd served as ship's master for six years before going to work for the Canal. "My day with you has really been an experience," he told us. He spoke too soon, but he didn't know that.

A northeasterly headwind was blowing about Force 6 or 7. We motored out of the last downward lock and met a three-foot chop. "It" roared at the top of its lungs but made little headway.

"If you give me permission, I'll sail her out of the Canal," Larry said. "Can you?" George asked dubiously. "Well, go ahead, we're blocking traffic either way."

So, under staysail and single-reefed main we short tacked. For the first time that day, *Seraffyn* seemed alive. We beat under the sterns of some ships and around the bows of others, and George had his radio always in hand. In the night, the ships loomed above us. We could tell each time a ship locked down, because we got a flush of current that shoved us to windward. Within an hour we were into the huge bay of Cristobal-Colon.

George radioed for a pilot boat to pick him up. The boat arrived and with some neat boat handling took George and Jim off while we lay hove-to in the chop.

As they backed off, George yelled to us, "You may not have a head, but sure do eat well!"

Wade sailed with us to the Panama National Yacht Club, and we had a good night's sleep after laughing over the events of the year's slowest Canal transit.

"See you in the week when I bring my boat through," Wade said as we walked him to the train depot the next day. "I'm glad I've got an engine—it will make things much simpler."

We spent a week puttering on the boat, returning the borrowed outboard motor, and catching up on our correspondence. On Saturday, we watched Wade and Connie sail in.

"Guess who we drew as pilot?" Wade yelled.

"George!" we said in unison.

"Yep, and he spent the whole trip telling our extra crew about the first trip he ever made on a sailboat," Wade said.

"Was your transit a little less exciting?" we asked.

"It was until the motor broke down and we had to anchor in the Gaillard Cut," Wade said, laughing.

"Poor George," we both said.

"I'm not so sure," said Wade. "He's thinking of getting a small boat and learning to sail."

9

Wind and Worms

IT'S JUST AMAZING what a difference an isthmus can make. From Balboa on the Pacific through the Canal to Colon on the Caribbean is only 50 miles. Yet the climates are completely different. In Balboa we had become used to morning calms, afternoon onshore breezes, a regular downpour at 1500, and hot, humid, calm evenings.

Now as we lay at the Panama Yacht Club in Colon, Caribbean trade winds blew at 25 to 30 knots, 24 hours a day. Eric and Susan Hiscock, whom we had met at San Diego, had warned us about the strong prevailing winds. In fact, Eric had said, "I spent more time running under bare poles in the Caribbean than anywhere else in the world."

So Larry set to work sewing a third row of reef points into our mainsail. We also decided to scrape our teak decks and do some other minor chores before we left the Canal Zone, where it was easy to find supplies.

We remained at a yacht club dock for three weeks, listening to the wind whistling in our rigging day and night. Every time I washed clothes, I had to use four or five clothes pins to hold each item. Anything we put on the dock had to be weighted down. Every day I looked forward to going away from the boat and into the center of town where I wouldn't have to listen to the moaning wind.

Some afternoons we walked to the Canal Zone Yacht Club to see if any new boats had come in, to check for mail and to sample the fine oysters. Almost every yacht that arrived from the Caribbean had hair-raising tales to tell. We saw even more broken spreaders, torn sails, and exhausted people than we had before crossing the Gulf of Tehuantepec. By the third week, I was a nervous wreck, snapping at Larry when he teased me, and lying awake at night. One evening it all came to a head. We started a real row, a rare thing in our little private world.

Larry finally said, "Lin, what's bothering you? You're not the fun-loving person you were. Do you want to quit sailing? You can fly up to the States if you want to."

I considered his words seriously, and gradually realized I was spooked by the wind, by the "sea stories" we'd been hearing, and by the prospect of beating to windward day-in, day-out.

Larry didn't laugh at me as I explained this, but reassured me. "You know *Seraffyn* can take it," he said. You helped build her. We've been in stronger winds than these. Look at the boats that have broken gear over at the yacht club. Most of them are big old charter boats, with rotten gear, that the owners are trying to sell because they can't earn enough to take care of them. Do you think I'd take you or

88

Seraffyn into a dangerous situation?''

We studied the charts for the Spanish Main and saw a string of anchorages not more than 30 miles apart, and Larry promised we would run back to Panama if it proved too rough. That seemed reasonable to me, and I felt better.

After the third week we were ready to start the 18-mile beat Northeast to Portobelo. Wade and Connie planned to meet us there. They wanted Larry to survey their boat because they were worried about teredo damage along their waterline.

We sailed to the Canal Zone Yacht Club to load duty-free stores. Opposite this club is a large fuel-bunkering dock, and although we took the precaution of covering our fenders with plastic bags, we still ended up with so much crude oil on our lines and hull we used a gallon of kerosene cleaning up—and we were only there four hours. If you draw five feet or less, you should go to the Panamanian Club (no oil there) where you can swim off your boat in clear water.

We got underway about 1400 one day early in February 1971, and beat into the huge swell outside the breakwater. About three miles out, the swell spread and the sailing became fun. By 1730, we were six miles from Portobelo and dark was falling. We didn't want to try and clear Salmenella reef at night with no navigation lights to guide us, so we ran back to Colon. In less that two and a half hours we were anchored behind the breakwater enjoying a hot dinner.

The following morning was squally and grey so we loafed in our big bunk, and then held the last half of our cribbage tournament. Larry cheats; I haven't figured out how yet, but he must, to win so consistently.

On the third day, we beat out of the entrance early in the day and, looking back, saw Connie and Wade raising sail on *Samburan*. That was a challenge. I can't help being competitive, and became so engrossed in helping Larry get every last bit of speed out of *Seraffyn* that I didn't even notice the 15 to 20 foot seas, and the Force 6 to 7 winds.

Six hours later we worked past the Salmenella reef into the history-filled bay of Portobelo. Wade and Connie had beaten us by about 20 minutes (with their 11-foot-longer boat), and as soon as our anchor was down we joined them for an exploring expedition ashore.

From the guardian reef, where Sir Francis Drake was buried in a lead casket, to the round fortress built by Columbus, we were completely surrounded by history. Here was the meeting place of explorers, pirates, exploiters—a bay which had held the ships of men such as Drake, Morgan and Balboa. From our foredeck, we could count six fortresses plus the ruins of a complete city. Now, only a small native village nestles among the ruins of an old treasure house on the western shore. A highway is under constrtuction from Colon, so probably the quiet of the beautiful port will soon be shattered by tourism.

On our second day in Portobelo, we packed a lunch, and the four of us climbed through the thick jungle toward the highest fortress. Halfway up we reached a dam built around 1600 to feed water to the middle and lower forts. The dam was completely covered with growth but still strong and full of fresh water.

We swam off the boat three or four times a day, but the first time we tried snorkeling, a launch came from the village and an official warned us: ''No skindiving allowed. All historical relics must be left undisturbed as the property of the Republic of Panama.'' So our masks and snorkels remained on board.

Although spring tides in Portobelo only range 18 to 20 inches, Larry thought it might be enough to allow him to survey *Samburan's* waterline. One day about an

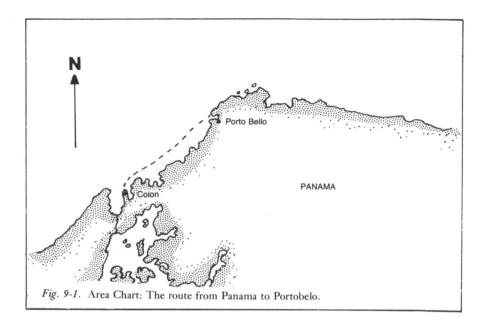

Fig. 9-1. Area Chart: The route from Panama to Portobelo.

hour after high tide, Wade set an anchor out astern, then powered *Samburan* ashore, slacking the stern anchor line until she grounded firmly on a patch of hard sand. As the tide slowly fell, he and Larry set two anchors from 300 foot lines that lead through *Samburan's* masthead blocks, and dug them into the sand directly off her beam to both sides. When the tide went down, she stood securely on her keel on the sloping beach, drying out to well below the turn of her bilges.

As Larry surveyed *Samburan's* exposed waterline, Wade's worst fears were confirmed. Worms had eaten into more than 16 planks, plus her stem and sternpost, in a four-inch-wide band running completely around the hull. Larry's knife went right through the mahogany planks in several places. You could see frames through others, as the soft wood left by the worm holes pulled away easily. Using a blow torch, Wade and Larry heated the wormy areas until they steamed, trying to kill any worms still in the wood. Then they mixed up underwater putty and filled the gaps: it took a quart of the two-part mixture. Finally they scraped off all of the loose enamel on the waterline, the cause of the problem, and applied a coat of antifouling paint.

After we had winched *Samburan* afloat on the next high tide, Larry and I discussed the cause of *Samburan's* problem. When Wade had first loaded her for cruising, she floated below her antifouling waterline and quickly grew weed on her enamel boottop. So, on the next haulout, Wade simply applied the antifouling paint over his boottop paint. Three or four months later, he had noticed bubbles along his waterline, but didn't think the condition important. By the time we met him in Panama, it was too late—the damage had been done. The constant immersion in salt water had caused the enamel under the antifouling paint to lift off the planking, allowing the worms to go behind the bubbles and into the planks. If he had scraped the boottop down to bare wood before raising his waterline by applying the antifouling paint, it would have soaked into the wood and bonded well.

Pho. 9-2. At Portobelo we walked out of the city to see the fortress.

We certainly were glad we had put creosote on *Seraffyn's* bottom when she was built. As we rowed back home, we stared at our waterline level. "Next time we haul, I'd like to scrape down our boottop and put creosote on that, too," Larry said. Even though we were floating a half inch above our waterline, another 300-400 pounds of stores, plus our weight, plus our dinghy, would make it close.

The day before we sailed from Portobelo, Larry and I rowed across the bay to walk through the ruins of the old city. The walls of the treasury still stood, and so did the wharves and granaries built almost 400 years before. The round fortress built by Columbus' men in 1493 had weathered the centuries but now, instead of deep water, river silt surrounded its piers. We strolled out of the city toward the fortress at the harbor's western entrance, and sat watching the surf break on the Salmemella reef. A tiny girl approached us shyly, holding out a string of seeds. She looked about six years old. "Will you buy these?" she asked in Spanish.

We looked at her beads, a single string of grey and blue seeds from some tropical plant strung on cotton line.

"I made them myself and they will cost you only five cents. They will bring you good luck," she said with a wide-eyed smile. We bought them and watched her running back toward her village clutching her nickel.

Back aboard I draped the beads three times around our barometer to get them out of the way. Twice during the next four years, I took the beads off the barometer and tossed them in a locker, and both times we had bad fortune, getting into trouble with *Seraffyn*. We're not superstitious, but the beads are draped around the barometer permanently as I write.

We set sail early the next day alongside *Samburan*. At the entrance to Portobelo, Wade and Connie turned to run toward the Canal Zone, and we prepared to beat northward toward Isla Grande where we heard there was a chance to practice chasing lobster again.

10

Across the Spanish Main

AS WE WORKED TOWARD ISLA GRANDE, I was amazed (and pleased) to find that Larry was right about beating across the Caribbean. We had sailed in heavier winds. If we kept just the right amount of canvas on *Seraffyn,* she sailed beautifully. If we didn't pinch her too much, she'd make 90° to 95° tacks, and foot along well. I had followed Larry's suggestion and prepared lunch before we sailed, so when we got hungry I only had to duck below to get the sandwiches and thermos of lemonade.

During the 20-mile beat, Larry tuned up *Seraffyn's* rigging. In the Pacific most of our sailing had been off the wind, so the rigging had been left slack to ease any strain on our hull and get better downwind performance. Now Larry tightened the shrouds until our mast stood perfectly straight. When the shroud tension was adjusted to Larry's satisfaction, the shrouds on the leeward side were slightly loose and those on the windward side were taut. The lower shrouds were left looser than the cap shrouds because they had less length to stretch. When Larry was finished, I stood by the mast on each tack and, sure enough, it stood straight as an arrow in the 30-knot winds.

We sighted Isla Grande easily—above its cluster of coconut palms stood a magnificient lighthouse. We rounded the eastern end of the island, surfing on 15-foot swells, then reached into a small bay on Isla Grande's southern side. A small group of huts hummed with evening activity as we lowered our anchor into the clear water.

When we rowed ashore after dinner, the villagers excitedly told us: "Tomorrow or the next day is a wonderful day."

"What happens tomorrow or the next day?" Larry asked.

"That's when the lighthouse tender comes. You do not want to miss that," an old black lady said as she cleaned fish. The youngsters playing in the sand near her nodded in wide-eyed agreement.

We spent the next day strolling along the shore and chatting with two natives who were hollowing out a mahogany log for a canoe. Their only tools were a one-inch auger, two cupped adz's with eight-inch handles, and a smoothing plane. They burned out most of the wood, then drilled holes along the bottom. By pushing a twig through the holes as a "feeler gauge" they were able to remove wood until the canoe was the thickness they wanted. Finally, the holes were plugged, and the outside of the canoe was smoothed and tarred.

"If you want to see a beautiful, really large canoe," the workmen suggested, "row across to the mainland to that little house." We went later and were rewarded by the sight of a 22-foot-long canoe with fine ends and a beautiful shape. Its builder, who walked over as we arrived, said, "This is for the boys' club in Panama. They will use it for their paddling race through the Canal."

We asked how much it cost. "I have to charge a high price because the tree for this canoe was two miles inland and five miles away from here. When the lighthouse tender comes, if he likes it, he will pay me forty dollars," the builder said. It had taken two months to carve the canoe.

On the third day at Isla Grande we rowed ashore and asked one of the villagers, "Where is the lighthouse tender?"

"Tomorrow or the next day, he'll be here. Don't leave yet. You'll be sorry if you miss him."

We noticed a sail on the other side of the island and walked across to watch it pass, a big event; we had seen only two yachts besides *Samburan* since leaving Panama.

The next day at noon, Wade and Connie sailed in and anchored just inshore of us—the two boats at anchor completely filling the cove. As we lounged on *Samburan* having a drink and playing with their cat, Tica, Wade told us he would have had to wait two months to haul out and replace his worm-riddled planking in Panama or Colon, so they had decided to sail to see if the work could be done in Cartagena.

Then we chanted the phrase we heard on each visit to the village: "Tomorrow or the next day the lighthouse tender comes. You won't want to miss that!"

For five days now we had been hearing about the lighthouse tender. The skindiving had been fair, but not great; or, to put it another way, we could catch all the fish we wanted, but we never saw a lobster. Larry was ready to move on.

"Let's wait just one more day," I said. "I'm so curious about this lighthouse-tender business, I'd hate to miss it. He must be a super person to cause all this excitement."

At mid-afternoon we looked ashore and noticed the village youngsters run-

Pho. 10-1 & 10-2. The 22-foot canoe was a beautiful piece of native craftsmanship. Destined for a boy's club in Panama, it cost forty dollars!

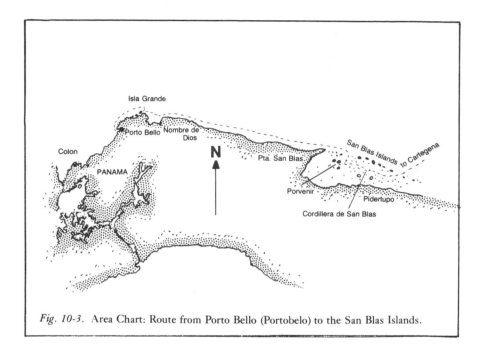

Fig. 10-3. Area Chart: Route from Porto Bello (Portobelo) to the San Blas Islands.

ning along the beach toward their canoes. Then we heard the thump of big engines astern and turned in amazement to see a vintage 300-foot-long ship heave into view in the narrow channel.

"Where can anything that big anchor?" Larry asked.

The answer came as the lighthouse tender *Atlas* dropped her huge stern hook overboard and powered straight along the channel, running out almost 2000 feet of cable. Then she slowed, dropped her bow anchor and, with her stern windlass, winched herself back until she settled snugly between the two anchors in 30 fathoms of water. The engines had barely stopped before 20 canoes full of youngsters and not-so-youngsters converged on the lowered boarding ladder of *Atlas*.

Wade and Connie rowed over and asked, "What do you think of that?"

We weren't sure what to think as we watched a canoe-load of kids sailing shoreward eating ice cream cones.

Connie and I couldn't stand the idea of being left out of the fun, and we couldn't persuade Wade and Larry to row over, so we went alone in two dinghies. As we approached *Atlas,* someone on board shouted, "We wondered when you'd come. Do you prefer martinis or scotch-on-the-rocks?"

We handed our dinghy painters to the crewman who met us and climbed up to the deck. What a sight! Two 12-foot trestle tables had been set up, each sagging under a load of ice cream, candy and cookies. Over 30 chattering native children were roughhousing with the crew and trying to eat a year's supply of treats all at once. More natives kept arriving, each one greeting the crew and captain of *Atlas* like long-lost friends.

After eating our share of ice cream, we were given cool drinks and climbed one deck higher to loaf in lounge chairs under the bridge deck awning, and chat with the captain and first mate. I think only then did Connie and I remember our men stranded on *Seraffyn*.

"It's too late for dinner and too hectic here, anyway." Captain Anderson said, "so I'll send a boat to pick you up for breakfast tomorrow at oh-nine-hundred. Meanwhile, do you have ice boxes on your boats?"

We both answered yes, and I asked why.

"You'll find out," the captain said, leading us down to the lower deck. There was a 50-pound block of ice in the bottom of each dinghy with a package of pork chops sitting on top. What a treat—there was no fresh meat on Isla Grande! We called our thanks.

Captain Anderson waved and yelled, "Until tomorrow," as he was surrounded by a new wave of villagers.

What a bawling out I got when I rowed proudly home with my prize of ice and meat!

"Look at the tar and oil on that dinghy," Larry said angrily. "Why didn't you tie it off the leeward end of the ship where it wouldn't have rubbed against her oily side?"

For the first time I noticed the heavy oil all around *Rinky's* dacron fender. "But I didn't secure her, a crewman did," I protested. "Damn it, Lin, you must be responsible for your own boat. You can't expect anyone else to take care of your equipment!" Larry thrust a bottle of kerosene and a rag at me and pointed shoreward. "Don't come back till that dinghy looks like new," he said, scowling.

I was in tears as I rowed to the beach, not because Larry was wrong, but because I had been careless. In the carnival atmosphere on *Atlas* I'd never once thought about the dinghy.

An hour later I rowed back, drawn by *Seraffyn's* warmly glowing anchor lamp. Larry was on deck to greet me. He put his arms around me and said, "Sorry I got so furious, but I had to sit here for two hours watching the dink bash against the side of that rough, oily ship, and I got angrier by the minute. Considering how proud you were to own that dinghy when she was the only sailboat you had, I never expected you to be so careless."

At 0900 the next morning a motor launch came carefully alongside with Connie and Wade already on board. The bustle of activity was completely different as we boarded *Atlas*. A 10-ton crane on the foredeck was lowering two motor launches and several rowboats into the water, while men on the afterdeck lifted an endless stream of oil drums from the hold. Captain Anderson met us in the dining room where the steward handed us a menu.

"Order as much or as little as you want. The waffles were especially good this morning," Captain Anderson said. We read the menu:

Tomato Juice * Grapefruit * Fruit Cocktail
Oatmeal
Eggs * Pancakes * Waffles
Sausage * Bacon
Fried Potatoes
Corn Fritters * Toast
Coffee * Tea * Milk

Not surprisingly, breakfast took two hours, and Captain Anderson described the ship as we ate.

"*Atlas* was the last ship built completely by the Panama Canal Company before World War Two," he said. "She's all riveted and shoal draft, so she can lift and set buoys anywhere in the Canal. We come out to Isla Grande twice a year to refuel, repaint, and repair the lighthouse and its equipment. The ship has a huge freezer room, and the cook is given extra funds for this trip because we can't go home to dinner each night. We use the extra money to buy treats for the kids. Every crewman here must have a baby or two named after him. If you like, I'll show you around *Atlas,* and then the lighthouse keeper has invited you to join him for a tour ashore."

After touring the ship, we went ashore with a boatload of of diesel oil drums. The lighthouse tender told a surprising story as we climbed the staircase that was cut into solid rock, passing a hut where mechanics were overhauling the three generators.

"About four years ago," he said, "the authorities decided that from then on all lights under U.S. jurisdiction would have to be powered by electricity instead of acetylene gas. So, instead of employing a local man to change the gas bottle each week, we had to install three generators, to guard against breakdowns, and now every six months we have to come here and ferry twenty-thousand gallons of diesel oil in drums ashore, through the reef, and we still have to employ a native to pull the switch each night. With the acetylene, we could just shove the bottles off *Atlas* and tow them ashore throught the surf." He shook his head.

"Then, there's the color of the light. With acetylene this light used to burn pure white, and it was visible for thirty miles. The electric bulb burns yellow, and you're lucky if you can see the light twenty-two miles away."

We arrived at the base of the 100-foot-high tower, and watched as three teams of men on scaffolds painted from the top of the bolted steel lighthouse downward.

As we climbed the spiral steps inside the tower, the lighthouse tender showed us the grandfather-clock-type winder with its 100-foot-long weighted chain hanging down the middle of the staircase. "The authorities also decided," the lighthouse keeper continued, "that we had to replace the old lens rotator with an electric motor. This light has burned since 1893, when the French built it here to guide their supply ships into Panama. It never missed a night in all that time. First month we had this electric rotator it broke down, and the light was off all night. The local lighthouse keeper had to use the old wind-up rotator until we came to repair the motor."

The lens of the lighthouse was a beautiful thing. Hundreds of hand-cut, hand-polished prisms had been made and assembled in Paris. The lens weighed hundreds of pounds, but floated easily on a sealed mercury bearing. The original mercury was till doing the work, 80 years later.

We stared down from the top of the lighthouse to the surging ocean almost 400 feet directly below us. The lighthouse keeper related how a sailing ship had brought the prefabricated sections of the lighthouse from France. The ship was secured in position in the small bay below the cliff, with four anchors and a system of wires and blocks was rigged to the top of the island to move each lighthouse section directly from the ship to the construction site.

We spent our daylight hours aboard *Atlas* for the next three days, and Captain Anderson spent his evenings on *Seraffyn* recounting stories of his younger years aboard lumber schooners on the U.S. eastern seaboard. On the fourth day, we were invited for a farewell breakfast. As the chief fired up the main engine of *Atlas,* and the crew hauled the last launch on board, we climbed into our two dinghies to find another block of ice plus a bag of frozen strawberries and a can of whipping cream in each. We watched and waved as *Atlas* lifted her anchors and steamed out. Then Larry shouted across to Wade and Connie, "Think we'll be on our way, too."

An hour later we sailed out of the anchorage toward Nombre de Dios and Cartagena.

The San Blas Islands are scattered along the Panamanian Coast from Punta de Las Mulatas to the Colombian border. We had met no one who had spent much time among these islands and we were curious. It seemed that since there were no navigation lights in these reef-strewn waters, most cruising boats from the Caribbean bound for Panama, with fair winds behind them, passed them right by. We were interested in getting to Cartagena where we hoped to haul *Seraffyn* and repaint her bottom and waterline.

So, as we approached Porvenir, the first island of the group, in the gathering dusk, Larry asked me, "Should we stop here or sail on through the night?"

I don't like night watches except when absolutely necessary so I answered, "If we can get our anchor down before dark, why not get a good night's sleep?"

We worked behind Chichime Cay and set our anchor just at dark. We must have been glad we'd stopped because we stayed for two months, and only left when we ran low on kerosene and food. The U.S. charts of the area are excellent. Reefs showed easily in the clear water, and if you counted carefully you always knew which of the 365 islands you were near. The islands range in size from large enough to hold about 10 coconut palms to almost a square mile; each one has its barrier reef and lies at right angles to the tradewinds, so you could beam-reach up and down the island chain in calm water.

But it wasn't the clear water and good sailing that fascinated us, it was the Indians. From the moment we sailed into the small entry port of Porvenir, we were fascinated by the 27,000 Cunas who lived there.

The Panamanian *Commandante* who signed our entry papers explained: "These islands are completely owned by the Cuna Indians, and they handle their own internal affairs. I am here only to represent the government of Panama. It is my job to assist the Indians with any external matters. You must follow the rules of the Indians during your stay. Don't take a photograph of a person unless you ask permission first, and don't tie your yacht to their piers after sunset. Foreigners are not allowed ashore after dark."

We stayed at Porvenir for several days, learning about the people from the *Commandante* and his assistant, who spoke Spanish and English and was a Cuna. On our second night there we finally caught the eight-pound lobster we had dreamed about since Baja, and didn't even get our hair wet. Instead, we wore old shoes (as instructed) and took gloves and flashlight ashore as soon as it was absolutely dark. We prowled along the barrier reef in knee-deep water until we saw a lobster feeding. Our flashlight shining in its eyes mesmerized it and, as I held the beam steady, Larry reached down from behind and grabbed it. The first lobster was our whopper, snapping its tail fiercely and gouging a dozen scratches on Larry's arm, but Larry just grinned with pleasure. I could see him dreaming of the grilled white meat dipped in drawn butter. That one lobster made us three delicious meals.

There is a tiny airstrip at Porvenir where four or five tourists arrived each day in a small airplane. Five or six Cuna Indian women in beautiful native costumes spent their days waiting for these potential customers, sewing busily on their gorgeous *mola* blouses as they chattered away—like any sewing circle anywhere.

These blouses, appliquéd completely on three to five layers of cloth, have designs ranging from fish and animals to free-form patterns, and each is the original idea of the woman who makes it. Each side of a blouse can take from two weeks to a month to complete. Since these blouses are worn every day, and a young girl must have 20 made by the time she marries, sewing is almost a full-time job. Add to this the fact that the Indians have discovered that tourists will pay up to four dollars just for one side of a blouse, and it's easy to understand why you see almost nothing but the bowed, red-scarved tops of Cuna women's heads from dawn to dusk as they stitch away with bright-colored bits of thread and cloth.

John and Nancy Ogden, young marine biologists, motored by one day and joined us for drinks on board *Seraffyn*. They had been doing research on these islands for six months under the auspices of the Woods Hole Oceanographic Institute in Massachusetts, investigating how the parrot fish had created these coral-sand islands by eating and digesting the live coral, then excreting the shells to form sand. Nancy and John had wandered extensively among the islands and told us not to be too impressed by the *mola* work we saw within five or six miles of Porvenir.

"Wait until you get farther away from the islands the tourists can reach easily," they told us. "You'll find *molas* that are works of art! Museums and art collectors in Canada and the United States are willing to pay incredible prices for the *molas* you'll see in the outlying islands. If you want to do some trading, try the islands farther east and buy the best *molas* you can find. You'll be able to sell them easily at three or four times their cost."

I asked why Indians living in the tropics, only six degrees from the Equator, wore such elaborate clothes.

John related the legend he had heard from a tribal elder: "A long, long time ago a blue-eyed blond giant sailed into these islands in a huge sailing canoe. He offered to teach the Indians on the mainland how to stop living like nude savages. One tribe accepted his offer and learned to plant crops and sew clothes and build canoes. The other tribe refused, and still lives like animals in the forest, nude and eating the fruits and nuts they pick from the trees. The Cunas, who accepted the stranger's advice, came to call themselves *Tullis*. They formed a strong matriarchal society, and built their homes on these islands away from the mosquitoes and diseases of the mainland. They became so strong that when the Panamanians tried to conquer the islands, the Cuna held them at bay for many months without losing a man, while the Panamanians, despite their guns and ships, lost twenty-seven men. The United States stepped in and arranged a treaty that allowed the Cunas to own the three hundred sixty-five San Blas islands and a parcel of arable land on the mainland, two miles wide and as long as the island group, on which to grow food and building materials."

John added that many anthropologists believe the blond giant might have been a Viking.

"Notice the puffed sleeves on the Indian blouses, and the embroidery," he said. "They are similar to the ones worn by Norwegian girls today. And then look at the upturned bow and stern of their sailing canoes, and the fine ends. That shape is as close to a Viking ship as you could carve out of one log. The Cuna language has many words that sound just like Norwegian, and their religion is based on ten rules that translate just like the ten commandments." At the Ogdens' suggestion we decided to sail 20 miles east to meet Tom Moody on an island named Pidertupo.

"Tom came here from the States several years ago and really gained the confidence of the Indians by bringing his small daughter and wife to live and work in the islands,'' Nancy told us. ''One of the families leased him a small island and he built a lovely little resort. He has really come to know the Cuna and they trust him.''

We anchored in front of Pidertupo and wouldn't have known it wasn't a Cuna Village if we hadn't spotted a wind generator on a water tower among the palm trees in the center of the 200-foot-by-600-foot island.

''Come ashore and have lunch, it's on the table,'' Joan Moody called out to us, before we'd even furled our mainsail.

We joined the Moodys and their daughter, Marijo, and their two guests, and were almost immediately caught up in the island life. Larry was soon working to help Tom repair the water-catching system on the roof of one of the seven guest cabins.

That evening as we all had cocktails aboard *Seraffyn,* Tom told us more about the Cunas: ''These Indians have one of the most interesting cultures in the world. In fact, I think they are the only Indian group in the Americas that have been in contact with the white man's system, and yet still retain their own customs, costumes, language, and lands.''

I asked Tom and Joan what they thought about the idea of buying some *molas* to trade when we sailed north.

Joan really became enthusiastic about the idea, ''Yes, and take Marijo with you. She knows all of the Indians in this area and speaks their language. She'll break down any barriers, and if you find any *molas* that are better than the ones I have, I might be interested in trading too.''

The next day Tom took us to the island south of Pidertupo in a small motor launch. Joan had been right about Marijo. Decked out in her own *mola* blouse and wraparound skirt, her blond hair glowing, the six-year old soon had her Indian

Pho. 10-4. Tom Moody (with Mary Jo on his lap) and his friends joined us for several afternoon sails aboard *Seraffyn.*

Pho. 10-5. In the 20′ by 50′ palm and bamboo lodge, a communal pot of food was kept bubbling constantly for any village member who might wander in hungry.

friends showing us some of their finest works. As we bargained with one girl who had some especially fine blouses, an old Cuna lady insisted we all come to her hut so she could make an ankle band to complete Marijo's costume. We walked over and were fascinated by the 20′x50′ thatch-and-bamboo lodge which we examined as the woman wrapped a 12-foot string of beads around Marijo's ankle.

From the hut beams, hung 20 or more hammocks, and a small fire in the corner heated a bubbling pot of food. As we watched Marijo's ankle bracelet grow, several Indians strolled into the hut, scooped up a bowl of food from the big pot, and walked over to a corner to eat.

I asked what was in the pot, and was told, "We put in anything we catch or grow and keep it cooking all the time. Then no matter when people get hungry they can have something to eat immediately. Today there is mostly rice, bananas, yams and fish in it."

The days sped by on Pidertupo. We joined Tom for skindiving, island-hopping, *mola*-buying and more work sessions. Tom and his guests joined us for afternoon sails on *Seraffyn,* and Joan and I came to know each other better as we worked together in her bamboo galley which was designed to let the cool daytime breezes blow through it, while the thatched roof kept the rain out. We borrowed books from their 2000-book trading library, and explored every corner of the island.

We really appreciated the fact that there were no generator noises on Pidertupo. Joan and Tom used butane for cooking and lighting and their silent wind generator to power the radio transmitter and washing machine. Rain water was collected from the cabin roofs and was pumped up into the water tower once a week. Guests arrived by airplane on a small landing strip on the mainland, and Tom met them with his launch. One day a small plane buzzed Pidertupo twice. I saw Joan running down to the beach making odd signals to the pilot. Minutes later, Tom came out to *Seraffyn* in his runabout.

"The market has just flown in. Need any food?" he asked.

We joined him and reached the airstrip just as eight or 10 sailing canoes full of Cunas arrived. The pilot opened his plane to reveal bottles of chocolate milk, store-wrapped bread, candy bars, green peppers, tomatoes, frozen chickens and ground beef. He sold out quickly, and the empty space was just as quickly filled with live lobsters the Cunas had brought in plastic tubs.

"I'll buzz you next time I fly by, if I have any food left to sell," the pilot said to Tom.

When we arrived back at *Seraffyn* we saw *Samburan* anchored nearby. Wade and Connie waved, and we invited them for dinner so they could share our fresh meat.

"Tica the Terror" made a great hit with Marijo, and we all learned Tica was aptly named. She liked to be the center of attention and when I put out dinner and we sat down to eat, Tica refused to move from the middle of the table.

We banished her to the dinghy which was trailing 30 feet astern. Five minutes later she was back on the center of the table, dripping wet and grinning. We were puzzled by how the two-pound feline terror got on board, so we put her back in the dinghy, let it drop back 30 feet, and sat there watching. She meowed in outrage for three or four minutes, then took a flying leap into the choppy water, and swam rapidly toward us. When she reached *Seraffyn* she wedged her back against the rudder, dug her claws into the transom, and climbed aboard.

We resigned ourselves to her presence, closed the dinner table, and ate off our laps.

When we were back in the duty-free Canal Zone we had made a decision about cameras. We had thrown away our third "cheapie" and we hated the idea of spending another $25 on a camera that wouldn't last long in the salt air. We had heard about one that was absolutely waterproof, spent several afternoons investigating this wonder, the Nikonos Calypso Underwater camera, and finally parted with $135.00 after carefully reading the brochures and studying the camera's construction. As I prepared to join Larry and Tom on one of their diving expeditions, I grabbed the camera. It took me 10 minutes to get brave enough to go into the water with a $135.00 camera around my neck. We've had that camera six years now and it has been a great and practical investment, even if we rarely use it underwater.

It was difficult, but we finally forced ourselves to leave the anthropological, gastronomical, and social pleasures of Pidertupo. In place of several cases of canned food below, we carried 35 beautiful *molas*, four live lobsters, and hearts full of memories.

I boiled the lobster tails as we reached out toward the Hollandaise Channel, and dug out the last bottle of duty-free wine from Panama. Just as I was about to serve lunch, we cleared the end of the reef we'd been sailing behind for two months and met the huge northeast swell that had rolled across the length of the Caribbean. Helmer steered as I lay on deck being seasick. I turned and glanced below to see Larry gorging himself on Pidertupo lobster dipped in drawn butter, accompanied by our last bottle of Chateau Neuf de Pape. "I wish he'd get seasick, just one time," I thought.

11

Cartagena

WE WONDER WHO IT WAS who first put out the crazy notion that cruising boats don't need good windward ability? Once you reach Panama, the odds are 9-to-1 you will have a beat no matter which way you're headed. It's a beat to the Galapagos, a beat north to California, and a beat to cross the Caribbean.

Our goal was the east coast of the United States and, until we reached Jamaica, not only did we have to beat, but we had to fight the Gulf Stream as well. The pilot charts show a 1.5-knot countercurrent running east along the Panamanian coast as far as Cartagena, and our observations confirmed this.

So, we beat toward Colombia in the strong northeast winds, urging *Seraffyn* to windward under double-reefed main and staysail. We needed this easting badly; it would help us lay north toward Jamaica later in the spring, when the trades swing more to the east.

We hove-to our second evening at sea, dropped the staysail, sheeted the main in flat and lashed the tiller slightly alee. Our running fix had put us only 20 miles offshore and just to windward of Boca Chica, the only navigational light for 60 miles, and we didn't want to approach a low-lying rocky coast in darkness.

Besides, it was our second anniversary: It was April 15, 1971, and we had been cruising two full years. As the boat rode easily, the decks drying gradually after the spray of the past two days, Larry mixed a rum punch and we sat in the cockpit watching the sunset.

"Did you realize we've only sailed five thousand miles in two years?" I asked Larry. "The Kennedy's on *Kelea* went all the way around the world in three."

Larry sipped his drink, a look of complete satisfaction on his face. "It's not the miles under your keel that count, it's the memories, the friends and the knowledge you gain."

We reminisced happily about the bit of Spanish we had learned—enough to let us communicate with the people we had met. Then there were the "fish feeds," the skindiving, and the wonderful sailing. We had half a guest book filled with the names of the people we had met, and that only included people who had been on board. I agreed with Larry when he said, "This is the pace for us, fast enough to offer a kaleidoscope of people and places, but slow enough to allow us to get to know and appreciate them."

At 0800 we raised sail and started moving again. Larry took a sight at 1000, came below and looked at his stop watch. It had quit working.

"No problem," he said, "I'll give you the chronometer and when I say

'Mark,' you note the exact time.'' He got our Bulova Accutron watch from the navigation locker, looked at it and let out a string of choice language. "The bloody chronometer has stopped, too.'' We checked the log and saw we had last replaced the battery a year and a half before—and didn't have a spare on board. By that time it was too late to take a morning sight because the sun was overhead.

"We'll use the WWV time-tick, Lin,'' Larry said. "I'll get the sextant adjusted as close as possible and you give me a countdown with the radio, and say 'Mark.' ''

At 1400 this technique worked perfectly. Our line of position ran right through the Boca Chica lighthouse. "That's great!'' Larry said, "Now we can ease sheets and run down that bearing till we spot the lighthouse. We've worked at least ten miles to windward of our rhumb line the past two days.''

Everyone who sails knows the deep pleasure of easing sheets, of feeling the ship lift her skirts and start to skim joyfully toward a new landfall. It was dark that evening when we anchored just off Boca Chica, the small village near the mouth of Cartagena's huge natural harbor. I hated to wait till morning to see what lay ashore, but I was too sleepy to suggest rowing in.

We were up at daybreak and drank our coffee on deck as we surveyed the forts on each side of the channel we had worked through the evening before. Then we started the 20-mile beat to Cartagena. What a scene!

A fleet of gaff-rigged dugout canoes, loaded well above their gunwales with fruit, charcoal and building stakes, were beating up the bay alongside us. Some of these canoes were schooners 40 feet long, their only ballast provided by two or three crewmen hiked out on long planks to windward. On each canoe was a metal charcoal brazier for cooking, filled with glowing coals. As we tacked alongside

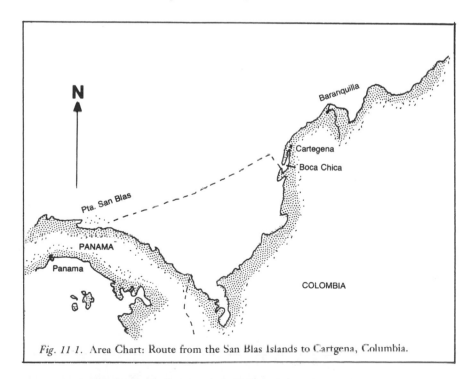

Fig. 11 1. Area Chart: Route from the San Blas Islands to Cartgena, Columbia.

Pho. 11-2. We had never seen anything like the fortified city of Cartagena.

one canoe we watched the three men on the outrigger plank walk casually inboard. As the canoe tacked through the eye of the wind, one of the men moved the outrigger plank to the opposite side, and the others bent down and lit their cigarettes on the coals. They chatted like Sunday strollers as they walked the plank and sat on the outer end, feet dangling. We later learned that these canoes with their flour-sack sails move 60 percent of the cargoes in Cartagena bay.

The *Club de Pesca de Cartagena* welcomed foreign yachts into one of the most beautiful settings imaginable. We were moored in front of a 16th century fortress, a cannon pointing at *Seraffyn's* masthead. The dock was crowded with cruising yachts flying at least 10 different flags. A Canadian flag flew from the stern of *Astrocyte,* a yacht from our own club in West Vancouver, British Columbia.

"I sailed on board *Astrocyte* years ago when she was first launched," Larry told me as we warped in alongside *Dawn,* a 42-foot trimaran sailed by Bob and Claudette Frawley whom we had first met in Mexico.

Claudette took our sternline and asked, "Do you want any fresh meat?"
"Of course," I replied. We had had almost two months of canned food and seafood.

"Okay, I'll wake you about oh-five-thirty and take you to the market," Claudette said. "Wear a mini-skirt and sandals."

"Why?" I asked, "Is the butcher a ladies' man?"

"You'll find out tomorrow," Claudette said.

As soon as we were moored, we went over to 50-foot *Astrocyte* to hear the story of Charlie and Ruth's five-year global circumnavigation, westward from Vancouver, British Columbia, via the Pacific and Indian Oceans, and around the Cape of Good hope.

They had a harrowing tale to tell: As they were running from Santa Marta (on the northern tip of Colombia) westward toward Cartagena, they didn't follow the *Coast Pilot's* advice to stay 50-miles offshore, away from the breakers and shoals caused by the river at Barranquilla. They were only 20-miles offshore, beam-reaching under the genoa, when a huge breaker rolled them over, mast under. They felt the mast hit bottom as a second wave swept over them. *Astrocyte* righted quickly, but their large deep cockpit and open companionway allowed the boat to fill half-way.

Miraculously, their diesel engine started right up, but seconds later all their electrical equipment blew out, including the bilge pumps. By hand pumping, and bailing with buckets, they kept the water level below the engine's air intake and it kept running as they headed offshore away from the danger area. Later, they spotted the lights leading through the shoals and worked up the Magdalena River into Barranquilla, still bailing. The wind-direction indicator, mounted on a ⅜-inch stainless steel rod at the masthead was bent at 45 degrees, proof that their mast actually had hit bottom. Their dinghy had been washed overboard. Ruth was bleeding badly from a cut caused by cases of food falling on her, out of the bilge.

They were so exhausted by the time they reached port that they didn't take the advice of the port captain and hire a watchman. Instead, Charley, who is a doctor, cleaned up Ruth's cuts, and they went to sleep.

By morning their decks were swept clean of everything movable: sails, winch handles, life preservers, etc. Everything the sea hadn't taken, local bandits had. It took them a month of hard work to clean up *Astrocyte* and buy back as much of their stolen gear as they could locate. Most of their time was spent trying to get electrical equipment working again. They had sailed to Cartagena a few weeks before we got there to finish up the work; they were tired of worrying about thieves and knew the *Club de Pesca* had an armed guard.

After hearing this story we asked Charley and Ruth, "Do you know a good restaurant? How about joining us for dinner."

They pointed to the yacht club restaurant—white tables in the shade of a banyan tree just inside the fortress walls, not 10 feet from the bow of *Astrocyte*. "The best in town," they said.

Dinner was a treat. A five-course meal, starting with oysters and ending with ice cream sundaes, cost $2.50 each, and the wine was fine.

At 0530 the next morning, I heard a rap on deck. I climbed carefully over Larry and joined Claudette.

"Bring some plastic bags," she whispered. I got some, and we walked toward town as the horizon turned sunrise pink. Horse-drawn carts rumbled over the 16th century cobbles. Canoes glided across the still waters and grounded next to the vast open market. Indian women sat beside their blankets, cutting and measuring their produce as customers bargained for half of a tomato, a quarter of an onion, a half of a cabbage, a spoonful of oil, or 100 grams of rice.

As we approached the meat market, we heard the "moo" and "oink" of meat on the hoof. Inside the clean, tile-lined building, Claudette's favorite butcher was just dragging the skinned carcass of a whole cow into his stall. He cut off the head and set it on a table to prove that his meat was fresh.

Claudette said, *"El fillette, por favor."*

The butcher attacked the carcass with a machete, and moments later he held out a long, bloody strip of red meat. Claudette dropped it into a plastic bag which she handed to me.

"I don't need that much," I protested, looking at the six-pound hunk of meat.

"It only costs twenty cents a pound, and you'll find lots of ways to use it," Claudette replied.

She asked for another fillet, and the butcher returned to his machete work. A few minutes later we left, each laded with a complete fillet for ourselves, plus two for friends who couldn't stomach the meat market. We also bought some lovely pork at equally low prices. As we walked home in the morning light I looked down at my blood-spotted legs, and understood why Claudette had specified a short skirt. The fillet kept well on ice, and Larry and I had steaks for breakfast, lunch and dinner. After four meals of steak, I used the rest of the meat in an Irish stew. Some cooks will think that was a waste of tender fillet mignon, but variety is the spice of life.

We've never known a friendlier or more helpful yacht club than that one at Cartagena. The secretary took care of all our needs; mooring charges were minimal; the docks were strong and conveniently arranged, and there were hot showers. Yet several yachtsmen from Europe and North America had displayed such bad manners that members of the club, too polite to complain directly to the offending visitors, were discussing the closing of the club to non-members. One of the complaints was that some visitors were completely rebuilding their boats or motors, and had spread engines and transmissions across the docks, dripping dirty oil on clean wood and blocking the walkways that led to club members' yachts.

Another Vancouver boat arrived a week after we did. As Lol Killams' 72-foot *Greybeard* was too deep to come alongside the club piers, we rowed out to pass on a warning from the club secretary. "Take your dinghy on board at night," we told Lol. "There's been a lot of thievery lately."

The next morning Lol yelled to us, "Can we borrow your cars? Our outboard and oars are gone."

When you consider that an outboard motor is worth a year's salary to a Colombian, it's no wonder theft is such a problem. The yacht club guard made life at the piers much easier.

Pho. 11-3. We arrived in Cartagena after a 20-mile beat up the bay in company with a fleet of gaff-rigged dugout canoes laden with cargo.

We've never seen anything like the two-mile-square fortified city of Cartagena. It has walls 20-feet thick. On a hill overlooking the city is the fortress of San Felipe which covers half a square mile. It is honeycombed with five-foot-high tunnels. We explored these tunnels with a torch, and learned from the guards that King Ferdinand of Spain built the city and the fortress to protect his fleet and his gold shipments, but his 16 million pieces of eight and the one million Indians who died during the construction went for naught when Cartagena—and its gold—were captured by English Admiral Edward Vernon.

One afternoon we decided to sail down the bay to photograph some of the working canoes. As we uncovered our mainsail, a man on the dock said to Claudette, "May I come aboard your trimaran?"

She said, "Sure" and the man, who was dressed in a grey business suit, stepped aboard, to stand looking at *Seraffyn,* studying her carefully.

"Are you coming sailing?" I asked him in Spanish.

He looked around and, finding no one else near, said, "Are you speaking to me?"

"Yes. If you want to go for an hour's sail, jump aboard."

His shoes and socks were off in seconds and, beaming with pleasure, he came aboard. As he worked out of the upper harbor, we introduced ourselves and found that Jaco Modiano spoke perfect English. After extending profuse thanks for the invitation, he told us a little about himself. "I live in Barranquilla, where I have a plastics business, and I come here to sail my Snipe. Tomorrow is the National Snipe Class Championships."

We had a wonderful run down the habor with our own guide, who made the passing scene more interesting. When we returned to the club about 1800, Jaco pulled on his shoes and said, "Don't leave your boat. I'll be right back!"

He returned 15 minutes later with two friends, one a boatbuilder, the other, president of the local Snipe Class. They insisted we join them for dinner at an

Pho. 11-4. A fisherman repairs his nets near Boca Chica.

Pho. 11-5. Anchoring out instead of staying at docks was not only cheaper, but gave us cooler sleeping, and kept *Seraffyn* cleaner.

Arabian restaurant where we ate lamb rolled in fig leaves, shish kebob, and a paste made of garbanzo beans mixed with garlic.

While we were eating, the president of the Snipe Class asked, "Would you be willing to use *Seraffyn* as committee boat for tomorrow's races?"

We thought that would be fun and agreed at once.

In the morning we arrived at the dinghy club and were each presented with a Snipe badge.

"Your boat is now an honorary Snipe," Jaco told us.

I was put in charge of the starting horn, and went around in the club's power launch helping to lay out marks.

Larry was the lucky one. He was invited to helm on one of the Snipes. Considering that he had never raced anything but keel boats, he did quite well in his own race, placing fifth out of 10 boats in 30-knot winds, even after breaking an outhaul fitting.

Later, at the *Club de Pesca,* we accepted Jaco's invitation to take the luxury bus to Barranquilla for a day's visit.

On Tuesday we rode through the desertlike countryside in an air-conditioned luxury bus at 10 times *Seraffyn's* top speed of six knots. In Barranquilla, Jaco greeted us and took us to his home for lunch. His handsome, redheaded wife, Eva showed us around their lovely apartment and then bombarded us with questions about *Sefaffyn.*

"It all sounds so wonderful, Jaco told me we could do the same in the boat Mario is building for us, but I didn't believe him until he brought you here."

After lunch we made arrangements for Jaco and Eva to join us on the weekend for some more sailing. Then Jaco took us to meet Mario at his boatbuilding yard and see the half-completed *Kathaleen.*

Larry and Mario got involved talking shop and Mario explained, "I have one advantage; I own a hotel so I don't have to worry about profits. I only build boats for my friends, for pleasure. It's also nice to keep my craftsmen busy."

Jaco's 28-foot double-ended cruiser hull verified Mario's words. The only thing that wasn't absolutely perfect was the mahogany planking. Since it was impossible to get mahogany over 12-feet long, each plank had two scarfs in it.

Next morning, we knew *Samburan* had arrived, even before we saw the boat or her owners, because we heard giggles of delight coming from the boats around us. We went on deck to see Tica sitting quietly on a dock behind a busy fisherman. The man was dropping his three pronged hook into a school of minnows. Each time he jerked his line upward he snagged a minnow, which he pulled off the hook, and dropped on the dock behind him. He never once looked behind him so he didn't see Tica gobble up each minnow as it arrived.

After 10 minutes and 10 minnows, Tica could barely crawl, and I could barely sit up I was laughing so hard. The fisherman coiled up his line, put it in his pocket, swung his feet up on the dock, and opened a plastic bag.

Only then did he look around to scoop up his bait. Tica didn't even have the decency to look ashamed. She sat there licking her chops, waiting for another tidbit. The fisherman nodded resignedly, unrolled his fishing line, and set to work again.

When we first arrived in Cartagena we planned to stay for two months waiting for the winds to shift to the east, as the pilot charts showed they did around the beginning of May. There was much to do around Cartagena—daysailing, fishing, exploring. Besides, we wanted to haul and paint *Seraffyn.* So we wrote to my folks, who were acting as forwarding agents for our mail, and asked them to send everything they had in one airmail package to the *Club de Pesca*. Then we looked for a place to haul. The club ways was too shallow to take us. The commercial ways was too busy. The fishermen's ways wasn't built to take sailboats. We were in a dilemma because our waterline was scrubbed almost down to bare wood.

Meanwhile, a two-pound package of mail arrived, and one letter had a shattering effect. When we had sold our business and possessions and left California, we had a bank balance of $4500—over half of what it had cost to build *Seraffyn*. We took the rest of our cash and, by occasional jobs of yacht delivery or boatbuilding, we had been able to cruise enjoyably on $200 to $250 a month, without touching our emergency fund.

Then we had got greedy. A stockbroker we met during our second year of cruising told us about "a real winner," and we gambled. For a year he watched our stock carefully as it slowly went up. And then he wrote, "I didn't check your stock for about two weeks, and by then it was too late." His letter went on to say that if we held the stock for another year or two he might be able to get 10 percent of our investment back.

Suddenly, there we were with $400 in our kitty and $100 in our U.S. bank account! We didn't like the situation, and had to do something fast.

Larry had already been asked to do a few jobs locally: fitting new engine beds in one boat, surveying another, but those would only meet our living expenses. We wanted some money in the bank again.

"As soon as we take care of our waterline, we'll head north to the U.S. and go back to work," Larry said. "It just isn't safe to cruise without a decent emergency fund. If we lost our mast or I broke my leg or something, we'd be in real trouble. I'd hate to lose the boat because we couldn't pay a hospital bill."

One evening, Dennis Nahum, the owner of the *Club de Pesca*, picked us up for dinner in his runabout. As we headed down the harbor, he gave a discourse on his life as an expatriate English gourmet running a restaurant in Colombia.

"It's great! Our little town has eight of the world's best eateries, with bargain-basement prices, all within walking distance—fabulous fresh food, and my wife is a wonderful cook, besides."

He turned into a narrow channel between some sand dunes and we flew into a perfect little lagoon. "That's the hotel your friend Mario, the boatbuilder, owns," Dennis said, pointing to a nine-story white building set in seven luxurious acres. "And *that's* the chief of police's office. He sits behind the big window facing the lagoon. Invite him for a drink some afternoon. He loves yachts. Once you're his friend, you'll be able to leave your boat safely anywhere in Cartagena." We drew alongside the small pier in front of Dennis' house, and his wife, Penny, greeted us.

She was just as interesting as Dennis, and worked as the UPI correspondent for the northern part of South America. With her fluent Spanish and understanding of local history, she was a mine of information. By the end of the evening, we were discussing a subject dear to her heart, writing. She gave us some invaluable advice when we told her we wanted to try writing about our cruise.

"Do it! Hundreds of people say they would like to write, but they keep putting it off till *mañana*. Just sit down and write! In fact, if you do it within the next day or two, bring your work over and I'll look at it—and give you any advice I can."

We asked Dennis if there was enough water to sail *Seraffyn* into their lagoon; our chart showed this area to be swamp.

"Sure, bring her in." he said. "There's fresh water on our pier and hot water in our showers."

Pbo. 11-6. Our fiberglass sailing dinghy was not only our water taxi to shore, but indispensible for doing work on the topsides.

The next morning we sailed *Seraffyn* to the lagoon entrance, dropped sails, anchored, and sounded the lagoon and channel with our lead line in *Rinky*. We found two inches more than our draft, and there was just over an hour to high tide. Back on *Seraffyn,* we set sail—and promptly ran aground.

Larry climbed back into *Rinky,* sounded, and said, "We missed the channel by four feet. We can kedge her over a two-inch hump, or wait for the tide." We relaxed on deck as the sails kept pulling.

A man waded out from shore and asked, "Why are you sitting there with all your sails set?"

"We stopped for cocktails," Larry answered, lifting his wine glass. "Come join us." Half an hour later, we were anchored in the center of the lagoon.

Early the next morning, we met the chief of police, who watched as we ran *Seraffyn* onto the hard sand just before high water, as we had done with *Samburan* two months earlier. The 20-inch fall of tide provided just enough room to sand and repaint the waterline. The creosote from the waterline down was sufficient protection for the area we couldn't repaint. The next day we were anchored in the lagoon again, with one major worry behind us.

Although we hadn't planned to, we remained in the lagoon for a week. Larry had complained of an earache the afternoon we hauled ourselves off the beach, and by that evening he had to take a codeine tablet. The pain continued, so we went to see a doctor recommended by Penny. But after four days, Larry still had no relief. We were invited to a dinner party ashore on the fifth day and Larry tried to beg off, but after taking more painkiller, he felt better and we went.

One of the men at the party, Jim, was the resident SCUBA diver for Esso. Larry immediately became interested, and we were soon deep in conversation about the diving around Cartagena.

"Only problem with diving around the bay is that it's easy to pick up ear fungus—really painful if you don't treat it properly," Jim said.

We described Larry's symptoms, and Jim felt they were definitely those of the ear fungus. "It's easy to cure," he said. "Just pour a solution of five percent hydrogen peroxide in your ear channel three times a day. Not many doctors know this, and they'll treat you with antibiotics as if you had an internal ear infection."

We started the treatment as soon as we got back to the boat, and Larry's ear pains were almost gone by the next day.

May was running out, the northeast trades were swinging more to the east, and our funds were getting lower, so we prepared for the 500 mile beat to Jamaica.

Meanwhile, Wade and Connie came by to say farewell. "As soon as we find Tica we're sailing for the States," Wade told us. "I don't have enough money to have *Samburan's* planks replaced here, so it's time to go back to work."

Tica had wandered off, or been stolen. The local police were looking for her, spurred on by the offer of a good reward, but Wade and Connie were still at the *Club de Pesca* five days later when we sailed. They seemed heartbroken. "We never thought two-and-a-half pounds of black fluff could mean so much," Connie said sadly.

As we lifted our anchor to run down the bay, I, too, worried about poor little Tica, lost in the big city of Cartagena.

12

Our Adversary and Our Ally, The Gulf Stream

I DREADED THE 480-mile beat to Jamaica. I worried about being seasick. I wondered what to do about feeding Larry. By the time we actually set off from Cartagena, I was annoyed with myself; I hated being a worrier.

Larry asked, ''Do you want to anchor for the night at Boca Chica and make sure everything's ready?''

''Nope,'' I said. ''I've got four days' food prepared for you and in the ice chest, in case I can't cook. Everything's stowed the best I know how. Let's get on with it.''

We reached through the quarter-mile-wide exit and then took down our working jib to set the staysail. We sheeted in and set *Seraffyn* hard on the wind. Once clear of the land, we put Helmer to work. Then we tied two reefs in the mainsail.

Seraffyn worked through the choppy seas at almost four knots with only 205 square feet of canvas spread. Spray flew across the foredeck. Our course to Jamaica was 350°. We had to lay about 10° to 15° higher than that—about 005°—to counteract the Gulf Stream and to avoid the unlit shoals to leeward of our rhumb line. But *Seraffyn's* bowsprit only pointed 340°.

''If the pilot charts are right, we should get a lift as we get around the top of Colombia,'' Larry said. ''It's probably the land that's causing the wind to blow from the north. Start me some dinner while I secure for sea.''

As soon as I went below, I felt queasy. Fortunately, getting dinner only meant pouring my pre-made beef stew into a pot and heating it. With frequent gulps of the fresh air through the open companionway, I got Larry's hot stew on a plate and managed to make a tomato-and-cucumber salad. I wedged myself firmly into place, one hand on a sea rail and my forehead against the cabin side. I listened to the sounds Larry made as he tucked a third reef into the main, heard him go forward to unshackle the anchor. He secured it in position on the bobstay and capped the chain deck pipe. Then I heard him unscrew the forward ventilator and cap it.

When he came aft and saw the hot plate of food I was holding, he stripped off his wet-weather gear and gave me a smile. ''Good work, Lin,'' he said. ''Now why don't you climb into the bunk and take the first watch off? You'll probably feel better when you wake up.''

I climbed into the sleeping bag and lay thinking. How lucky could I get? A ship without a leak, a husband who not only didn't get seasick, but was considerate when I did. I vowed to be extra patient next time Larry teased me, slapped my bottom, criticized my sail-handling, or refused to go shopping.

Larry brought the oil lamps below and lit them. "Go to sleep, green eyes," he said, "we're starting to get a lift now. Our course is almost three-five-oh and the seas are easier, too."

By morning I was still seasick. I'd stood my watches, as Helmer guided *Seraffyn* over the high choppy waves, watching fishing boats and freighters pass, and breathing a sigh of relief as our bowsprit pointed ever closer to our desired course.

We shook out the third reef at dawn, then I climbed into my bunk and stayed there except to make Larry's meals. Larry kept busy. Frequently he pressed me to eat a biscuit or drink some fruit juice. Every half hour, starting at 0900, he took a sun sight. I marveled at his accuracy. I can take a sight on calm days when we are reaching or running, but we were hard on the wind, waves over 10 feet high and spray flying across the deck. Yet each half-hourly line lay true and accurate on our Caribbean chart.

After taking the fifth morning sight, Larry showed me our track on the chart and said, "We're being set to the west about a knot and a half. See these LOP's? They run parallel to our course because the sun is almost due east of us. We'll have to stay higher than we thought. The perfect course would be to zero-one-two, and we're almost laying that now.

By the end of the second day, we were able to ease sheets a few inches and still lay 015°. My seasickness never went away completely. My head felt heavy if I wasn't lying down, and food didn't interest me, though I could eat dry salt crackers and drink apricot nectar occasionally. At night my watches dragged as I lounged on the settee, going on deck every 10 minutes to scan the horizon for ships, check our course, and inspect the oil lamps that cast their red and green glow on our cabin top.

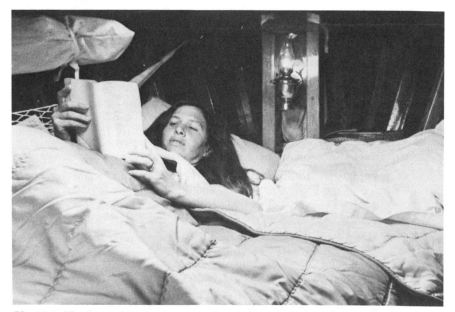

Pbo. 12-1. The forward bunk was cozy and warm in cool weather when in port.

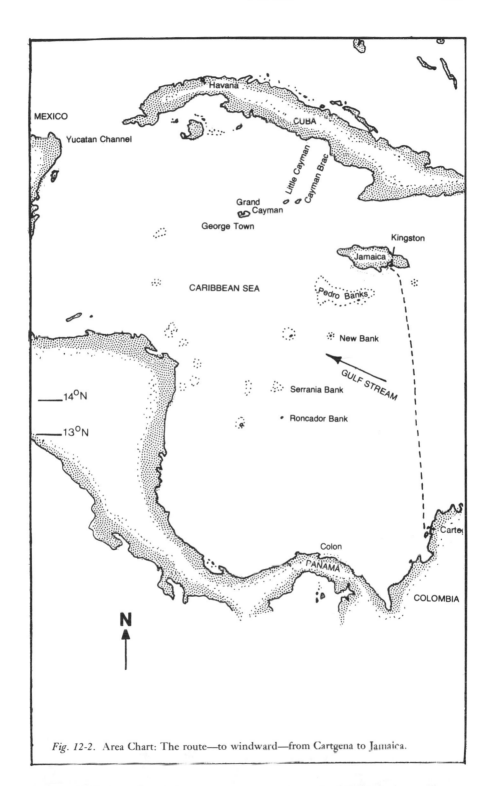

Fig. 12-2. Area Chart: The route—to windward—from Cartgena to Jamaica.

On the third day, a boil formed on my elbow. I thought I'd worn out Larry's sympathy, but he teased me as he thumbed through our medical guide. "Looks like I might be able to practice the carving my father taught me in his butcher shop," he said. "The guide says to lance your boil when it gets a white head." I hoped my boil would heal itself.

Larry took his morning sight. "Guess what, Lin, we're in the main steamer lane from the Windward Passage to Panama." He put his navigation books away and went on deck. Spray still flew across *Seraffyn's* foredeck but her cockpit was almost dry. "Yup, there's a ship, Lin," he called down to me.

I yelled to him from my bunk, "Stop joking." We hadn't seen a ship for two days.

"Don't believe me, but it's altered course right for us."

I rushed up from my bunk. There was a ship! Someone else was using our sea! *President Harriman* approached and from a mile off, we could see her bridge deck covered with people.

"You might consider putting on some clothes, Lin," Larry said.

I looked down at myself, rushed below and grabbed Larry's jacket. *President Harriman* made a wide, sweeping turn 200 yards off our bow.

Her officers and crew waved cheerily as we set our Canadian flag. We waved back and watched as they turned back onto their original course. Seconds later, we sailed into the smooth wake of the huge ship, and for the first time in three days it felt as if *Seraffyn* were on a mill pond. Fifty feet later we slammed back into the Gulf Stream seas, and 15 minutes later we were completely alone again.

Two days later, Larry lanced my boil with one of the scalpels from our medical kit. Then he checked our taffrail log. "Twenty miles to Jamaica, Lin," he announced.

At noon he yelled, "There it is, land!"

I climbed on deck, carrying the *Coast Pilot,* and we identified the White Horse Cliffs, three miles east of Kingston harbor.

"Okay, Lin, ease the staysail," Larry said. "I'll ease the main."

My headache went away instantly, as *Seraffyn* straightened up and gained speed.

"The worst is over, Lin," Larry told me. "Now it's fair winds all the way to the U.S, with the Gulf Stream pushing us. It wasn't so bad, now, was it?"

I had to agree. I was five pounds lighter—all the weight I'd tried to lose during the previous year—and my seasickness was only a memory.

Larry prepared the anchor and chain. I cleaned the cabin and stowed our wet-weather gear. Five days and 480 miles of beating were behind us. We had averaged 95 miles a day hard on the wind.

Jamaica's green mountains showed clear and beautiful as Larry hauled in the spinner of our taffrail log, and we rounded into Port Royal Harbor—and dropped anchor. We unlashed and launched the dinghy and rowed ashore, turning to look at our sturdy ship.

Who could ask for more? we wondered aloud while eating a wonderful meal of turtle steaks and baked potatoes in a restaurant right across from the church where the pirate Henry Morgan had stored his treasure

There is a beautiful resort, restaurant and swimming pool at Port Royal, run by Lady and Sir Anthony Jenkins. They made us feel welcome and joined us on board for dinner that night, bringing one of their hotel guests with them. During dinner, we described the San Blas Islands, the highlight of our cruise so far.

Pho. 12-3. The next morning Elio met us with his car and took us for a ride into the blue mountains behind Kingston.

Elio Guoitolini and Lady Anthony asked to see my *mola* collection and were as excited by them as we had been. They asked their price. I didn't know what to charge for these beautiful things and tentatively suggested $15.00 each.

Elio said, "Oh no! they're worth at least $25.00! Besides, they're something special. They've been imported by sailing ship."

I was staggered at the thought of making 10 times my purchase price.

The next morning, Elio picked us up in his car and drove us into the mountains behind Kingston. There, 4000 feet above the sea, amid cool breezes and pine trees, we sat in an English garden and had high tea. I could just see *Seraffyn,* a tiny white speck in the huge bay lying below us.

On our way back we stopped at Kingston University. Its grounds are famous and so is its bookstore. We spent most of what Elio had paid us for two *molas* on new paperback books and one hard cover, *The Life and Times of Horatio Hornblower* by C. N. Parkinson.

As we were leaving the University grounds, we saw a sign: MEDICAL CLINIC OPEN. I wanted Larry to see a doctor because he was getting a boil on his neck. A half-hour later, we had described Larry's boil, his earache, and my boils to a doctor.

"You two have been in the tropics too long," he said. "You need a change of climate, some cold weather. That will kill the bugs you've picked up. Meanwhile, Larry is going to be very uncomfortable for a while. He's developing a carbuncle on his neck and there's not much we can do for it—just antibiotics and painkillers."

For two weeks Larry suffered while the whole back of his neck swelled, and then burst into a cluster of five boils. The carbuncle left him irritable and exhausted, even when he was just lying in his bunk reading, and he preferred to be alone.

So I filled my days with sightseeing, swimming, and water-skiing with people I had met at the Port Royal Hotel. Then, one day Larry suggested a walk on shore: He was getting better. That evening a squall blew off the land. A 20-foot fiberglass sloop dragged anchor and blew down on us, its crew dashing frantically around the deck. We fended them off, then tossed them a line. "Hang onto us," Larry yelled, "our anchor is holding well."

Ten minutes later it was calm again, and we invited the boat's crew, Peter and Nicole Rurdon, and Julie Clymo, and their five children on board for drinks.

"Why don't you sail up to the Royal Kingston Yacht Club?" Nicole asked. "It's really nice, and from there we can easily take you to our house for dinner tomorrow. We're having a party."

The next morning we sailed to the clean, protected club basin. At the guest dock, the club secretary apologized when he asked for our yacht club membership card. He said, "We have had several visiting yachts leave here without paying their bar and restaurant bills. None of them left forwarding addresses. Now we have to record your club affiliation and address before we can offer you a mooring."

In the two and a half years we had been cruising that was only the second time we'd been asked if we were members of a yacht club. But we learned later that most American and European yacht clubs have a "Members Only" rule.

As we sailed into our slip, we noticed oysters on the concrete pilings, beautiful tiny clean oysters. We packed a bucket with eight dozen of them, and took them to Nicole's dinner party. They were a hit!

While Larry was recuperating, we were invited by members of the Royal Jamaica Yacht Club to join them for racing and, since we were the only visiting yacht there, so many members extended invitations that we had to split up and go on different boats. I learned a lot being on my own. In one race, I was in charge of the foredeck on a 34-foot sloop! And what racing! A mixed fleet from Dragons to 43-foot ocean racers, all setting spinnakers in the gusty 35-knot winds of Jamaica Bay.

The club manager offered us the use of the marine railway to haul and scrub our bottom when he noticed we had two inches of weed below the clean waterline we had painted in Cartagena. He explained the charges for members and said that if we could finish our work in one day, we could consider ourselves "temporary" members. We were sure we could do it.

As we sailed onto the ways car, Larry said to me, "That sure is a steep incline. I think I'll tie a safety line just in case *Seraffyn* starts to slide back on the car. Her bottom is awfully slippery with all this weed on it." He took a ⅝-inch line and tied it to the bottom of the front cross-bearer on the cradle. Then he led it through an aft fair lead and forward to a sheet winch.

The yard manager teased him. "Don't you trust our cradle?" he asked.

"Doesn't cost anything to tie a knot," Larry answered.

At 1700, our work done, we prepared to go back into the water. I was in the galley, and Larry was on deck. Buster, the yard manager, was in the water shoveling sand off the tracks. George, one of the workmen, began unwinding the hauling cable from its winch. When he had 50 or 60 feet loose, he joined a third man in pushing *Seraffyn* and her cradle toward the edge of the flat area of track. The boat and cradle began gathering speed. The two men tried to stop the boat, but couldn't. Instead of stopping at the edge of the incline as planned, *Seraffyn* kept going.

A shout went up. George ran to the winch, and, instead of releasing the brake

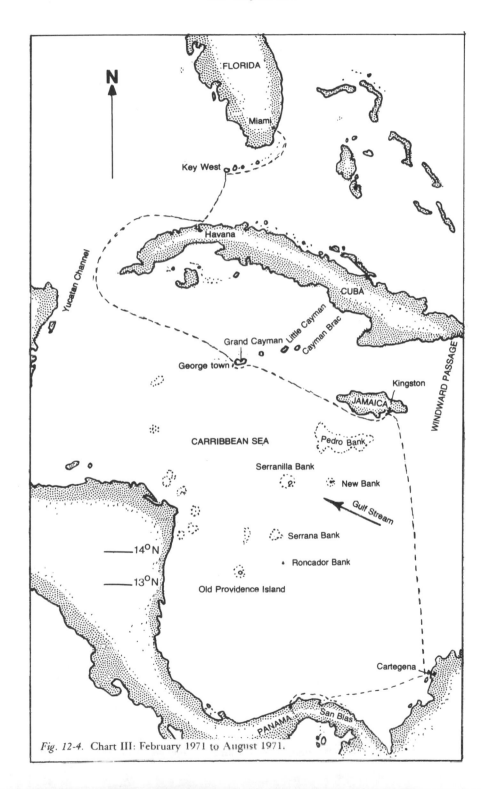

Fig. 12-4. Chart III: February 1971 to August 1971.

and letting *Seraffyn* rumble on right down into the water, he tried to take in the slack cable.

We came to a grinding, banging halt. I was tossed off my feet against the settee. Larry kept his footing, but let out a roar of outrage as he heard the sound of groaning timbers.

Seraffyn was standing almost upright, quivering, and Larry climbed down gingerly. She had slid back in the cradle four feet, bending both of the six-inch steel I-beam uprights down 30 degrees. Only the safety line Larry had tied on kept her from sliding further aft, and right off the cradle! The rope was bar tight, holding her on the cradle as she leaned on one forward support. Larry grabbed a seven-foot long baulk of lumber that lay near the tracks and heaved it as far as he could, cursing. Then, trying to regain his composure, he set to work with Buster to build temporary supports and reposition *Seraffyn* with the use of a hydraulic jack.

"The club will pay for any damages," Buster told us as he pulled *Seraffyn* back up onto the flat working area. Larry started surveying the boat. He found no problems other than six angry red 5/16-inch-deep gouges cut in the mahogany planking by the metal after supports.

"There's no structural damage," he said. "Give me a day out of the water and a piece of mahogany. With some graving pieces and paint, you'll never know it happened."

I thought Larry was merely being polite making that estimate, but by the next afternoon when we went back in the water (with two safety lines) you could barely see the damage. After another coat of paint applied the following day, it took a really close inspection to find the scars.

Larry's carbuncle had kept us in Jamaica far longer than we had planned, and our funds weren't growing, so we were anxious to get moving north. But before we left, we wanted to take some of our new friends for a sail—our way of saying thank you.

Peter, Nicole and Julie arrived with the five kids and a picnic lunch. Five adults and five youngsters, aged four to 12 set off on 24-foot *Seraffyn*. Kids were popping out of the forehatch, climbing under the cockpit, crawling into the chain locker. When we dropped anchor at Lime Key, five miles from the club, they slithered over the side into the water like a herd of seals. On the sail home, they cuddled blissfully in the double bunk and slept like angelic sardines.

The next day we took another friend for a sail, and afterward he almost ruined the day by saying, "Will you sell *Seraffyn?* I'll pay you nineteen thousand dollars for her!"

Larry turned white before answering quietly. "Would you sell your child?"

And then, two days later, we were on our way again.

Running, beautiful running—the breeze astern, the sun blazing, the taffrail log whirring merrily. That's what we went cruising for. Now the long-feared beat across the Caribbean was behind us, and all was right with my world.

The first signs we saw of the Cayman Islands were wrecks. We counted the hulks of 10 ships as we sailed past the south end of Grand Cayman. The island lies in an area of fluky currents, and its highest point is the new lighthouse that stands 50 feet above the sea.

In 1785, 10 merchant ships sailed from Jamaica toward Yucatan Channel, bound for England. On board one ship was a prince, and to make sure he was kept safe, an admiral of the Royal Navy had been attached to the fleet. The leading ship was to fire a flare as soon as it had located Grand Cayman and was clear. In the dark

Pho. 12-5. The first signs we saw of the Cayman Islands were gaunt wrecks jutting out of the water from the reefs.

of night the ship struck the reefs, and its commander started shooting flares, hoping to warn off the other nine ships. Tragically, one after another, each ship mistook the warning, piled up on the reef, and foundered. The Cayman Islanders came out to the reefs in small boats and instead of plundering the ships—a common practice in that era—saved the prince and all the crews except for one seaman. For this act of "bravery and honesty" George III of England exempted the Cayman Islands from all taxes and wartime conscription forever.

We saw the effect of this tax concession the moment we set foot ashore at Georgetown. Small, one-office buildings proclaimed: "World Headquarters of. . ." They were banks, oil companies, construction firms, each with one man in an office to meet legal requirements.

Everything on the island except seafood was flown in from Miami, so prices were exorbitant. We were planning to anchor only for the night, but once we had rowed ashore for a walk we immediately met people with whom we had friends in common, and we accepted an invitation from Peter Milnehouse and his wife to watch an afternoon cricket game the next day.

That evening, the four of us drove out of Georgetown bound for a "house-addition dinner." Huge land crabs scurried across the road, caught momentarily in our headlights. Peter explained the dinner. "When a native woman wants to earn extra money for something, like adding a room to her house, she invites everyone to an eat-all-you-can dinner, and charges about a dollar twenty-five each."

The woman who gave the dinner we attended, served us trays of deviled crab, pickled fish, lobster salad, and wild fruit on her candlelit kitchen table. She got the crabs by riding her motor scooter down the main road after dark.

We sailed from Georgtown a week later, and were careful with our navigation. We had been warned by friends on Grand Cayman that the Gulf Stream could be very unreliable, and we didn't want to be swept onto the shores of Cuba. We ran through Yucatan Channel without seeing land, then turned northeast toward Key West, Florida.

"Know what I'd like to do, Lin?" Larry asked me over cocktails one evening. "I'd like to sail up the East Coast and find a quiet river somewhere, with a little shipyard. Maybe I could find some boat-repair work and maybe we could find a boathouse to put *Seraffyn* in for the winter, so we could give her a real refit. Then we might rent a cottage with a big fireplace. You could try writing and maybe we could get an occasional yacht-delivery job.''

"Sounds good,'' I said, "if you add a big furry carpet in front of the fireplace.''

When the sun rose the next morning, I went below to make coffee. *Seraffyn* slipped happily along under main and lapper. I came back on deck to see a fisherman frantically paddling his canoe out of our way. I had looked just before going below and don't know how I missed him. I guess I was only watching for ships bigger than us.

As the sun rose higher we saw the twin chimneys of the Hershey sugar mills one mile east of Havana. We had been swept 60 miles east in 24 hours by the Gulf Stream. We tacked and headed due north. By nightfall we were becalmed over the American shoals.

We anchored for the night and in the morning sailed into Key West. The American customs officials seemed glad to see us. One of them said, "Three small yachts have recently sailed too close to Cuba and been confiscated. The owners are in jail in Havana, and we're trying to identify them. Friends of yours called us and said you were a month overdue. Your boat fits the description of one of the three reported in Cuba.''

"But we never said we'd be here on any set date,'' Larry said.

"Your friends read your letter to us over the phone,'' the official replied. "It said, 'Heading north directly for Key West the last of April.' ''

We had written that to Annabelle and Gordon Yates, who were cruising the east coast of Florida in their new boat, but they were cruising folk, too, and we thought they would know that Larry and I can't pass up islands. If there's one anywhere near our route, we have to explore it.

13

Earning Freedom Chips

ERNEST HEMINGWAY'S SPIRIT seemed alive in the quiet tree-lined streets of Key West. The subdued colonial atmosphere was a perfect reintroduction to the United States. We rested a few days, enjoying steak and ice cream again, and then slid along the Gulf Stream-washed Florida Keys, past a wonderful system of navigation lights and buoys, designed to keep even the most careless seaman off the reefs and shoals. We didn't stop to explore the Keys as we had a three-month accumulation of mail waiting for us in Fort Lauderdale, and we wanted to go to work. But first there was Miami.

The closer we came to Miami, the busier the sea and sky became. Speedboats buzzed by throwing rooster tails of spray; there were tour boats with glass bottoms, sailboats, sportfishermen, seaplanes, jets. We tacked through the village-planted-on-stilts that lies on either side of the channel which cuts the reef protecting Biscayne Bay from the Atlantic. It was startling to see palatial homes sitting on the water eight miles from land. Instead of driveways and garages, they had docks and boathouses; instead of gardens, unlimited acres of water, two feet deep and filled with the vibrant, diverse life of coral reef and subtropical waters.

We sailed into the Dinner Key channel—what a sight! Hundreds of boats, eight to 50 feet, plus people and cars in numbers we had not seen for two and a half years.

Three people stood on the yacht club dock, waving violently. We waved back and prepared to tack toward the guest dock. Larry put the helm down, but *Seraffyn* didn't come about. She couldn't; she was stuck in the mud, right in front of the yacht club.

Two people from the dock came out in a small powerboat, and came aboard. We exchanged introductions with ''Suds and Carol.'' Suds said, ''We were trying to warn you that there are more docks here than when your chart was drawn. But never mind, the tide will only fall another foot, then you'll have a two-foot rise to float you off. Meanwhile, we've brought you a cocktail. Where are you coming from?''

Suds and Carol had a little cruising boat and plans for a cruise someday. We sat on *Seraffyn's* gently tilting deck discussing cruising dreams and reality. Suds pointed to a 30-year-old, 50-foot ketch that he said a young couple was trying to refit with almost no money. ''What size boat do you think is right, now that you've been cruising for two years?'' he asked.

I went below and got the graph we had made from the 67 Ideal Cruising Boat

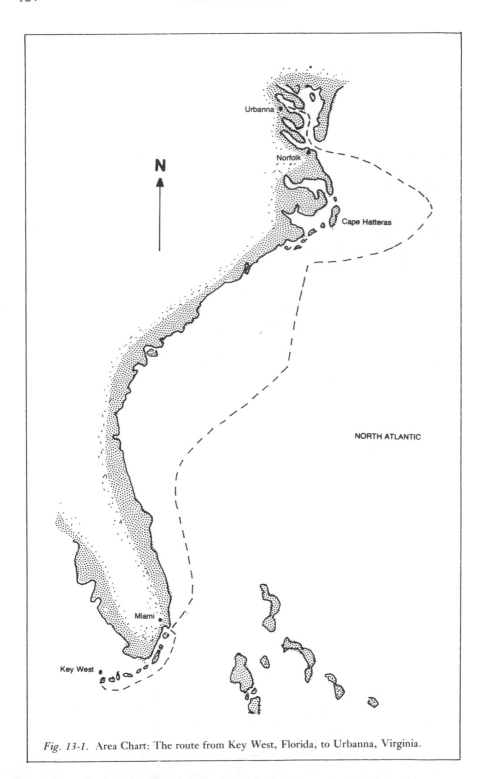

Fig. 13-1. Area Chart: The route from Key West, Florida, to Urbanna, Virginia.

surveys we had completed during the previous year. "We questioned the people on every yacht we met who had been cruising foreign waters for over six months," Larry explained. "People who had cruised for more than one year had boats that averaged thirty feet on deck; the ones who had cruised for over two years, without any independent income, had boats that averaged twenty nine feet. That's not just our opinion, but the actual statistics supplied by people who are doing the cruising."

Carol studied the chart and said, "We've watched dozens of heartbreaks right here. I'll bet not one person in a hundred who buys a big cruising boat ever goes off for more than a month. And those people over there, they'll never have enough money to outfit that fifty-footer, let alone take off."

Seraffyn slowly floated upright as the tide returned. Suds and Carol left for dinner, and we launched *Rinky*. Larry rowed a 300-foot line to a cleat on the guest dock. We wrapped it around our sheet winch and cranked. *Seraffyn* went flying sternward through the darkness, right past the startled crew of a 40-foot powerboat at the end of the guest dock.

"What kind of motor is that quiet?" Steele Reeder asked us, climbing off the powerboat. After he had helped us to tie up, Steele called to his wife, "Babette, set two more places for dinner."

There's nothing like cruising to discover real hospitality. The next morning we dug out a phone number given to us by the owners of Beckman Lumber Company in California at the time we bought the teak for *Seraffyn's* decks. "My son loves sailing. Call him when you get to Miami," Howard Beckman had told us.

I dialed the number. When George Beckman answered the phone, I said, "You don't know me, but your father supplied most of the lumber we used to build our boat, *Seraffyn*. Would you and your wife like to join us for a drink some evening?"

"I don't believe it!" George said, when I finished talking. "My father must have told two hundred people to look me up when they reach Miami, but you're the first one who's ever called. I'd love to get together with you."

An hour later George rushed down the dock. "I'm in a real hurry," he said. "Here are my car keys. It's the yellow Datsun in the parking lot. Use it to get whatever you need. I'll be back for it—and that drink—this evening." He dropped the keys on deck, turned and ran off, leaving us open mouthed.

We saw a lot of George and his family. He was a jet pilot and owned a 38-foot charter yacht in Miami. By chance, he needed a qualified captain to handle a one-week charter. So, two weeks later Larry sailed off on another boat: this time his crew was six young chemists from Chicago.

We really weren't quite ready for the rush of Miami. Just 200 yards from *Seraffyn,* outside the gates of the yacht club, was a highway, roaring cars, and a major metropolitan city moving at a hectic urban pace.

We tried to hold to a slower tempo, but our social life became a real whirl as we met boating people from everywhere, including one friend who had migrated from California. Bob Riggs had been on hand to help the day *Seraffyn's* keel was lifted in place. Now he was selling boats in a used-car-lot atmosphere of a marina two docks away. After a great reunion, he, too, asked us our plans. "I'm looking for someone acceptable to the insurance company to deliver three new boats to their owners," he said. We sent a resumé of our experience to the insurance company—and suddenly we needed a calendar to keep track of all the work: one charter and three deliveries lined up for the winter months. But it was still summer, and we wanted to start our "freedom chip" account on its way up right now.

Another new friend drove us to Fort Lauderdale where our mail was waiting, and there, Waldon Jones, a yachtsman we had met in Costa Rica, welcomed us as we walked into his office.

"Sail up here," he suggested. "There's lots of work to be had, and good safe places to keep your boat, too." He grabbed his jacket and spent the rest of the day showing us the city with its canals, yacht basins and shipyards. Fort Lauderdale was even more hectic than Miami.

The drive back to Miami was beautiful under warm, clear skies, followed by a beautiful sunset. We arrived at the Coral Reef Yacht Club and strolled through the tropical darkness to the boat. We climbed aboard *Seraffyn* where she lay absolutely still at the guest dock. Then something caused me to look down at her fenders, and I couldn't believe my eyes.

Between the chainplates, where the channels had gleamed white that morning, was a mass of ground pulp! Larry came running at my shout, and we pulled *Seraffyn* away from the pilings to look. We couldn't figure out what had torn the oak apart, but scraps of wood hung from the pier pilings.

We surveyed the mess, and Larry took out his bosun's knife to cut away some of the shreds of wood. "Only a day's work to have this fixed," he told me. "no structural damage. I'll just have to grave in a piece of wood then putty and paint."

We were too tired to put the cushions out in the cockpit that night, so we slept in the double bunk forward with the stars shining through the open hatch. We both awoke at the same instant. Heavy thunder rumbled in the distance. Cracks of lightening lit up the sky. Larry closed the hatch over us just as the first drop of rain came through. Then the squall hit.

Seraffyn surged heavily against the docks, her fenders squealing as the wind shoved against her exposed side. The water around us started to boil, and our fenders leaped from their places, exposing our damaged channel once again to the grinding, tearing pilings. We were both on deck in moments, completely nude in the pouring rain. I cried with fear as I tried to keep the fenders in place. Larry worked feverishly, shouting encouragement to me over the thunder. He grabbed our warping line, tied it to the sheet winch, then dove overboard and swam through the chop to a dock 150 feet to windward. When he reached the dock, a man who had seen our predicament, took the line from Larry and secured it. I cranked the winch as I never had before. *Seraffyn* pulled slowly away from the destructive dock, and finally lay safe as the squall blew itself out.

Larry thanked our helpful friend and swam back. "That was the fellow we met at the club yesterday," he said, climbing aboard. "He recorded fifty knots of wind in the first gust."

We went below out of the rain, dried off and had hot chocolate. The mystery of the chewed-up channel was now solved, and our distrust of Miami summer weather increased.

Dave, the dockmaster, moved us to a more protected dock the next day. Then Larry set to work chiseling out the damaged wood and shaping a graving piece.

"She's a cruising boat, Lin," Larry said as he worked. "That's why she's strong and painted white instead of varnished. If we can't take a few bumps without worrying, we won't have much fun." Five of our C-clamps held the new piece of oak in place while the waterproof glue dried. Then we relaxed in the cockpit and had an early dinner.

Pho. 13-2. An even more elaborate meal in the cockpit, using the cabin table.

The people on *Yellowbird,* the 40-foot ketch tied just astern of us, Dick and Florence Clark, were busy taking off their roller-furling jib. Somehow their jib halyard had got loose and the bitter end went up to the masthead. Larry offered to climb their mast and retrieve it. He was at the masthead a few minutes, then he called down, "Have you inspected this mast lately?"

"Sure, the boat just came back from the shipyard two weeks ago," Dick replied. "They put a coat of varnish on both masts."

When Larry came down, he hoisted Dick aloft in the bosun's chair, and Dick was shocked to discover that the clear fiberglass covering of the mast had cracked, and that the wood beneath it was turning black—first sign of rot.

We had a long discussion about the problem, and ended up with us quoting a price to remove the mast, repair it, inspect all of the rigging on both spars, and put one more coat of varnish on each. We went to work for one of the nicest employers one could hope to find. Dick Clark wanted everything done right, the strongest way and the best way with the best materials.

"Why skimp on outfitting a boat? You may be risking your life," he said over breakfast in the café down the street, where we met each morning to discuss the day's work.

As with any working people, our boat stopped being a long-distance cruiser then and became a weekender. The first weekend trip was with Steele and Babette. We sailed out the Dinner Key channel—one mile of 60-foot long tacks! *Seraffyn* touching twice when we delayed tacking a second too long. Steele didn't complain about the blisters he was getting hauling jib sheets and cranking winches until we got back to the dock that evening. Then he said, "How come we didn't reach out the southern entrance?"

"What southern entrance?" Larry and I shouted together. Steele took our chart and showed us a channel six-feet deep out across the shoals.

The work on *Yellowbird* progressed well. Then Larry took off the second week to play charter captain, as scheduled. When he got back it was my turn to leave. My mother was coming east to North Carolina for a conference of the National Association of Educational Secretaries, and I went north to visit with her for a week. When I returned, I found we were part of "the system." We now owned a car, insurance, the whole catastrophe. Larry had bought a 10-year old station wagon to carry his tools. So, having wheels, we had to travel.

The following Friday we drove across Florida to visit Annabelle and Gordon Yates in St. Petersburg. We spent two days with them, reminiscing about Baja California and getting to know the 23-foot fiberglass sloop they were living aboard.

"Where are you headed next?" they asked us.

"North or east, we're not sure," Larry said. "But one thing I do know is that I don't like the summer climate here. I don't like hearing a hurricane warning almost every time I turn on the radio. And I don't like feeling *Seraffyn* isn't safe in the marina if a hurricane does come. We'd have to rush back there to take her up the river if we got a warning now."

We told them about our dream of a farm on a creek with a fireplace.

"You ought to go up to Virginia, then," Annabelle said. "We spent a winter there, and it's just what you're looking for."

A man was standing on the dock taking photos of *Seraffyn* when we woke up one Saturday morning. That afternoon he came back with a friend. We were only too glad to talk to anyone who admired our boat that much.

"I own a small shipyard on Chesapeake Bay," Joe told us. One hour and three cups of coffee later, Joe made a suggestion: "Why not take off a few days and drive with me up to my place in Virginia. I'm way behind on a 56-foot power yacht I'm building, and I'd sure appreciate some skilled help." He described his creekside shipyard, and a boatshed his neighbor owned that seemed just right for *Seraffyn*.

There was so much good work available in Miami that for once we decided to be cautious. As much as we wanted to escape Florida's humid summer weather, we didn't want just to pack up and set sail. Instead, we took the cushions out of *Seraffyn,* plus our primus backup stove, a few pots, some cans of food and a thermos, and set out northward through the swamplands of Florida in our station wagon, *Green Machine.*

We fell in love with Virginia. An hour after we arrived at Urbanna on the Rappahannock River, we knew we were hooked. Then, on a sail downriver and across to the other side, we knew we had found "our" boatyard, on a creek. Farms spread their green fields down to the water's edge. Oysters waited along the banks, juicy and salty, ready to be downed in one gulp.

We went to the post office at Urbanna, a town of 600, and spoke to the postmistress: "We are planning to sail our boat up here from Miami for the winter. What address shall we use?" Our new address is beautifully simple: Lin and Larry Pardey, Urbanna, Virginia. We drove straight back to Miami to get *Seraffyn.*

But, we had complicated our lives. No longer could we just buy a few extra stores, lift anchor and go. First, we had to finish the work on *Yellowbird.* Next, we had a car to move to Virginia. Then there were the hurricanes.

We had a real reason to worry about them. Without an engine, we couldn't take *Seraffyn* up the inland waterway, so we would have to sail the 800 miles north in the open sea and around storm-ridden Cape Hatteras. The trip would take eight or nine days, and, other than Charleston, South Carolina, there are few safe ports along the wreck-strewn coast.

The work on *Yellowbird* proceeded quickly; the car problem was solved by our friend Waldon Jones. "The way you rave about Virginia makes me want to take a holiday," he said. "As soon as you get up there call me; I'll take a week off to drive your *Green Machine* north."

The hurricanes remained bothersome. Each morning there were radio reports: Tropical storm Beth. Course 215 degrees. Position—Yucatan Channel. Winds—Force 10."

Three boats down from us, Dr. Simpson, head of the Miami Hurricane Research Bureau, heard about our concern. He walked over one day and said, "If you can be ready to go with half a day's notice, I can tell you when there will be a good eight-to-ten day clear stretch for your voyage."

September is the height of the hurricane season. The hurricane map up at the store showed two tropical storms, two hurricanes, and a depression fanned out across the Atlantic and the Caribbean on the evening Dr. Simpson told us we could go.

"Don't worry about those hurricanes," he said. "The one near Bermuda is dying, the one near Colombia is traveling at only six knots, so it would take twelve or fourteen days to get here, even if it came this way. The two near the Cape Verde Islands are even farther away. I can just about guarantee ten days of easterly winds, but it will be winter when you get to Cape Hatteras."

His advice sounded completely logical, so we had a quick farewell breakfast with Dick and Florence and left. We cleared Dinner Key and anchored in the clean water of Biscayne Bay where Larry went overboard with his mask and fins to scrape the barnacles off our keel. We wanted all the speed we could get. Then we set our lapper, staysail and main, sailed out to the Atlantic, and went on a close reach to the north-northeast.

I felt as if we were being chased by invisible demons as I listened to the hurricane reports three times a day. Sure enough, the one over Bermuda dissipated, the one 600 miles south of us did turn north, but only traveling two knots faster than we were. The Gulf Stream was on our side. We got a 60-mile boost the first day, and about 20 miles a day for the next four.

When we reached the Cape Hatteras area we discovered the doctor was right—it was winter. All day we reduced sail. First, down staysail; then a reef in the main. Each time we took something off *Seraffyn* we put something else on ourselves. First, a jersey, then, pants. It was really cold! By mid-afternoon on our sixth day out, we were beating east in 50 knots of wind under triple-reefed main and staysail, wearing sweaters, jackets and wet-weather gear.

"Do you think it's worth it?" I asked Larry from my warm sleeping bag when he stuck his dripping head below to check the time.

"Yup, if we are living in a place we really like, we'll work harder and get cruising again sooner. Remember those oysters?"

When we had cleared the dangerous shoals of Cape Hatteras by 50 miles we went onto the other tack. *Seraffyn* fought looming seas, her log registering three knots through the water despite the 50-knot winds. Every hour for two-and-a-half days I blessed the strong rigging and watertight decks that let us punish *Seraffyn* that way without her making a sign of protest.

Just after nightfall on our eighth day at sea, a ship approached, searchlights playing on our reefed sails. The ship loomed larger and larger until we could see its seawashed decks as it rolled heavily. We both stood on deck watching it, praying it wasn't going to try to rescue us. In those heaving seas, *Seraffyn* wouldn't have

Pho. 13-3. We loved everything about Virginia, especially the pretty little sloops we saw on the Chesapeake.

stood a chance against that great steel hull. But the Japanese "fish factory" was just curious. They circled us 100 yards off then steamed southward into the dark.

Through the night the wind eased and by morning we were able to set more sail and reach into the Chesapeake Bay with all plain sail set. We anchored in calm water off the entrance of the York River. We had made 800 miles in eight days, beating all the way.

It took us two days to cover the last 60 miles up the Bay. We anchored both nights and never once turned on the hurricane reports. Then at last we sailed into Robinson's Creek to anchor in front of Joe's shipyard.

We looked around us at the flaming leaves of the oaks lining the riverbanks. A beautiful Chesapeake sloop tugging at a mooring nearby was *Seraffyn's* only neighbor on the slow-moving waters.

Joe called out to us, "The postmistress will send your mail down with the next person who comes this way," he shouted. "It should be here as soon as you come ashore for a shower and the southern fried chicken Eleanor is making at home."

In the morning Rudy Shackleford, one of Joe's workmen, roused us. "Hurricane coming," he said. "Better move in to the pilings, and secure your boat."

That evening the winds began. By morning, the water in the creek was washing over the small jetty as winds up to 60 knots churned the river into a froth. *Seraffyn* tugged at the eight ¾-inch mooring lines holding her firmly in the center of four strong pilings. Larry worked contentedly in the shop, building a box for his tools. I sewed next to the fire in Joe's home, mending some of our winter clothes and watching the rain lash the windowpanes.

Dr. Simpson had promised us eight or ten days without a hurricane. We'd had eleven. Now we were safe and sound for the winter.

14

Virginia

WE HAD JUST FOUND our cottage when we got a letter from Lyle Hess, saying that he and his wife, Jeanne, were coming east to the Annapolis Boat Show—only 90 miles from Urbanna. We drove up to meet them and had a great reunion. Going to boat shows is always fun, but having a skilled architect and shipwright as your companion makes it doubly interesting. Afterward we drove Lyle and Jeanne back to Urbanna, the four of us talking incessantly, swapping news of friends in California—sailors, boatbuilders, and the old Newport Beach waterfront crowd. Lyle wanted an evaluation of *Seraffyn's* cruising performance. It took us four days to explain what could have been said in two words: "She's perfect."

Waldon Jones arrived from Florida with *Green Machine,* and joined Larry and Lyle for a sail on *Seraffyn.* They came back chilled, but Waldon was beaming. He had just asked Lyle to design him a larger *Seraffyn.*

"Aren't you ready yet for something a bit bigger?" Lyle asked us that evening.

"She takes us and all our stuff where we want to go," Larry said, "so why stop sailing for two or three years just to build a bigger boat?"

I passed the plate of grilled oysters as I said, "When it's too cold to live on *Seraffyn,* it only costs us seventy to eighty dollars a month to rent a cottage like this. For that amount we couldn't even start to build a boat big enough to have a fireplace. Besides, I wouldn't be able to sail a boat much bigger by myself, since I only weigh ninety-eight pounds."

"And then there's the cost," Larry said. "We only have to work about three months a year to pay for cruising in a twenty-four footer. If we went to a thirty-five footer, we'd be working four or five months for money, plus a month extra on the boat. I like sailing, not working, so I'll stick to little *Seraffyn.*"

Lyle and Waldon promised to keep us up to date on the *Super Seraffyn* by sending us drawings as they evolved. We hated to see the Hesses and Waldon go, but the void they left was soon filled with new people, the country folk of Virginia.

What amazed both Larry and me about that part of Virginia was the lack of crowds. We expected it to be jammed with people. We imagined highways and cities. But Middlesex County, larger than Los Angeles, had only about 10,000 people. It was our first taste of American small-town life and we loved it.

Joe introduced us to Mrs. Carlton who owned the property on which his shipyard was located. Her house overlooked Joe's place on one side and a round pond connected to the river on the other. On the pond was a boat shed.

On the day we went to visit her, Mrs. Carlton insisted we use the shed. "Pay me? Don't worry about that," she said. "It's nice to have people around. No one's used the shed since my husband died." She poured tea, served us delicious homemade pie, and then showed us the diploma she had just received from the University of Richmond. "I drove sixty miles there every morning, sixty miles back every evening, and graduated with honors at the age of sixty-eight," she told us with pride.

We removed *Seraffyn's* mast using the boatyard sheer legs. Then we rowed her through the 20-foot-wide mouth of the pond and into the shed. She fit it as if it had been made for her; even the tip of the bowsprit was protected. We stripped the boat of everything, bunkboards, stores, chain, hatches, the deck box, the locker doors. Then we scrubbed the inside of her hull with soap and water—our regular annual cleaning. Shorn of her finery, our elegant cutter looked tiny and forlorn. I went by her every day for the first two weeks to assure myself that she was safe and secure.

We settled in. I borrowed a bicycle. Larry drove to Joe's each morning. At "home," I wrote, played house and explored. Virgil Gill had rented us a cottage that had once been the slaves' quarters of Remlik Turkey Farm. It sat beneath a large mulberry tree half a mile from the main house. On one side was a pasture with a spotted pony. Downwind, 500 feet away, was the pig pen. About 1000 feet to the right was the cow barn, and on our left, down the slope with its covey of mallards, was the river. I was given a gallon of fresh milk each day, and Helen Gill showed me how to make it into butter and yoghurt. On one of our evening rides home through the woods, we startled a buck deer. It stood in the glare of our headlights a moment, then bounded off, into the brush. Somehow it was a symbol of what we loved about Virginia.

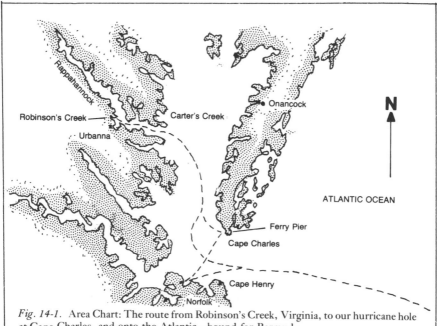

Fig. 14-1. Area Chart: The route from Robinson's Creek, Virginia, to our hurricane hole at Cape Charles, and onto the Atlantic—bound for Bermuda.

A month later we had to fly to Miami to deliver the first two of the three boats we had agreed to handle. It was a jolt to fly from the cool rural atmosphere of Urbanna straight into the heat and humidity of Miami without the "padding" of a sailing voyage in between. Then there was the shock of delivering a new production boat. I'd been on several delivery jobs before, but all of them had been racers, tested and outfitted by their owners, or motor cruisers on their way home against wind or current after a long cruise.

To step aboard a new, fresh-from-the-factory boat and take it to sea is frightening. The ads look great, but they don't tell you that much of what you see in them are "options." Our first boat had no anchor, no bucket, no chain, no door latches, no bilge pumps, loose hose clamps (leaky hoses), no cotter pins in the rigging. It took us two days of shopping and inspection to get that boat ready for sea.

The owner had bought the most boat $35,000 could buy; to us, it was no bargain. We made a 1200-mile beat in her, in winds up to 50 knots, and by the time we reached Puerto Rico we had a list of 28 broken items, including poorly installed chain plates, a structural bulkhead that fell out when we started going to windward, and household electrical fittings that got damp and shorted out after three days at sea.

The second delivery was a different boat from a different builder, but the same story. It made us feel that when you buy any new boat, particularly production fiberglass, it's a case of buyer beware. A beginner, buying a boat for the first time and lacking experience should certainly hire someone who really knows how a boat should be put together, to survey the boat beforehand. It may seem like an added expense, but what the buyer learns will save him money and help him get a good boat.

As soon as we flew back to Urbanna, we drove over to check *Seraffyn,* then went to our little cottage. Larry lit a roaring fire while I clutched my sailing jacket tightly around me. As the fire warmed our tiny living room I cooked hamburgers on the grill in the fireplace. By the glow of the fire we ate and discussed our future.

"Well, Lin, looks like we'll have enough freedom chips to sail again by April," Larry said. "Where do you want to go?"

"I'd love to see England, the Thames, 'Falmouth for Orders,' and boats that look like *Seraffyn,*" I said.

"But what about Nantucket, Cuttyhunk, Newport and Mystic Seaport?" Larry asked.

"Yes, and then there's Maine and the St. Lawrence," I added.

"England does sound good, though, Lin," Larry said. "We could go up to the Clyde and see Fife's old yards and Ireland's rocky coast."

"But what about Bristol, Rhode Island—Herreshoff country?" I asked.

"How about flipping a coin?" Larry suggested. "Heads for England, tails for New England."

The penny flashed in the firelight and its copper glow revealed our fate: heads—east to England, to the Old World for new adventures.

I pedaled my bike down the country lane with Larry's lunch in the basket. At the road to the boatyard I paused, then decided to continue into town to get our mail. The first letter I saw was from *Boating* magazine. Well, I thought, at least they've got around to rejecting my two articles. I had prepared myself for this. (I had a friend in California who received 50 rejection slips without having one piece

Pho. 14-2. Our table, which slides under the cockpit, serves equally well for eating or typing.

accepted.) I walked out of the post office, stopped and opened the letter:

"A check will be sent to you sometime this week. Would you like to write a short series of articles for us?"

I don't remember pedaling back to Joe's. When I got there, Larry was just walking out of the shed where he was lofting a 38-foot powerboat.

"We're *rich*–we're writers!" I yelled to him.

"How about some lunch? Then you can tell me what all this noise is about," Larry called back.

We spread lunch on the dock next to *Seraffyn*. Then I showed him the letter. Before we'd finished eating, we spent the check seven times.

"Well, Lin," Larry said, "I vote we have a good dinner to celebrate, then take the writing money to buy you a decent typewriter that will fit on *Seraffyn*. I wonder if I could write some of the ideas I've come up with?"

A big freeze-up came just after Christmas. We had spent a day exploring Colonial Williamsburg, the atmosphere of 1770 seeming all the more realistic in the restored village as young boys carried in armloads of wood to stoke the roaring wood fires of the kitchens in the Governor's mansion.

When we returned to our 1820 cottage, the ground was frozen. We needed an extra blanket on our bed even with the gas heater going full blast. We woke up at 0200, shivering. The gas line had frozen, and the heater had stopped. The thermometer outside the window registered –2°. Larry volunteered to climb out of our semi-warm bed and start a fire. I saw the flicker of the fire start and dragged our sleeping bag and blankets into the living room. We cuddled close, next to that roaring fireplace, remembering humid nights in the tropics.

Morning came, bright and cold at 6°. A temperature 26° below freezing was something really new to us. All the plumbing for the cottage, including the toilet, was frozen. Later, Rudi and Barbara Shackleford drove up and unloaded birch logs, saying, "Figured you'd need some slow-burning wood to see you through. Come over to our place if you want a shower. We built our house for these temperatures." Virgil arrived next to tell us there was water available at the main house. So we were back to boat conditions for four days—a bucket for a head, and a jug for water.

By February our freedom chip account was healthy, with one more boat delivery to top it up, and a bit of writing income due to put icing on the cake. Since we were sailing for Europe and might not be back for years, we decided to pack *Green Machine* and drive west to visit our folks. One of the men at Joe's promised to keep an eye on *Seraffyn* for us.

We started off with a foam ice chest holding eight gallons of yoghurt and ten pounds of fresh butter as homemade gifts for our friends in California. We had a snow storm in Texas. We were awed by the colors of the Painted Desert. We visited my folks in Los Angeles, and friends in old Newport Beach. Then we drove through the flood of the Columbia River to the Pend-Oreille River, and up to Vancouver, British Columbia, where Larry's family and friends overfed us, and finally wished us fond farewells. We drove back east to New York, then south to Virginia. In six weeks, we covered 9000 miles.

Spring was arriving when we reached Virginia. *Seraffyn* was covered with bird droppings and feathers. There must have been 10 birds nesting in the rafters above her.

"Clean me, rig me, sail me," she seemed to say, and we were listening.

We stripped the old varnish from *Seraffyn's* mast and boom. Then, while I applied six coats of varnish, Larry took on *Rinky Dink*. He removed her debonded seats and filled them with new foam. While he reglassed the seats in place, he filled the gouges and dents. In four days she looked like new. *Seraffyn* got more comfortable backrests on her settees, an extra hawse pipe for our nylon bow warp, and a new teak sill for the companionway.

In the evenings Larry spliced new wire rigging. We had bought first-quality American stainless steel wire for *Seraffyn* when she was built. Now, only two years later, it was rusting, and some the of the strands were unlaying. In Jamaica we had been moored next to a 10-year old English yacht whose stainless-wire rigging glowed like new. Larry wondered why ours wasn't like that and, on a hunch, took a magnet from our portable chess set. Our wire grabbed the little magnet and held it; the English wire didn't attract the magnet at all. So we took the magnet with us when we drove to Norfolk to look at wire in various chandlers. All of them offered wire that grabbed the magnet. Finally, in disgust we ordered 300 feet of quarter-inch 7x7 stainless rigging wire from Jeckells of England. Five years later, that wire is still like new.

In three weeks all the in-the-water jobs were done. A few car trips to Richmond and Norfolk took care of purchasing the stores we needed and the charts for our proposed route: Bermuda-Azores-English Channel-Falmouth. Our butane tank was repaired and the only job left was to deliver one more boat, and then haul *Seraffyn* for a paint job.

This time we arrived in Miami and found a completely outfitted 35-footer. The owner had spent a month on board and ironed out the bugs of a new boat. As he wrote us, he had "spent twenty six thousand on the boat then five thousand more on extras to get her ready for sea."

We powered up the Intercoastal Waterway, 1100 miles to Virginia, in 14 days. It's a scenic and interesting route, but one that better suits a powerboat with lots of time than a sailboat in a hurry. When we turned her over to the owner, we were practically home.

At high tide one day in early May we rowed *Seraffyn* out of the boat house and across the pond to the boatyard pier. Joe's ways were full, so we loaded *Seraffyn's* mast, boom and dinghy on deck and towed her downriver to Ben Benson's Boat Yard, six miles away on Irvington Creek.

Seraffyn was lifted out on a travel lift and put in a cradle on top of a bed of oyster shells. As we stripped her topsides and waterline down to bare wood, new friends arrived. Dr. Walter Tilden, the 85-year-old owner of a 25-foot Folkboat brought us a basket of the first strawberries from his garden. "Sure would like a sail on her," he said, admiring *Seraffyn*.

Frank Mann hauled his Folkboat *Hetara* into a cradle just 100 feet from us and he set to work stripping paint, too. "Soon as we get our boats back in the water let's go for a short cruise together," he said.

Seraffyn sat quietly as we refurbished her. I gold-leafed her name anew and varnished her bilges and hatches. Larry painted creosote on her newly wooded waterline to within a half-inch of the topside paint. Then he applied our standard three coats in one hot day. "Now I don't have to worry about worms as much ," he said. We worked like devils for two weeks and relaunched a like-new *Seraffyn*, glowing in white, varnish and blue.

After transferring our possessions back to the boat, we added up our hours of work—almost 500 hours. If a shipyard had done the work, it would have cost nearly $3000—over a year's cruising expenses. Materials came to $400, including

Pho. 14-3. Hauled out and seen in profile, *Seraffyn* shows her modest forefoot and large rudder, which allows her to come about quickly, even under main alone.

hauling charges. Once again we blessed our small boat, which we could maintain ourselves.

Before the Atlantic crossing, we had one final important job. Virgil Gill had taken us on a walking tour of his farm one day, and pointed out some trees just coming into bloom. "That's locust," he said, "best timber in the world. Used it for fence posts for sixty years—never rots, stronger than oak, impervious to bugs once it's seasoned. If you're really plannin' to build another boat some day, you can cut down these seven trees—as long as you clean up afterward. An' you can put the wood in the old barn over by the race track, to season." In payment for those trees, Larry rebuilt the toilet on Virgil's power cruiser. Some day we may want a new *Seraffyn,* and the 1500 board feet of two-inch locust flitches that Larry cut and stored will be dry and ready for us.

It was good to get back on board. Just living on the boat gives me the feeling that I own the world, and now there was the added excitement of an ocean crossing ahead—50 or 60 days if we were slow, 40 if we weren't. We spent days collecting books. I made shopping lists, bought items, crossed them off, started new lists. *Seraffyn* settled to her lines, lockers jammed with canned and packaged goods.

One day our friends, Rick and Susan Blagbourne arrived from Vancouver, unannounced. They often did that to us. "Couldn't let you sail off without a good farewell committee," Rick said. The two of them joined us on day cruises up the

Pho. 14-4. Rick and Susan Blagbourne arrived from Vancouver, British Columbia.

river, and helped us check our gear one last time.

I found a copy of Lloyds registry of yachts and got the address of a yacht club in Falmouth, England. I wrote the secretary and asked if they would hold our mail. A Mrs. Muirhead wrote back, "Of course." So instead of simply "Urbanna, Virginia," we now had a rather grand address: "Yacht Serrafyn, c/o the Royal Cornwall Yacht Club, Greenbank, Falmouth, near Truro, Cornwall, England."

We had written our farewell letters, taken Dr. Tilden and his wife for a sail, refitted our boat, explored the creeks of the Corrotoman River, cut our timber, and eaten our fill of oysters. All we had to do was buy our fresh food and leave; there was nothing more to do.

"We can't go without some kind of thank-you to the people around here," I said to Larry, and he agreed. In our moment of need, Joanne and Lou Siegel and the Rappahannock River Yacht Club generously offered us their pier for a dock party.

Next to *Seraffyn,* we set up a table with a huge bowl of our special rum punch, a bucket of ice cubes, a bottle of bourbon, a bowl of oysters, several loaves of fresh bread, and several platters of cold cuts and sweets. People drove 40 miles from Urbanna to say farewell—people I'll never forget, like Mr. and Mrs. Bristow, owners of Urbanna's country store. Mrs. Bristow had spent hours helping me with my manuscripts.

Barbara and Rudy Shackleford arrived in their little speedboat. Barbara had hand-embroidered a set of linen napkins for *Seraffyn*. As the last guests were leaving, Virgil Gill called over his shoulder, "Better clean out your oven."

I opened the oven door and found a 20-pound turkey, "Compliments of Remlik Hall." Virgil had supplied half our fresh meat for the voyage.

Rick and Susan helped us lug aboard 100 pounds of ice, 25 pounds of potatoes, 25 pounds of onions, 144 eggs, fresh meat, and fruit. They took possession of *Green Machine* and agreed to put it on blocks next to our locust in Virgil's old barn.

At noon the next day we untied our mooring lines. No one was around to send us off. But downriver at the mouth of the creek there was a surprise waiting for us: Four boats from the Rappahannock River Yacht Club were waiting to accompany us on the first leg, Susan and Rick among them.

We put Helmer to work and sat on *Seraffyn's* side deck as she worked to windward. We shouted across the water, "Come on, get a boat and sail to England, too."

Rick called back, "Someday. Don't worry, we'll join you someday."

One by one the boats turned back and we were alone again and on our way, our next planned stop, Bermuda. *Seraffyn* was ready, and we were ready—but the weather wasn't.

15

Hurricane

AS WE SAILED toward the ocean, Larry said, "Well, Lin, it's the big moment. A penny for your thoughts."

I watched the last of our friends sail back under the Rappahannock River Bridge and said, "I remembered the extra toothpaste."

Larry gave me his familiar what-a-nut-you-are look and asked, "Are you worried about crossing the Atlantic?"

"Not if you aren't. Remember what you said the day I met you, when you took me for a sail on your charter boat? 'Stick with me, baby, and you'll go a long way.' Well, I hate to admit it but you've kept your promise, and it's been a pretty good life so far."

Larry adjusted the windvane and eased the jib sheet just a touch. Then he looked up at *Seraffyn's* rigging before answering. "We've sailed through some pretty rough weather without breaking a single piece of gear yet, so I don't see any reason to start worrying now," he said. "The *Pilot Chart* shows good weather for the crossing. I just wish this wind would back a bit. I can't see any good reason to start beating across the Atlantic."

The wind held steady from the east-southeast. We tacked across Chesapeake Bay and reached along the Eastern Shore. In the next few hours the barometer fell and the sky became overcast. We anchored near shore for the night, and I roasted the turkey for dinner. We went to bed early.

We turned on the morning weather forecast before we lifted anchor: "Southeast winds, 20 to 25 knots . . ." Larry got out the chart. "The chart shows a harbor about fifteen miles south of here," he said. "Let's reach down there and anchor till this thing blows over."

We hauled up the anchor and set the main and staysail. I turned on the radio again at noon: "Southeast winds increasing to 28 to 35 knots by evening." Before I clicked the radio off, I heard something more: "Hurricane Agnes, situated near Cuba, has been down-graded to a tropical storm, with winds of 45 to 50 knots." I forgot about that as the entrance to the abandoned Cape Charles Ferry Harbor appeared ahead.

We sailed through the 200-foot-wide entrance—two breakwaters formed by rows of sunken concrete ships. The line of ships stretched toward the shore, but ended about 200 yards short of the beach. Straight ahead was a deserted ferry terminal with a T-shaped dock. A 32-foot double-ended, gaffrigged cutter named *Juno* was anchored in the center of the harbor. We sailed past her and anchored near the protecting shore, just northwest of the pier. The wind was gusting off the

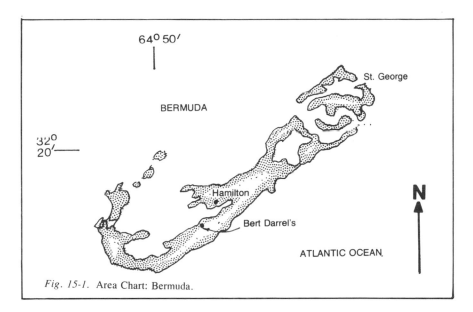

Fig. 15-1. Area Chart: Bermuda.

land at 20 knots, but our 25-pound CQR grabbed well in the sandy bottom at 18 feet. Larry paid out 100 feet of chain as we had plenty of room astern of us.

The barometer kept dropping all night. By morning rain squalls came tumbling over the point of Cape Charles. The wind increased to over 30 knots. We lay comfortably, only the slightest swell distrubing our anchorage. I turned on the radio every two hours. "Possible wind shift to the north or northwest at 18 to 20 knots, then decreasing," was the report at 1500.

The barometer was low—29.30 and still dropping slowly. We had plenty of scope out, and good protection from every direction but the west—the 200-foot opening of the entrance. We slept soundly that night in spite of the whine in the rigging; at midnight the wind quit.

Seraffyn woke us as she rolled slowly to the swell we had felt earlier. When we were head-to-wind, the swell rolling under our stern hadn't disturbed us, but now with no wind *Seraffyn* lay in the trough. We slid open the hatch: a starry sky and calm night.

"Well, Lin, we can probably start for Bermuda tomorrow," Larry said.

I went to get a drink of water and tapped the barometer as I drank: 28.70—and falling.

Then the wind hit again, the first gust swinging *Seraffyn* violently to the end of her chain. Rain slashed down through the open hatch. Larry rushed past me to the deck. I heard the rattle of chain playing out through the screech of wind in the rigging.

I grabbed a torch. The ferry dock, with its T-shaped concrete-and-steel arms, had protected us from the southeast winds, but now it rose over us menacingly, only 100 feet away.

Larry came below, drenched. He said, "She's holding, Lin, it's probably just a squall. Turn on the radio." Country music blared over the sound of wind and rain.

Seraffyn lunged against her 5/16-inch chain, and the seas started to build. The wind didn't come from north-northwest now, but directly from the west, right into the harbor entrance—and we were right in its path. Larry put on his foul-weather gear and went on deck again to put a nylon snubbing line on our chain.

I listened to the radio as the announcer broke through the music: "Warning! Hurricane Agnes has reformed over the Virginia capes and southern Chesapeake Bay. Cape Charles reports winds of 85 knots." We were three miles from Cape Charles.

Larry came into the cockpit. "It must be blowing sixty out here," he yelled. "I can barely stand on deck."

I yelled back at him, "It's blowing eighty! We're in a hurricane."

A flash of light hit Larry, and we looked up to see the owner of *June*, 200 yards to windward of us, on deck, paying out chain for an extra anchor. We couldn't do that as we were too close to that pier to let out any more scope. It was impossible to launch the dinghy. Even if we had launched it, no one could have rowed against that wind and sea. I looked around and started to cry.

"Lin, get into your wet gear," Larry ordered. "and we'll rig *Seraffyn* so that if we start to drag we can leave the anchor and sail out the southern entrance."

The barometer was still dropping. Under the pressure of the fierce wind, the waters of Chesapeake Bay were being pushed southward—right through our harbor. The current must have been five or six knots, and it held us beam-to the building seas—parallel to the ferry dock.

I crawled forward along the deck, tasting the salt of tears or spray, I didn't know which. Larry had to shout instructions right into my ear. *Seraffyn* rolled her bulwarks under, first one, then the other. And then the ⅜-inch nylon anchor-chain snubber snapped!

Larry let out more chain. We now lay to a scope of 11:1. Together we rigged a line that would let us turn *Seraffyn* stern to wind if we decided to slip our anchor chain. Larry rigged an anchor buoy to throw over if we did leave, so that we could return for our ground tackle later. Then we triple-reefed the mainsail. What a job that was: it would have been impossible without lazy jacks!

Another flash of lightning revealed that terrifying pier just 100 feet away. Row after row of waves paraded through the harbor entrance, hitting us smack on the beam. I went below and tried to warm milk for hot chocolate. I didn't finish;

Pho. 15-2 & 15-3. The ferry dock, with its T-shaped concrete-and-steel arms, had protected us from the southeast winds, but now rose over us menacingly.

instead I rushed on deck to vomit.

Larry came below. He held me and said, "If the anchor chain parts, or the anchor starts to drag, we may be able to run out of here now. We can set the reefed main or the staysail or do it under bare poles. If *Seraffyn* goes aground, we'll tie a long line between us and swim ashore together. Swim with the seas. There aren't many rocks on shore. Once you're in the water, forget the boat and worry about yourself."

My stomach surged and rebelled. Larry told me to keep my wet gear on and lie on the cabin sole. He went out on deck again to get a long safety line ready. When he came into the cabin 10 minutes later, blood was running from his forehead, down the front of his jacket and onto his trousers.

I forgot my stomach and grabbed a towel.

"Don't know what I hit," he said, as I swabbed his head.

I managed a slight laugh when the "gash" turned out to be a nick less than a quarter-inch long. A Bandaid took care of it.

Still *Seraffyn* rolled and lunged, solid green water sloshing first up one cabin side, then the other, the rigging shrieking, chain crashing in its chock, dishes bashing, and books shifting.

At 0300 the radio reported: "Hurricane Agnes is now moving north, with winds to 75 knots. The barometer is rising."

I tapped ours. It was rising, too! As for the wind, we couldn't tell if it was worse or better. *Seraffyn* still rolled abominably.

Keeping busy, Larry crawled out on deck once again to take down the remains of our windvane cover. He came back in, holding the torn bits of dacron and the remains of the counterbalance. "We're holding well, Lin," he said. "Try not to worry too much."

"Are you frightened, Larry?" I asked from the cabin sole, as he poured himself a shot of brandy.

"Yes," he said, "I've never been so scared in my life. But I think the worst is over. Try to sleep. I'll do everything I can." He tapped the glass. "Look at the barometer rise," he said. It had jerked up from 28.50 to 28.60.

Pho. 15-4 & 15-5. Dawn showed the unmistakable marching ranks of hurricane clouds. The wind was dropping, but *Seraffyn* still rolled and lunged violently.

The grey dawn showed the unmistakable marching ranks of hurricane clouds. The wind was dropping, but *Seraffyn* still rolled and lunged violently. Larry could now face the wind when he stood in the cockpit. The rain stopped and Larry yelled down to me, "The guy on *Juno* is taking photos of us. We must look a sight."

By 0930 the wind was down to 45 knots. The rolling had not eased, however, and the pier was still only 100 feet away.

"Come on, Lin," Larry said. "Let's try to sail to Norfolk, and find a more comfortable anchorage. If we can't lay Norfolk harbor, we'll come back here and anchor in a better spot."

Our anchor had started for China. We had the chain straight up and down and heaved as hard as we could on the 9:1-ratio winch. Each lunge of the boat broke another few links loose, and it was 30 minutes before we finally broke the CQR free.

We ran out the south entrance under double-reefed main and staysail, and hit a confused sea. The current had changed. Now the water was rushing north, back into the bay, as the huge depression passed. We couldn't lay Norfolk—the seas were too rough and the wind was still gusting to 45 knots. So we ran back and anchored close to the western breakwater, a much better spot.

What bliss! *Seraffyn* only rolled slightly in the swell. I could stand up and didn't feel seasick. The wind dropped steadily but the swell where *Juno* was didn't. We saw one man struggling to raise an anchor. Larry suggested he take the dinghy and try to help.

As Larry rowed off, keeping close to the sheltering breakwater, I yelled, "Bring him back for lunch, there's plenty of turkey."

I turned on the radio and heard reports of floods, ruined crops, deaths, and the entire city of Richmond without drinking water. Our losses were minor. It had been a really bad night, but all we suffered was a blown-out windvane cover and a broken counterbalance support.

Larry and Ray Bashum arrived for lunch after moving *Juno* closer to the breakwater. Ray told us how lucky he was to have room to set two anchors after being hit by the first 85-knot gusts. "My God, how you rolled!" he said. "You sure looked uncomfortable."

"We were," I said.

Ray said he would send us copies of the photos he had taken that morning. "It was only blowing 65 knots on my indicator when I took them, but I could still see most of your rudder and bilge when *Seraffyn* rolled. I saw how close you were to that pier and I tried to float a line down to you on a buoy. If it hadn't been for that current, I could have reached you, and pulled out another anchor to hold you head to wind."

Ray was headed home to Solomon Island after a single-handed voyage from the Bahamas. "I'm sure glad I came in to wait the storm out," he said as he climbed into the dinghy to leave.

We sailed to Norfolk the next day, under clear blue skies and on quiet seas. The only reminder of our encounter with Hurricane Agnes was our bare windvane frame.

A friendly but very busy sailmaker was kind enough to let us sew up a new vane cover on his machine. So, two days later, with more ice and fresh food on board, we tried again: Next stop, Bermuda.

A light northerly forced us to short-tack out the Little Creek entrance. We were halfway out when Larry said, "Look behind us, Lin."

An aircraft carrier, a destroyer and two escort vessels were chugging slowly down on us. "Discretion is the better part of valor," Larry said, and he eased sheets and ran back in the narrow channel to let the huge ships pass. I unrolled our Canadian flag and let it fly as the carrier passed. Every man on board saluted, and their ensign dipped. When the last ship passed, we hardened sheets again and once more started beating toward the entrance. A light southerly breeze came up, and wispy fog covered the horizon as we beat out of Chesapeake Bay toward the Atlantic.

For two days we sailed in light shifting headwinds, using our big genoa. Then we found our old friend the Gulf Stream. The barometer dropped and grey clouds started to build. Working fast we got the genoa down and the mainsail reefed before the first squall hit. The wind rose steadily from the southwest, and the seas built until we dropped the triple-reefed main, and reached along under just the staysail in 40 knots of wind.

The Gulf Stream kicked up an ugly sea. One wave broke under our windward bilge and rolled *Seraffyn's* leeward deck down until the cockpit filled. My plastic wash basin was in the cockpit with the forward-cowl-vent top and the bag for the spare taffrail log spinners in it. We watched them all float away, and decided it was time to heave-to.

We lay hove-to for 12 hours. "I hope it's not another hurricane," I told Larry.

"No, Lin, just the Gulf Stream," Larry said, but I turned the radio on every hour to get weather reports.

We set sail again when the skies cleared. Soon we were reaching along at six knots under double-reefed main and staysail through a starlit night.

At 0600 Larry called me, "Come see this huge squall." I climbed out of the bunk. To windward, rushing toward us was a huge cloud, thunderbolts bursting

Pho. 15-6 & 15-7. The squall hit as a sheet of wind. *Seraffyn* heeled 20 degrees, but rode comfortably. The rain and wind hit so hard the seas went flat.

out of it from every angle, rain hissing down, and a froth of white water in front of it like the bow wave of a huge ship.

"Quick, Lin, get the camera!" Larry said.

"Larry, let's get some sail down," I answered, jittery with worry.

"You get the waterproof camera, I'll heave-to. But hurry!" Larry said.

I dug out the camera, and *Seraffyn* came close to the wind with only her double-reefed mainsail still pulling.

The squall hit as a sheet of wind, and Larry laughed with glee as he snapped photos. *Seraffyn* heeled 20 degrees, but rode comfortably. The rain and wind hit so hard the seas went flat. By the time the squall passed, the seas were nearly calm again and the sun came out. The wind died and 20 minutes later we were cautiously setting more sail, bit by bit. Two hours later I wrote in our log: *Beam reaching under lapper, staysail, mainsail. Speed five knots, perfect sailing.*

From the log:

Sunday, July 2, (1972) 1200. Noon-to-noon run, 112 miles, Bermuda 150 miles off. Fantastic sailing.

Monday, July 3. 0800. All same. Perfect.

But those log entries don't tell the whole story. We had dinner on the foredeck, our wine glasses steady on the deck while we ate baked potato, roast beef and tossed salad. Our stereo recorder played Beethoven's "Moonlight Sonata." After dinner we lounged against a sailbag, arms around each other, trying to identify stars from our *Bowditch* star chart.

Our three-hour night watches went swiftly. We read in the cockpit by the light of a small battery lamp, and *Serrafyn* slid through the phosphorescent seas at an easy five knots.

Who needed Bermuda? We had our own perfect world.

Tuesday, July 4. 0030. All's well. Beam reaching. 0330. Identified light on Bermuda, approx. distance offshore 15 miles.

Larry tacked to the south while I prepared to go on watch. "Hi, Sweets," he said, "I'm working a bit to weather so we can make our landfall in the morning with lots of sea room." He went below to sleep.

Within an hour I could no longer see the light.

When Larry came on watch he wasn't concerned. "We must have been at the extreme edge of the light's visibility," he said. "When we tacked, we moved out of its range." He tacked again to the east, and I went below for three hours' sleep.

When I awoke I rushed on deck to see Bermuda. It wasn't there. I searched the horizon. "There it is, way over there," I said, pointing to a smudge south of us.

"That's not Bermuda, Lin, it's a cloud," Larry said. "Bermuda should be slightly north of us from our dead reckoning. The log is probably reading slightly wrong. We'll spot the island in an hour or so."

I waited a while longer and then said again, "That's Bermuda."

Larry got angry. "How the hell could we end up north of the island?" he said.

At 0900 Larry took another sight; it put us north of Bermuda. He couldn't believe it. It made no sense at all on his dead-reckoning track, but it did coincide with my cloud. We turned on our Zenith. It was not equipped to do direction finding, but we dialed it to the Hamilton Station and swung the radio until we got a null. The radio lay across Larry's line of position. The cloud was Bermuda.

We spent the next five hours beating to North End Light. We had been set 20 miles north of our course. Although we had pleasant winds for the sail, we were full of nagging doubts. How had Larry made a 20-mile error in navigation? He had never been more than a mile off on our landfalls, even in the Gulf Stream. Our sextant had been recently adjusted, our chronometer had been checked daily against the radio, our compass had been swung just a week ago. Larry searched through our *Pilot Charts* and *Ocean Passages for the World* for any mention of magnetic anomalies. Nothing there.

(We didn't get our answer until three weeks later when we were sailing with Bert Darrell out of Hamilton. He was telling us about the wrecks that line the reefs of Bermuda. "It's the current that does them in," he said. "One day it runs north at two to three knots, the next day it may run south at four, and then, some days there's no current at all. Depends on the mood of the Gulf Stream.")

The fragrance of island flowers reached out to us as we approached the Georgetown Cut—the scents of hibiscus, honeysuckle and roses mingled and were wafted two miles out to sea. After six days at sea, we reached through the 100-foot-wide gap into the protected harbor of St. George.

We got a signal to approach the town quay, and tied up next to six other transatlantic-bound yachts. The crystal-clear water alongside our boat was tempting. We could see bottom 15 feet below.

Larry and I worked together furling the mainsail, then Larry said,"The hell with it. "Let's dive overboard and cool off. We'll straighten out the boat later."

So we dove in and cooled off, even though we were in the center of town.

Then, sticking to a custom we follow each time we make a passage longer than three days, I put on my favorite dress, and Larry took me to dinner.

The first leg of our voyage to England was behind us.

16

The Long Leg

WE DIDN'T PLAN TO STAY in Bermuda a month; it just happened.

All we wanted was a brief rest, a look-see, some fresh food, and a check we had ordered from our bank. But Bermuda is a sailing crossroads, a pink and green delight set in the Atlantic.

We stayed at the dock between Ordnance Island and St. George for two days. By that time we had made enough new friends both ashore and on yachts to keep us in a constant social whirl. It was great. People—that's what cruising is all about.

But we couldn't take the heat, so we moved away from the dock and sailed out of the harbor to anchor 100 yards away. The islands of the bay protected us from any swell, and the cooling breeze rushed down our windsail into our cabin. We often prefer to anchor out, and we've found very few places where we couldn't anchor for free. Rowing ashore is a small price to pay for all the benefits: It's cooler; people from shore don't track oil and sand onto our teak decks; the water around us is clean, so we can just dive in for a swim. And, it's easier to anchor than tie to a dock: no fenders, no mooring lines, no chafing gear. Anchoring off is quieter, too: No one tries to bring his boat alongside or tramp across your deck at midnight. But mostly, we like the privacy. It's disconcerting to have dockside loungers staring down your companionway as you change into your swimsuit. More than once, when we've been trying to sleep, we've heard someone on the pier say, "I wonder if anyone lives in that boat. Do you think they really sailed from Canada in that?" (I always want to rush on deck and shout, "Yes!")

We invited our new friends over for drinks. When they saw how cool we were, three other cruising boats joined us at anchor. We had met Nick and Gerry Shoenwolf on their trimaran *Gudrun* three years before in Acapulco. When two yacht wives get together they usually discuss the galley and food.

"Be careful of your pressure cooker," Gerry said.

"I don't have one," I answered.

"Maybe that's a good thing. Look at these burns," Gerry said, lifting her blouse. Her entire midriff was covered with healing, but still red, scar tissue.

"I was cooking rice as we reached along toward Bermuda a week ago," she said. "I took the pressure cooker off the stove and put it in the sink in cool water for about five minutes. The top felt cool enough to open, but when I unscrewed it a blast of steam hit me. Now Nick won't let me in the galley in a bikini. I have to wear an apron or long blouse."

Nick has a good point. When you are braced against the lurch and roll of a sailboat, you just can't react as quickly as you do ashore. And, you are closer to your pots and are usually wearing fewer clothes in a ship's galley than in a kitchen.

I am always amazed at how much interest people express in what type of stove to use, and how little they worry about preventing burns at sea, probably the most frequent medical problems on a yacht. I know of one woman who was deep-frying some food on a gimbaled stove. The boat lurched and threw her against the stove. It tilted toward her, and the pot tipped the boiling oil into the front of her wet-weather gear. She had to be flown out by a helicopter to get treatment for third degree burns. She was lucky; the accident happened during a transpacific race and there were escort vessels nearby to render assistance. On a small cruiser, sailing alone, there may be no help available for weeks.

The best safety precaution, we feel, is a proper galley layout. A stove located so that the cook faces fore or aft as she works is much safer than a gimbaled stove. When the boat rolls, any spilled liquid will go to port or starboard and not on the cook. Deep pots will do as much good as gimbals, and reliable pot clamps will free the cook's hands for other work. Good handholds for the cook, lots of hot pads on a handy hook, a sink right next to the stove for quick disposal of overflowing pots, a safety harness to hold the cook in place, and a niche at the galley to keep the crew from bumping into her—these are all worth having. I've been very lucky so far—only such minor burns as any shoreside cook might suffer. *Seraffyn's* galley, without a gimbaled stove, is extremely well-planned for safe and convenient cooking.

We learned that the 14-foot Bermuda dinghies were going to race the following Sunday, we invited four friends to join us under *Seraffyn's* sun awning for a ringside view of the event. Three dinghies arrived in tow from Hamilton, three more emerged from the sailing club sheds in St. George. Each of these dinghies had its own collection of three complete rigs! (The towing vessel looked like a spar shop.) One rig was for heavy weather, another for medium, and a rig—almost 40

Pho. 16-1. Seraffyn's galley, without a gimballed stove, is extremely well-planned for safe and convenient cooking at sea.

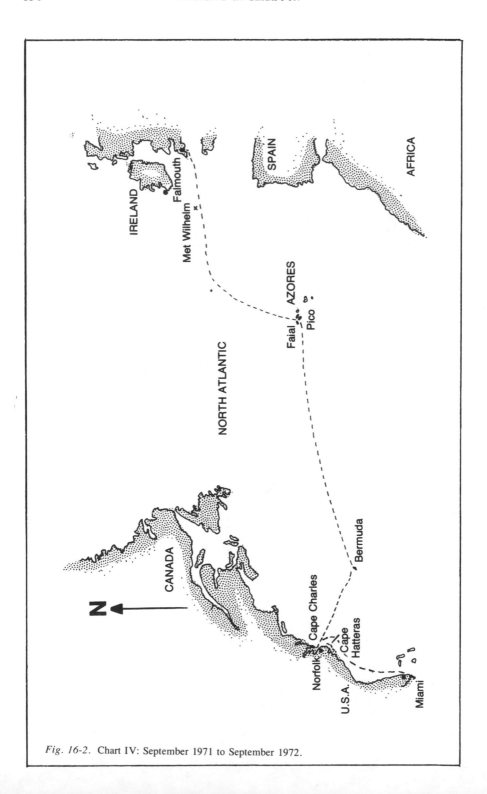

Fig. 16-2. Chart IV: September 1971 to September 1972.

feet tall—for light winds. There is no limit on sail area permitted for these open boats.

It was a light-air day and we watched the six dinghies (crewed by six men each, with 12-foot bowsprits, and long, overhanging booms) as they raced around a windward-leeward course. A young boy bailed furiously with a plastic basin from the leeward side of each dinghy. They held two races, each of three times around the course. On the final leg of the second race, one dinghy didn't clear the committee boat and its bowsprit punched through the committee boat's topsides. The owner of the committee boat, looking down at the hole the bowsprit had left, commented, "Good place for another portlight."

After two weeks we forced ourselves to leave the good life of St. George and sail over to Hamilton to check for mail. Larry hove-to in front of the Royal Hamilton Yacht Club, and I rowed ashore, and went up to the club.

"Sorry, no ladies allowed," the doorman said.

I fumed and became an instant Women's Libber, but I held my temper. "How can I get my mail?" I asked coldly.

"Wait here," the doorman said, and went off down a dim hallway. He returned with our letters on a silver tray.

We anchored across the bay from the club, in front of a small shipyard. We had been given a letter of introduction to the owner, Bert Darrel, and when we met him we had an instant friend. Bert is the person you see if you have an equipment problem with your yacht in Bermuda. What a mine of information! Bert taught Larry a splice he had invented that worked on 1x19 wire. Then he showed us a room full of natural crooks of Bermuda-grown cedar. "There's enough here to build two thirty-foot boats if you ever come back to Hamilton," he said.

Bert asked us to crew with him on Saturday, aboard Laury Brangman's

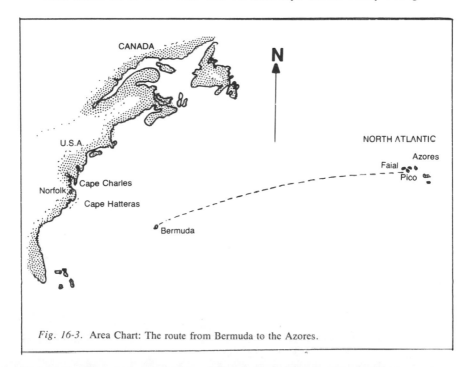

Fig. 16-3. Area Chart: The route from Bermuda to the Azores.

Pho. 16-4. We had planned only a brief rest and resupply for the Atlantic crossing in Bermuda, but we ended up staying a month—anchored out 100 yards from the shore.

27-footer. Both men were in their late sixties, and we've never seen keener sailors or a tougher course. We raced a triangular course through the maze of coral reefs. I was given a pair of Polaroid sun glasses, and lay on the foredeck watching for coral heads. We beat up to them until our bow almost touched, then tacked, watching for the next one and trying to make sure we didn't end up in a *cul de sac* of coral heads.

Three weeks slipped by. It was the middle of July and we had at least 3000 miles ahead of us, so we ran back to St. George and restocked with fresh food. With a 1900-mile voyage ahead (to the Azores), I was especially careful in my selection of fresh vegetables. I bought green tomatoes and wrapped them in newspaper, and did the same with lemons. I bought four cabbages, six cucumbers and more onions. We still had eight dozen farm-fresh eggs from Virginia, and I turned over each carton every three days so they stayed perfect for three months. I found some canned Camembert and Brie in the market; we came to consider the cheese a real treat. We filled up our tanks with water, butane, and kerosene.

We called our new Bermuda friends, Rick and Sheila Wenyon, to say goodbye. Rick said, "Wait right there, we have a gift for you." They arrived an hour later with a copy of the English publication, *Reed's Nautical Almanac.* The book made great browsing. Sheila and Rick roared with laughter when I read aloud the section on delivering a baby at sea. But it was a godsend. The tidal charts and light lists for the coast of England became dog-eared during our next year's cruising.

Our duty-free stores arrived just after Rick and Sheila left; one case of scotch, one of rum, half a case of cognac, and a case of wine. The log for that day reads: *Stores aboard and ready for sea, Thursday, July 20, 1972 at 1300.*

The St. George cut points directly at Fayal in the Azores. At 0800 we reached through the harbor and were on our way under mainsail and lapper. I helped Larry prepare for sea: We sealed the chain locker, secured the anchor, and lashed the tiller. It was lovely sailing.

"How about a glass of lemonade?" Larry asked. I went below, and was instantly seasick! Something below smelled bad! There wasn't enough sea running to make me feel that queasy, and I knew I wasn't pregnant. I went on deck for air, and a whiff of the odor came with me. Kerosene!

Somewhere in the boat there was a kerosene leak. I checked each lamp. All secure. Then I crawled into the forepeak where our kerosene gravity tank sat over the chain locker. Each dip of our bow as we surged along sent a small spray of kerosene up through the top of the stainless steel tank. There was a large crack in the solder around the filler hole.

"What do we do now?" I asked Larry, feeling queasy and discouraged.

"That's easy. We turn back and get it fixed," he said again.

So, we came back and were in St. George again three hours later. Larry rowed ashore to borrow two five-gallon cans to hold the kerosene. Removing the empty tank proved to be much more difficult than getting it fixed. After it was out, we just carried it to the nearest garage where they said they would solder it at once.

"Don't rush." Larry told them. "Tomorrow's Friday, and we can't sail, so tomorrow afternoon will be soon enough."

The welder was a sailor we had met before, and he asked, "Why can't you sail tomorrow?"

"I'm not superstitious," Larry said, "but I don't ask for trouble. I won't start a voyage on a Friday."

Bob and Gail Perry were tied up at the quay on Friday as we returned with our tank. We spent the evening on their boat, *Pelagic,* trading cruising stories. Bob and Gail were waiting for a friend who was due in the morning to sail with them to the Azores. "See you in Horta. We're leaving on Monday," they called as we rowed back to *Seraffyn.*

The wind was fresh, blowing right out the channel toward Horta the next morning, so we sailed with main and lapper wing-and-wing. Our rhumb line course for the Azores was 095°.

The wind increased as we cleared the land and we decided to reef the mainsail. One batten pocket ripped as we lowered the sail against the shrouds. Larry sat on deck mending the sail and cussing. He said, "I'm going to get a sail without battens as soon as we reach England. Look at this! I've mended the same batten pocket five times." The mainsail was getting pretty "ripe." We had never covered it, and the bottom panels were weakened from constant exposure to the ultra-violet rays of the sun. But the most vulnerable area was unquestionably the batten pockets.

By midnight the wind was up to Force 7, dead astern. We dropped the lapper and its pole and set the staysail. Then we settled in to the routine of watches, three on, three off, running dead downwidnd, Helmer keeping *Seraffyn* on course. For the next 14 days we never touched Helmer! Sometimes we raised a bit more sail, a few times we reefed, but always *Seraffyn* kept moving along at five knots. We had daily runs, noon-to-noon, of 138, 120, 130. What a boat she is! In spite of the big following seas and force 5-7 winds, she let us live comfortably. Spray usually kept the cockpit damp, so we spent our days below, reading or playing cribbage. Nothing changed much. Larry took one sight in the morning and another at noon, and our daily position X's on the chart inched along toward Fayal. Our five-minute time ticks from station WWV gradually faded, and we switched to the BBC which gives a time-check every six hours.

After a week at sea, our dirty clothes became a nuisance. Neither of us wore anything during the day, but at night we needed a sweater and pants. Dirty towels and bed-sheets became damp with salt and never completely dried. I couldn't stand their smell and worried about mildew. Then Larry came up with a good idea: He put them in a sailbag which he dipped overboard once a day. Then he stored the completely wet bag under the dinghy. It never dried, and nothing mildewed.

On August 1, I baked bread to celebrate my 28th birthday. We had been at sea 10 days and we had run out of ice and fresh meat, but I conjured up a lasagne out of canned stores and cheese. *Seraffyn* still swooped along at over five knots in the 30-knot breeze. The seas rolled up under her stern but my bread and lasagne baked without problems, wedged in the oven with extra bread tins. I put a damp towel on our slide-out table to keep the dishes from sliding. Larry searched the bilges for a bottle of red wine.

"Lin, can I ask a favor?" he said as he uncorked the bottle. I nodded. "Don't get upset, but would you dress for dinner?"

I looked down at my bare body. I couldn't help but smile as I dug in my locker for a bikini. A change is as good as a rest, my grandmother always used to say.

After dinner we held our wine glasses and lounged together on the settee.

"Could be worse," Larry remarked. *Seraffyn* heeled and surged along. Spray spattered the canvas companionway cover. A fresh breeze funneled below through our skylight hatch as Helmer held us unerringly on course. The glow of the setting sun was reflected on the mahogany cabin sides.

"You know what I like best about cruising?" Larry said. "Having so much time to read. What other way of life would let me read a book like the *Rise and Fall of the Third Reich,* cover to cover, in a week?"

I tried to imagine what it would be like if we didn't love reading. The motion in a Force 7 sea was enough to keep us from doing any jobs that weren't essential, and the spray kept us off the deck. It was most comfortable lying in our bunks. Our library was being rapidly and enjoyably depleted.

So it went, our log showing daily noon-to-noon runs of 130, 120, 128. On the 13th day Larry looked up from his chart. "This could get boring," he said. Our lives had fallen into a routine. Watches from 2100 to 0900, three hours off, three hours on. On watch you carefully opened the hatch every 10 minutes or so to search the horizon for ships; then back below to your book. Breakfast was fruit, toast, tea or coffee. We would compare notes on our night watches, clean ourselves up and start the usual daytime routine: Larry's morning sight, lunch, a noon (or afternoon) sight, a nap; then dinner, clean, fill and light the oil lamps, and back on night watches.

Larry's comment about almost being bored seemed to change the weather. Squall clouds formed on the horizon, though the wind remained dead astern, driving us at over five knots.

At midnight I woke Larry. "I'm going to heave-to," I told him. "There's a vicious-looking squall coming down on us."

Larry looked out the hatch and agreed. The black cloud blocked the stars from horizon to horizon. Great flashes of lightning lit up its rolling grey face, and thunder rumbled toward us. I headed into the wind and dropped the staysail. The cloud reached us and passed overhead. The wind dropped as it passed, and for all the noise and fuss, the cloud did nothing but suck our wind away. The seas lost

Pho. 16-5. In the middle of July we ran back to St. George, restocked with fresh food, filled the water tanks, washed clothes, and got ready for sea.

their crests and before Larry crawled back into his bunk he helped me set the genoa and full mainsail.

By morning we were barely making three knots over an absolutely flat sea. Still, it was a pleasant change. We emerged from our turtle shell and gloried in the dry, sun-drenched warmth.

I set out a batch of bread to rise and we lounged on settee cushions in the cockpit. We made love in the sunlight and perfect tranquility of our own special island. We listened to the sounds of the gurgling wake. It seemed a miracle that two average people like ourselves could experience such a moment of perfection in this world. What other kind of life could offer us so much variety; such changes of weather, such an intimate look at the moods of the sea, such variety of towns and cities and deserted coves. What did it matter if occasionally I was seasick? A bout only lasted a day or two. Who cared if we met some storms? They were only the smallest part of our sailing. We had the world in the palms of our hands. We had each other, we had our 24-foot playpen, and we had the time to enjoy whatever came: lots of time and no schedule at all.

At noon that day, we set the spinnaker and stuffed ourselves with the aromatic fresh-baked bread before it cooled. At 2000 we were becalmed. We doused ourselves with salt water and scrubbed with Head and Shoulders Shampoo, which lathered beautifully—the best salt water soap I've found. Then we each rinsed off with a gallon of fresh water, and felt wonderful.

By my watch, at 0200 a breeze sprang up and we were running wing-and-wing again as the breeze became a wind and the wind increased until it was blowing 30 knots.

"Should see Fayal in the morning, Lin," Larry said. "It's high enough to sight from forty miles away."

At first light I rushed on deck. Clouds and drizzle—what a disappointment. We bowled along at five knots and I kept staring toward the east. At 1500 a watery sun pierced the clouds. Larry shot it and said. "Ten miles to the west end of Fayal. Then, at 1530; "I see it! It's right there," I yelled, pointing. I was filled with a thrill such as Columbus' lookout must have felt when he saw San Salvador (in the Bahamas) appear on the horizon. Through the haze, the island filled in—black, green and blue volcanic rock. Hydrangeas bloomed along the edges of manicured fields and as we drew nearer, white-washed houses and roads appeared.

We ate dinner in the lee of the land, beam reaching toward Horta. At 0300 of our 16th day at sea, shore lights winked a welcome and we beat into Horta's harbor, anchoring in five fathoms of water.

Larry put his arms around me and held me tightly. "Well, little girl, you've sailed across the Atlantic" he said. "What do you think of that?"

"It's hard to believe," I answered. "*Seraffyn* sure has a charm."

She really has. Only 22 feet on the waterline, she had sailed 1900 miles in 15 days, 18 hours, averaging over five knots (and we had been becalmed for half a day).

We put our last set of clean sheets in the sleeping bag on the double bunk forward, and the first time in over two weeks, slept the whole night together, my head against Larry's warm shoulder. *Seraffyn's* anchor was securely dug into the bottom, attached to the first bit of the Old World we had come to.

17

Horta
or
Peter's Blue-Water Sailor's Reception Center

"WELCOME TO HORTA," someone yelled down our companionway. Larry rubbed his eyes and scrambled out of the bunk to look for his trousers. "It's only six A.M.," he moaned to me quietly. A pilot boat lay alongside, and the pilot stood in our cockpit. "I let you rest till eight o'clock, but I must move you now," he said in excellent English. "This is not good holding ground." We had forgotten to set our clock ahead to the local time of each zone as we sailed east, and so we had lost two hours.

"Where shall I move?" Larry asked.

"Don't worry," the pilot said. "We'll tow you. Do you want to be against the seawall or on a mooring?"

Larry looked and saw three yachts surging against their mooring lines at the seawall. "I'll sail to that mooring," he answered.

"No, you are our guest," the pilot said. "I insist on saving you the work. We will tow you. There are no charges. It is our way of making you welcome."

"*Seraffyn* is a pretty heavy boat to tow. When she gets moving she doesn't want to stop," Larry said.

The pilot raised his eyebrows. "I have been towing visiting yachts for thirty years," he said somewhat disdainfully.

Larry lifted the anchor. He put two turns of the towline around our anchor winch and said to me, "Lin, hold this line and be ready to cast off and drop the anchor if I say so." He went aft to steer.

The wind on our stern caught *Seraffyn's* rigging. She gathered speed behind the pilotboat. We rushed down harbor toward a stone ramp.

"Cast off, Lin, I'll round up at that mooring," Larry called. The pilotboat roared into reverse and barely missed the seawall. Larry reached over the side and grabbed the mooring pennant. We were secured to it before the pilot came alongside.

"Sorry," he said "there was more wind than I thought."

"No problem; no damage done," Larry assured him.

The pilot pointed to a blue-fronted shop on shore. He said, "Peter has a drink for you at his Café Sport. He will take care of any problems you have, even laundry. Have a pleasant stay in Horta. Use the mooring as long as you want. There is a bathhouse over there." He pointed to another building on shore.

We packed our clean clothes, bath kits, and dirty laundry, and went ashore. What a bathhouse! Polished brass fixtures, gleaming bathtubs and plenty of hot water—all for 15 cents. We emerged, scrubbed pink, 45 minutes later. Then we

157

walked to the famous Café Sport.

We had first read about Peter and the Café Sport in Eric Hiscock's cruising books. The famous Peter met us at the door and welcomed us in good English. He led us to a table, poured two glasses of local burgundy and handed us his guest book of cruising people. We proudly signed at the end of a list that included Alain Gerbault, Susan and Eric Hiscock, Peter Pye, Carleton Mitchell: names famous through almost 50 years of cruising history.

Peter's father first maintained the book, from the 1920s through the 1950s. Then Peter had taken over. The future list-keeper, Peter's brown-eyed, eight-year old son, took our formidable bag of laundry and disappeared around the corner. The clothes reappeared three days later, sparklingly clean and perfectly ironed—at a cost of $3.00.

Pho. 17-1. We had first read about Peter and the Café Sport in Eric Hiscock's cruising books. The famous Peter met us at the door and welcomed us in good English.

The Café Sport is a tiny room decorated with whale's teeth, sailing pictures and soccer team photos, and holds six small tables. We were the only patrons until a man rushed through the door and yelled something in Portuguese to Peter. Peter translated for us. "This is my friend Anton," Peter said. "He has spotted two yachts rounding the island."

Anton was an interesting man. He didn't just speak Portuguese. He spoke French, German, English, Dutch, and a smattering of a half-dozen other languages as well. He carved and polished whale's teeth for a living, and had once taught the art of scrimshaw as guest of a museum in Newport, Rhode Island. He joined us and answered an avalanche of questions about Horta. After about an hour, I signaled to Larry that not only was the wine rushing to my head with devastating effect, but also I was starving.

"Can you suggest a good restaurant?" Larry asked Anton. "Lin deserves a dinner ashore after cooking for sixteen days at sea."

Anton and Peter didn't hesitate. *"Graciosa,"* they said together.

"You must let me guide you," Anton said. "You would never find the restaurant by yourselves."

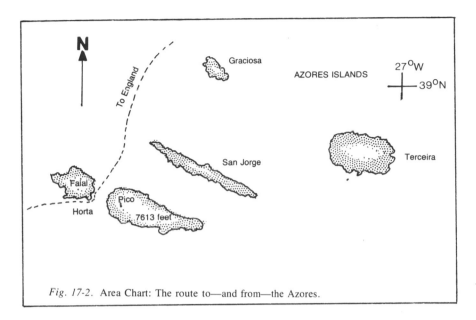

Fig. 17-2. Area Chart: The route to—and from—the Azores.

So we set off, first along the waterfront toward town, then under an archway, down a alley, around a flock of chickens, through a doorway with no sign, past a kitchen hung with onions and garlic, and finally into a room with four long tables. Anton sat with us, and a lady put a loaf of hot bread and bottle of local red wine on the table. Anton chatted with her for a minute and then said, "I've taken the liberty of ordering for you."

A platter of what looked like tiny chickens appeared just before we had completely demolished the loaf of bread. The birds were surrounded by French fries and sliced tomatoes. Larry told me they weren't chicken but pigeons—like the ones we saw strutting around the waterfront. No matter, rubbed with garlic, stuffed with sage and covered with a sauce made of cream they tasted wonderful. After that came goat's cheese, and more delicious bread and grapes fresh from the vine. Best of all, I didn't have to wash the dishes.

We tried to ask in sign language for the bill. But Anton had already taken care of it. "You can invite me aboard your boat sometime, in exchange," he said.

While Larry and Anton wandered off to look for oil-lamp wicks, I browsed through a few shops that were open and then returned to Peter's café, just in time to see *Pelagic* being made fast to the seawall. She had made a good voyage. But at 40 feet overall, she had taken only one day less than we did. A big blue boat was docked in front of *Pelagic*.

"*British Steel*," Peter said, putting down his binoculars.

The café slowly filled with people from the new yachts. Peter introduced me to the crew of *British Steel*. Brian Cooke, the skipper, was returning to England from his second single-handed transatlantic race. I joined him and his crew for a drink, but had tea instead of the potent wine. Two more yachts hove into view.

"*Strongbow* and *Architusus*" Brian told us. "They're also on their way home to England from the single-handed race."

Peter was really excited. He said, "Last year only sixteen boats stopped in Horta during the whole year. Now we have nine boats here all at the same time.

Wonderful!'' He rushed out to the back room for more glasses.

Larry and Anton walked through the door, and when Anton spotted Brian, he ran over to embrace him like a long-lost brother. Then the introductions began again. Brian Cooke took charge: "Larry, this is my crew, Eric, Michael and Mike, and this is Lin.''

Larry's blue eyes twinkled. "Yes I've met her," he said, "She's my wife.''

A roar went up, and Peter arrived with the glasses and a demijohn of wine. By evening the café was filled with deep-water sailors from France, America, England, Canada, and Australia. Sea stories and smoke drifted out over the peaceful streets of Horta.

Brian Cooke called for a moment's quiet. "Anton has suggested we climb Mount Pico,'' he announced. "Anyone who wants to go, be here tomorrow at noon. Bring something to eat and a blanket. We'll be gone overnight.''

We looked across the five-mile strait to Mount Pico, and saw its 7800-foot-high peak poking up through the perpetual cloud. There was no safe harbor over there, so Anton suggested we take the ferry. "Don't worry," Anton told the group, "You will only have to walk up the last three thousand feet to reach the top.''

We left the café trying to remember which people belonged to which yacht. The seawall was almost full of racing yachts that had been designed for or converted to single-handed sailing. The assortment included the 59-foot *British Steel,* built for strength and a Cape Horn challenge: *Architusus,* a 50-foot trimaran with four staterooms, and *Strongbow,* 60 feet long. In the middle of the harbor was diminutive *Seraffyn.*

Fourteen of us showed up the next day at noon for the climb. The three

Pho. 17-3. Seraffyn sat in the middle of the crowded harbor, surrounded by all the large visiting racing yachts.

Frenchmen had brought plastic jugs, and Peter filled them with wine. The English all wore sailing hats, the Australian had a hunting knife on his belt, and Larry, representing Canada, carried a sleeping bag. I was the only female and vowed to demonstrate women's stamina by reaching the top no matter what. Anton escorted us to the ferry.

We joined a goat, a cow and 40 Azorians on the 50-foot ferry, and arrived at the picturesque 100-foot-long harbor of Pico an hour later. Anton had made preparations by telephone. Three taxis were waiting, and drove us on an hour-long tour of the black volcanic coast before taking us to the vineyards of Anton's friend José, who was providing us with two guides. Before we set off to make the ascent, we had to taste the products of José's vineyards. We sat under a canopy of grape vines, and first we'd taste the grapes fresh from the vines, then José would pour each of us a glass of the wine made from the grapes. This went on for four or five hours.

Our guides found us in a very relaxed, more than slightly inebriated state. They tried to sober us by explaining we would have to climb for two hours before sunset; then, at midnight we would climb the last 2000 feet, arriving at the top for the sunrise. "Only about two hundred people a year reach the top," they told us.

We climbed into the waiting taxis and rode half way up the steep volcanic mountain. At the end of the road the drivers stopped, and we tumbled out. The taximen agreed to come back the next afternoon to pick us up. Eric, the English bank manager off *British Steel,* was acting as accountant for our expedition. "They'll be back," he said, "I didn't pay them."

We started off, one guide in front, the other in our wake. The songs of the first hour reflected the various nationalities: Sea shanties from the waterfront of Marseille, "Waltzing Matilda," "Canadian Logger," "The Sloop John B." But

Pho 17-4 We sat under a canopy of grape vines. First, we'd taste the grapes fresh from the vines, then a glass of wine made from the same grapes.

in the second hour of climbing, over the steep green meadows toward a crater that never seemed any closer, nationalities were forgotten, and occasionally "It's a Long Way to Tipperary" would burst from the throat of anyone with energy to sing.

We made it to the top, all 14 of us. We scrambled over rough lava, through shale, and around shrubs. The torches of our two guides barely lit the faint path. Every hour our guides would stop and set a shrub afire. We learned later that this was a signal to a watchman on Fayal that all was well. From the still steaming, volcanic top of Mount Pico the sunrise was glorious. But a heavy cloud moved over, and wearily we headed down, unable to see even 20 feet ahead.

On the way down, five of our party wandered off the path in the heavy mist. Our guides put the rest of us in an old blowhole, out of the mist and wind, and went searching for the lost lambs. The slopes rang with the guides yodels as they combed the mountainside until finally they heard the answering shouts of the lost climbers. After a six-hour downhill slide, we arrived at the green meadows at the end of the road—exhausted, knee-sore sailors, but filled with memories of a conquered mountain.

Our taxis arrived on time, and the guides rode with us down the rest of the 7800-foot mountain and joined us for a celebration lunch of local wine, cheese and ham. They poured us on to the ferry and waved goodbye, saying, "Come again next year and we will try to reach the top faster."

As the ferry slid across the silken sea toward Horta, Eric added up the expenses: The ferry ride, taxis for two days, lunch, guides, wine, and tips came to $5.00 each. Little wonder cruising seems to return 10 times the value of its cost.

Fifteen minutes after we got to Horta, the bathhouse was full of soaking, scrubbing climbers. Yet there was a seemingly endless supply of hot water. At least three of the expedition, including my captain, Larry, had swollen knees.

Pho. 17-5. We looked across the five-mile-wide-strait to Mount Pico, and saw its 7800-foot-high peak poking up through the perpetual cloud cover.

Sailors are notoriously poor hikers because at sea their legs are the least exercised parts of their bodies.

There was one distinctly different thing about Horta's small harbor that evening: A 210-foot Dutch salvage tug was anchored in the middle. Half of the climbers met aboard *British Steel* for dinner, and the tug was the center of our conversation.

"How would you like to tour it?" I piped up.

"Can you arrange that?" Mike asked.

"Let's row out and ask," I said.

Larry gave me a slightly disapproving look, but the *British Steel* crew was already pumping up their six-man rubber dinghy.

"I'll stay here," Larry said. His knees were bothering him. Brian Cooke stayed behind too. So six of us rowed toward the big black vessel. No one greeted us as we approached.

"Row all the way around it," I suggested, glad I was the only woman there and not obliged to take a turn at the oars. On our second circuit, a blond man came on deck and yelled, "Hello."

It was my turn: "Hello, do you give tours?" I called.

"Of course," the man on the tug replied. "Come alongside. The captain has asked me to invite you for drinks in his cabin."

Nick de Jonge took us from one end of the 11,000-horsepower tug to the other. He showed us the 40-foot-long drive shaft with its variable-pitch propeller, and the fuel tanks that would carry *Rode Zee* from Horta to China non-stop. She was "on station," waiting for any emergency calls that might come from disabled ships at sea. "As long as we're here, you are welcome to use our laundry," Nick said, showing us three washing machines, two driers, and an ironing board that were provided for the crew of 21.

As he led a thoroughly dazzled group of small-boat sailors to the captain's quarters, Nick made the familiar request of blue-water sailors: "If you have any good books to trade, bring them over. Our library is getting boring."

Captain Kalkman had commanded Smit Tugs for 25 years, although he was only 45. What tales he had to tell! We sat and listened, fascinated, for two hours, depleting his liquor and ice supply. Then I mentioned Larry and Brian back on *British Steel*. "Bring them over for dinner tomorrow," the captain said.

The next evening we were back aboard *Rode Zee*. Crews from most of the 10 yachts in port were on board, chatting with crew and officers and filling the laundry room. Captain Kalkman was quite serious at first. "I worry about you people on small yachts," he said. "It's so hard to see your lights at night. If I were you, I would keep a very good watch. Even with a man on watch on a ship's bridge, you are still in danger. If that man only turns to fill his coffee cup while the ship is moving at sixteen knots, your lights can be missed. You must stay out of the ship's way. In fact, if I were single-handing or had a small boat, I'd have a big white flashing light at my masthead no matter what the International Rules of the Road say. All ships would avoid you, then."

Somebody asked, "Don't most ships stay in the shipping lanes?"

Captain Kalkman laughed before answering. "Shipping lanes were designed by men behind desks," he said. "What prudent captain would take his ship through the fog and icebergs of the North Atlantic when two hundred miles south he could have clear sailing? No. Shipping lanes or not, you keep a good watch at night. Sleep in the daytime; a sailboat is easy to see then." The conversation turned to stories of salvage jobs, towing and the sea.

I invited the captain, first mate and chief engineer to lunch on *Seraffyn* the next day. Then, since several boats were preparing to sail, I asked, "Do you happen to have a weather report?"

Nick de Jonge replied, "We don't listen to weather reports. When it is time to go, we have to leave—whatever the weather—so knowing what it will be like before we go would just depress us."

At lunch the next day we received a typed copy of the latest shipping forecast for the North Atlantic, gathered from ships actually at sea. Each day thereafter the radio officer of the "Yacht Club *Rode Zee*" (as we came to call her), distributed a daily forecast to the yachts in harbor.

Strong northeasterly winds blew for the next week, so no yachts left, but no one cared. Visitors flowed from yacht to tug and tug to yacht, with Peter's Café, Anton's workshop, and the *Graciosa* as way stations in the tours.

A single-handed sailor entered the harbor in a beautiful, 35-year-old, English racing-cruising cutter, *Mouette,* and took the mooring next to us. I watched the world's most-patched rubber dinghy being launched by a tall, lanky, dark-haired man wearing sea boots that rivaled his dinghy for patches. The boots had patches on its patches. As Brian Craige-Lucas rowed past us, we yelled, "Where did you come from?"

"Cape Verdes!" he shouted. Brian had done the passage on one tack in his engineless 32-footer, and now he was headed back to England for the winter to replenish his cruising funds before heading for Brazil. We had dinner on his boat and added another fine book to our shelf—*The Shell Guide to the South Coast of England.* We saw why Brian said he knew it by heart: The book was held together by a rubber band.

Brian joined the happy roundabout ashore. Then the barometer rose. The wind started to veer to the southeast and Brian Cooke and his crew were the first to leave. He had offered to be our mailing address in England, and as *British Steel* sailed passed us, he yelled, "Come spend the winter in Poole. We'll take good care of you."

We remained in Horta to put a coat of paint on our bulwarks and relax a few more days. Anton had promised Larry a chance to go whaling in one of the 40-foot sailing longboats the Azorians still use for that purpose. But for three weeks no whales had been sighted, and the canoes lay unused on the beach.

Rode Zee stood ready to go in the middle of the harbor and we rowed out to say goodbye. "We'll miss you," Captain Kalkman said. "Almost all of the yachts are gone now, and it has been fun to join your parties."

As the end of August approached we thanked Anton and Peter for their hospitality, had one last *Graciosa* dinner and stored our gifts of local wine and whale's teeth in preparation for the beat out of Horta on the final leg of our Atlantic crossing—to England.

Author's Note: *As we were doing the final editing of this book with our publisher early in 1976, we learned of the sad loss at sea of Brian Cooke. After our arrival in England Brian became our mail drop and helped us with many kindnesses. When he went missing, the world lost a wonderful sailor and we lost a good friend.*

18

The Other Side

IF WE'LL ALWAYS REMEMBER our passage to the Azores for its constant wind and speed, we'll also remember our trip from there to England for its variety. Personally I'd prefer to forget that voyage altogether: Head winds, calms, gales, calms, storms. To cover 1180 miles we sailed 1412. The only consolation we had was learning later that *British Steel* and all the other eastward-bound yachts had the same conditions.

We departed Horta in good spirits. Sailing close-hauled, we headed due north, looking for the northwesterlies shown on the pilot charts. We started on the new books we had traded for. Larry read to me from Thoreau's *Walden:*

Remember thy creator in the days of thy youth. Rise free from care before the dawn and seek adventures. Let the noon find thee by other fields and the night overtake thee everywhere at home. There are no larger fields than these, no worthier games than may here be played. Grow wild according to thy nature, like these sedges and brakes that will never become English hay. Let the thunder rumble, what if it threaten ruin to farmers' crops? That is not its errand to thee. Take shelter under the cloud, while they flee to carts and sheds. Let not to get a living be thy trade, but thy sport. Enjoy the land but own it not. Through want of enterprise and faith, men are where they are. Buying and selling and spending their lives like serfs.

How well it expressed our lives, our feelings! I copied the lines into our log so we could refer back to them.

As we worked northward, the breeze began to die. Only 48 miles from Horta we were becalmed; in fact, we've never been so becalmed. The jettisoned scraps from each meal remained floating around us for hours. The sails didn't slat—there wasn't enough motion even for that. For 27 hours there wasn't a ripple of wind, and our noon sight put us only six miles closer to England.

Although there was no wind, we felt a chill in the air. I used the calm weather to dig out winter clothes; we were glad to put on sweatshirts and slacks. Larry sewed some more patches on the mainsail, and I simmered a pot of stew. We could still see the tip of Mount Pico, 60 miles south of us.

As the third morning wore on, completely windless, I read the entire log and discovered that the lack of an engine had hardly slowed our passages because we had rarely been becalmed. In our three years of cruising we had been entirely without wind for less than 65 hours. Larry pointed out that we would have spent that much time just servicing an engine—changing filters and lube oil.

Just after lunch Larry put the mainsail back on the track and hauled it aloft to

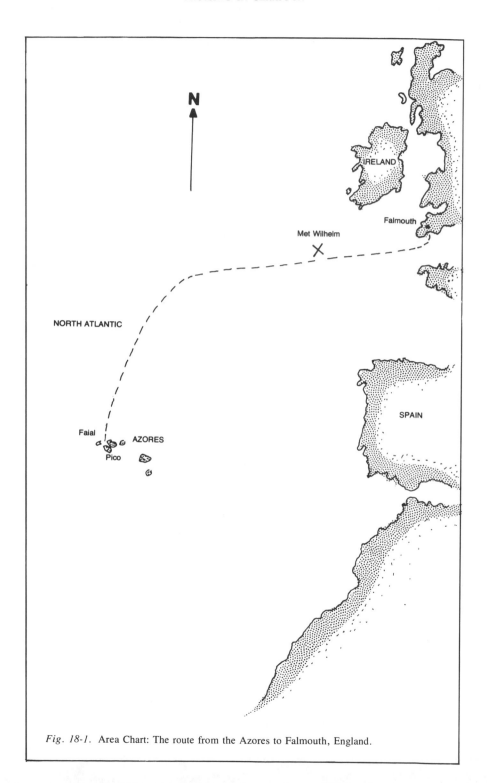

Fig. 18-1. Area Chart: The route from the Azores to Falmouth, England.

admire his handiwork. A lovely L-shaped patch covered the newest hole in the foot.

"Good thing we have reef points, Lin," he said. "Even though the foot of the sail has rotted from the sun, all the area above the first set of reef points is in good shape. If the foot blew out completely, we could easily sail with one reef tied in."

A breeze stirred the sail. We set the lapper which had lay in the jib net for the past 27 hours. Wing-and-wing we ran away from our garbage, directly toward England at nearly five knots.

We made 115 miles noon to noon, then 125 miles the next day as the winds grew stronger. We shared the last of Peter's wine in the cockpit at sunset. "We're really going to England," I said. "Just think, London, the Royal Ballet, fish and chips."

Larry had different thoughts. "I wonder if we'll see boats like *Seraffyn*, English working cutters?" he mused. "And what about Cowes and the Solent? While we're this far north we should go to see Lief Moller in Denmark."

At his mention of Denmark I got out the World Almanac. The sun set behind us, and *Seraffyn's* sails were brushed with gold against a purple sky, as we traced the map of Europe with our fingers. "I'd like to see Finland. Look at all those islands," I said to Larry, my fingernail etching a route across the North Sea, past Denmark and Sweden.

"I wonder if we could get a visa to visit Russia," Larry said. For an hour we discussed possible routes through the endless maze of sea and land that makes up Europe. England was still 900 miles away, and already our thoughts were on the next voyage.

We were too sure of ourselves, and we paid for it. Slowly the wind backed through the night, and by morning we couldn't point toward England. The seas and clouds built up. We reefed the main, doused the lapper, and set the staysail.

Our distance-covered figure dropped: 60 miles noon-to-noon, 62 miles, 40 miles, 60 miles—always hard on the wind, pointing north, fighting strong north-easterlies where the *Pilot Chart* indicated we should get northwesterlies.

Our log for September 2 reads: *Frustrated crew. Wishing for any wind but easterly. 740 miles to go.*

Nine days at sea—cold and often overcast. Rain squalls forced us to shorten sail three or four times a day. Wind strength changed sharply from hour to hour —and so did our tempers. "If we had any brains we'd turn south and reach to Spain," Larry muttered angrily.

"But all our mail is waiting in Falmouth," I answered, watching the compass point toward Iceland.

I wasn't in any better mood than Larry, but I resorted to one of my mother's cures for the blues—cooking. I rummaged through our can lockers until I found the last can of Brie. We had cheese and crackers with a drink. Then I made a frying pan full of corned beef hash with eggs on top, Larry's favorite. For breakfast I fried up Spam and scrambled eggs with tomatoes. And each of us took a multivitamin pill. It worked. Larry came below from reefing the mainsail yet another time, pulled of his dripping foul-weather gear and said. "If it's this much work, it really must be worthwhile." We laughed together, and it broke our bad mood. Two days later the wind shifted to the south. We eased sheets and settled back smugly, our bow pointing straight at England which now lay almost due east of us. We were still chuckling as the wind died again.

"Oh, well," was my comment, "what else can you expect?"

Larry turned on the BBC to hear the 1800 weather forecast and get a time check. A news bulletin blared forth: "Eleven Israeli athletes murdered at Olympic games in Munich by Arab terrorists."

Larry snapped off the radio and turned to me. "Everything out here makes sense," he said. "The sun crosses our meridian at an exact time. The stars and the moon rise when the *Nautical Almanac* says they will. Then you turn on the radio and hear something like that, and it makes no sense at all."

In the morning the wind blew from the north. With our usual optimism we set a full mainsail, staysail and lapper. All through that day we reached along with the wind growing slowly, and with us tying in one reef after another. By morning we had covered 119 miles, and we were down to staysail only. The radio from Cape Finisterre, Spain, reported north winds, Force 10. *Seraffyn* slammed into the seas, heeling to the gusts. Life below became miserable.

"I'm going to heave her to, Lin, "Larry said. "You stay below. No sense in both of us getting wet."

Larry uncleated the staysail sheet and handed it to me through the companionway. "Let it go when I yell," he said. I listened to the howl of wind in the rigging, the sound of breaking, rushing seas and spray. I heard Larry yell and let go of the sheet.

Snap! Crack! The flogging staysail shook the boat from stem to stern, banging like a cannon gone mad. I froze, and my mind went blank with fear. Tears rushed to my eyes as *Seraffyn* rolled sail-less in the trough of crashing seas.

The noise diminished when Larry hoisted the triple-reefed main which pointed *Serraffyn* into the wind, and tied the tiller slightly alee. I mentally caught hold of myself as our motion eased and the noise died away.

Larry came below and found me crying, "What's wrong?" he asked.

I managed a smile. "The noise scared me," I said.

The motion hove-to, as always was wonderful. Maybe it's just the contrast but it feels like sudden peace after a long war. Instead of a one-pot meal, I made a dinner of an onion omelet, boiled potatoes, and a tossed cabbage salad. After dinner we played cribbage and listened to the English weather reports: "Force 10 winds for all sea areas."

Larry went on deck to check the oil lamps while I washed the dishes. As I stood in the galley, I glanced around me. What a wonderful home we had! Larry had been right when he told me, "Buy the best gear you can for the boat. It may cost a bit more but it will be worth it." So I'd paid the extra for new Revere ware pots and pans, strong handsome ironstone dishware, wine glasses and stainless utensils. With our big oven, running water, and ice chest we really could live nicely, not just camp out. True, our home was small, but we had the luxury of a good stereo cassette player and down sleeping bags with percale sheets. We had our library, scrapbooks and typewriter. Larry's navigation locker was just an easy reach from the chart table, and held a small Sestral sextant, our Accutron watch, chronometer and a stopwatch. There was a three-cubic-foot locker full of his favorite woodworking tools right at hand. I had my sewing box, and the stores lockers were full of over 600 pounds of food. Everything we needed was there, all contained in a beautiful, finely finished boat. The light from our brass oil lamps gleamed off the highly varnished teak, mahogany and oak of our seagoing home. I wiped the bare maple drain board dry, then polished the chrome stove top. Before I climbed into the snug quarterberth I checked to make sure all the pans were secure in their racks. No noise from loose galley ware, no rattles from on deck. Larry came below, and all was well in our world, although the wind shrieked through the rigging.

We lay hove-to for 30 hours, and then finally the wind eased and we set our staysail to match the triple-reefed main. We were now within the area covered by BBC's weather reports, and their predictions of Force 4 northerly winds were accurate. We rushed on toward England all that night. Larry spotted the lights of two ships close by during his watch.

"I'm glad," I said when he described the ships. "I had the strangest thought last night: What if we reached England and it wasn't there?" Larry often doubts my sanity, and added that remark to his evidence as he climbed in to the bunk.

The sun was peeking over the horizon the next morning when I went on deck to look around. "Why didn't you tell me there was a yacht out here?" I called down to Larry.

Larry grumbled, "Let me sleep. I don't want to hear any more fantasies."

"Don't believe me," I retorted, hardening the sheets and resetting Helmer to work toward the schooner. That maneuver convinced Larry. He came on deck and looked at the tiny mound of canvas off to windward of us. "Set the staysail, Lin," he said.

We raced *Seraffyn* over the calm seas, carrying all the canvas she could take. People! Another yacht crazy enough to be 300 miles from land! We drew closer, and Larry went below to sleep again. By noon we had caught the 49-foot schooner. Her crew were just as anxious to talk as we were. We slid alongside, 30 feet off their rail, and dropped our staysail to keep pace with them.

"Where you coming from?" I yelled, noting as we came up to her that she

Pho. 18-2. After several hours we overtook the 49-foot schooner *Wilhelm* and spoke to the crew as we sailed alongside.

was the *Wilhelm*.

"San Miguel, Azores, twenty days out!" a crewman called.

"We're out of Horta, sixteen days," I called.

"We're almost out of stores," one man yelled. "No cigarettes, no booze."

"Throw us a line," Larry shouted. The man tied a sailbag to a line and heaved it, as both boats reached along at four knots. Larry put a bottle of rum in the bag and tossed it back into the water. The four men on *Wilhelm* cheered as they took it out of the bag—and each took a slug straight from the bottle.

"Hell of a storm," the man at the wheel yelled. "We were almost to England when it blew up. We lost two hundred miles running before it."

We had lost only 18 miles lying hove-to in the same storm.

The 49-foot *Wilhelm* didn't have the sail area to keep up with *Seraffyn* in the 10-knot breeze, so we waved goodbye and set the staysail as they dropped behind. Three hours later they were hull-down on the horizon.

The sea grew crowded as we crossed the continental shelf: porpoises, ships, fishing boats, bottles, plastic bags, trash, fishing floats. It was mostly the jetsam of civilization. At midnight, 19 days out of Horta, we spotted the light that has welcomed sailors to England for centuries, Bishop Rock.

We sailed past the Scilly Islands in the morning.

"Shall we stop?" I asked Larry.

"Hell, no!" Larry said. "I want to get our mail—It's been four months."

So we pressed on, past the Scilly Isles and into the English Channel; then, through the tidal overfalls near Land's End, past Penzance, Mount St. Michael and the Lizard, ticking them off one by one.

At noon we headed north into Falmouth Bay and got our first taste of English tides. We beat into the lee of the land, pressing hard to gain the last 20 miles. The wind gusted down off the green cliffs, and we were registering three or four knots on the taffrail log, but barely one knot over the bottom. The beat seemed endless. Then, almost abruptly, four hours had passed and the tide changed. We fairly flew over the bottom and reached in under Pendennis Castle as the dark of evening fell. A car parked on the hillside turned on its headlamps. The beams caught Larry as he took down our Canadian flag.

"Welcome to England," a Cornish voice called across 200 feet of water.

Tears came to my eyes. I helped Larry short-tack up the bay. We rounded up in front of the Royal Cornwall Yacht Club in Falmouth, England, and put down our anchor.

I put a casserole in the oven, then went on deck again to help furl the sails and study the lights of shore. The breeze died and the still harbor waters reflected hundreds of stars.

"We're here, Lin," Larry said.

Seven years after Larry lofted *Seraffyn,* three years after we left Newport Beach, nearly four months after we left Virginia, and 20 days from the Azores, we had finally made it.

England. Europe. The end of a voyage. The beginning of a new adventure.

THE END

Afterword

The First Flame Never Dies

Yes, even after 17 years, I'd choose her again. *Seraffyn* is a remarkable 24-foot boat. I can't think of any better small boat for a young couple of modest means who want to set off on their first cruise. During the 11 years we lived on *Seraffyn*, we had no surprises or gear failures. She never failed to tack, even in the strongest winds or roughest seas. With her 4'8" draft she made no noticeable leeway even when we drove her in rough conditions to windward. She sailed beautifully in light airs, hove to easily with a double-reefed mainsail (winds up to Force 8). She had a few faults, but none of them was vital.

The interior appearance is small due to her 24-inch-wide side decks and flush deck forward, but these large clear deck areas are a treat to work and sail on. The interior looks confining to people accustomed to modern production boats. But this was because the interior is plugged with storage lockers. We put deep bins under the bunks and settees and everywhere else we found space. *Seraffyn* has more storage space than many 28-footers.

In retrospect I would have liked more ballast for *Seraffyn,* maybe 3,600 pounds of lead instead of 2,720. We had to reef our sails sooner than on 29'6" *Taleisin* or on the 28-foot Bristol Channel Cutters we have sailed (all designed by Lyle Hess). This extra ballast would give *Seraffyn* more drive to windward. The immersion factor on *Seraffyn* is 630 pounds per inch. So if 880 pounds of lead were added, she would float about 1.4 inches lower. But this, in my opinion, would be a good trade-off due to the extra sail-packing power you would gain.

To compensate for this extra ballast you might be able to save some construction weight by using diagonal straps instead of the numerous heavy pitch pine lodging and hanging knees I built into *Seraffyn*'s deck. I chose Philippine mahogany for the double sawn frames back in 1965 when I was a neophyte boatbuilder with only six years of repair experience behind me. Now I would prefer a stronger wood, one like oak or black locust. Three of *Seraffyn*'s sawn frames had to be repaired when she was three years old because a fastening coincided with the futtock butt joint and the frames cracked at this weakened point.

One other change I would have made if money had been less of a consideration back then would be to use teak cabin sides instead of the Honduras mahogany we used on *Seraffyn*. Teak is easier to maintain because it does not bleach out with the sun, nor waterstain like mahogany is prone to do. With these changes I feel *Seraffyn* would make the best all around 24-foot long-distance cruising cutter in the world.

APPENDIX 1

Update for 1992 Edition

THE MAJOR CHANGE we found as we reviewed *Cruising in Seraffyn* for this 1992 edition is that inflation has made our cruising cost survey figures appear optimistic in the extreme. But if you update the figures using the following factors, you can still get an accurate estimate of today's costs.

Most of the boats included in our original survey were purchased during 1965-1972. To purchase the same boats now, you would have to pay about four times as much for a new vessel. But there are bargains galore to be found in second hand boats. One sailor we met in the Marquesas had been cruising for two years on a 50-year old, 34-foot wooden boat he bought and outfitted for $19,000. Two different cruisers showed us on board Rawson 30's they had bought and outfitted for under $30,000. In both cases, the boats were 20 years old, but definitely seaworthy and sea-kindly.

Outfitting, exclusive of electronics, still costs 25% in addition to the purchase price, unless you find a boat that has been outfitted by someone whose cruising dreams faded before they got a chance to fulfill them. Then, outfitting might cost as little as 15% of your purchase price. Though some electronic gear costs have fallen, a wider, more enticing array is now available. Even a simple solar powered system can add ten percent to your outfitting costs.

Cruising costs have risen from 100% to 150% above our 1975 figures. We still meet families of four out enjoying life on $500 or $600 a month in French Polynesia or along the east coast of Australia. We even met one couple with two young sons who have been out for almost three years on $330 a month, but by their own admission, their lives could best be described as spartan, to the extreme.

Insurance costs are still 1.7% of the boat's value, for experienced cruising sailors, on well found boats with at least three crew on board during passages. But with boat values up to four times higher, insurance can rarely be considered for any but well heeled sailors. Some cruisers, including ourselves, are now buying savings bonds equal to an insurance premium each year instead of insurance. That way we have a growing, affordable, all purpose emergency fund we can use — even if we never have a catastrophe.

Haul-out costs have doubled, and sail prices have almost quadrupled.

The optimistic side of the coin is that wages have almost tripled and in some places gone even higher. In French Polynesia and American Samoa, we met cruising men earning $1500 a month or more on construction sites. Cruising women working as teachers, nurses or sail makers are earning $1500 to $1800 a month in parts of the South Pacific. Skilled boat repair people are still in demand and here in Australia earn from $12 to $25 an hour if they work short term on contract. Best of all, work for skilled boat people is still available worldwide, in spite of economic upheavals and political change. When employers in remote places meet the creative, energetic workers who have the skills and knowledge to successfully set off and continue voyaging, they can usually find ways to hire them that comply with local immigration laws for short term work.

1976 Cruising Cost Survey

Wherever we stop we hear the same questions: How can you afford to cruise so long? How much does it cost?

When we started out we had the same questions, but there was no reliable place to find answers backed by facts— no books to lay it out for us. We learned to live within our cruising income, but we kept meeting people who were "overboated and underfinanced."

We now know exactly how much we spend each year. But we're just one cruising couple and our tastes and habits certainly vary from others. We eat out about once a week, but Larry resoles my sandals. We entertain frequently, and have steak and wine dinners aboard, but we have no engine, no head, no electronics. So our $300 to $340 per month budget (1975) reflects only our boat and our cruising style.

In the Azores, we met a couple on a 30-footer who had left England for a year's voyage to the Caribbean and back, with $500 in cash and a boat full of stores. Ten months later they still had $170 and enough food left for their return voyage. They never ate out; they ate the food they had brought along or what fish they could catch. The wife said to us, "I'd love to go to a café with you, but we can't afford even a glass of wine." (Wine cost 8 cents a glass.) She went on, "I'm glad we made this cruise but I know that we will need more money the next time, so we can buy a bottle of local wine and entertain a bit."

To arrive at reliable cost figures, we devised a questionnaire designed to give a true picture of cruising costs. We decided to survey only people cruising away from home for one year or longer. We did not include people who remained in one area to charter, or boats with professional crews—only people actually cruising. The data we got are not opinions; they are facts.

We started our survey in the summer of 1974 and stopped in the spring of 1976. It was cut off at that point for this book. Our first surprise was to find that of the hundreds of boats we met, only 32 had been cruising for over one year. True, there were dozens underway six months and longer, with intentions of continuing for two or even three years. Admittedly, these were only the boats we met, but they do seem representative. We sent surveys to cruising friends and received answers from as far away as the South Pacific, the Caribbean, the United States, England, and the Mediterranean.

The 32 yachtsmen who had been cruising for over one year had 551 years of sailing experience among them, and 86 years of cruising away from home. Their boats ranged from 24 feet to 50 feet. They came from six countries, including England, Australia, the United States, Germany, France and Switzerland. Only 12 of those surveyed had private incomes. Twenty crews earned money as they

171

TABLE 1

Price of a Cruising Boat

The prices of cruising boats shown below are located in the price bracket that reflectes the purchase price (or building cost) *plus* cost of outfitting. All prices shown here are for purchases made before 1974 because all people surveyed had already been cruising at least 12 months. Prices have risen drastically in the past three years and it is quite possible some of the prices shown below might have risen to nearly double what is shown in this table.

NOTE: Exceptional cases (*) are explained below Tables 2 and 3.

COST	\	\	\	\	\	\	\	\	\	\	\	\	\	\
LENGTH OF YACHT														
	24′	26′	28′	30′	32′	34′	36′	38′	40′	42′	44′	46′	48′	50′
OVER $50,000														NW
50,000							NW	NW					N ST	
45,000								NW						
40,000							NG	SW						
35,000						SG								
30,000						NG			BW					
25,000			NG		SG	NG		SW₁₉₅₅ SW						
20,000							NG		SW	BF**				
15,000		BW		S ST SG	SW₁₉₃₇									
10,000	BW	SW	SW	SW₁₉₄₉				SW₁₉₅₂* SW₁₉₃₄						
5,000	NG			SW₁₉₅₂ SW₁₉₃₀	SW₁₉₃₈									

Fig. AI-1. Table 1: Price of a Cruising Boat.

We have listed the year of construction next to any boat that was built before 1960. It is still possible to buy a boat over 25 years old at a low price, but our impression is that maintenance and parts replacement are difficult when cruising in them.

SYMBOLS:

B   Backyard Built   G   Fiberglass
S   Purchased second-hand   W   Wood
F   Ferro-Cement   N   Purchased New
ST   Steel   *   Exceptional Case

cruised. The crews broke down this way: 22 couples, four single-handers, two families, and four pickup crews.

WHAT DOES A CRUISING BOAT COST?

From our survey the cost of a cruising boat, not surprisingly, turns out to be directly related to size. Clearly, it costs less to buy and outfit a small yacht; it costs less to cruise in a small yacht. We considered the "cost" of the yacht as its purchase price plus outfitting, our survey revealing it costs 25 percent above purchase price to prepare a boat for long-distance cruising.

Acquiring a yacht under 33 feet long cost our respondents an average of $13,000—whether the boat was new, second-hand, backyard built, steel, wood or ferro-cement. But boats over 33 feet long cost an average of $36,000! The survey showed that small, second-hand boats are the "best buy." Eight second-hand boats under 33 feet were purchased and outfitted for under $12,000 each. But the seven second-hand boats over 33 feet cost an average of $21,000 each.

Boats cost by the foot (and the pound) today. The longer (and heavier) they are, the higher the purchase price. Bigger boats cost more to fit out, too. For instance, a 30-footer's mainsail will be around 250 square feet, and a 40-footer's around 400 square feet. At $1.60 per square foot, that's $400 for the 30-footer and $640 for the 40-footer.

Then there's the storm anchor. A 30-footer needs a 50-pounder, a 40-footer needs one of about 85 pounds or more, and anchors sell by the pound. Line for jib sheets sells by the foot, and the bigger boat requires jib sheets that are longer and of greater diameter than those needed by a small boat. Since cost is a factor of size, every dollar you can save when purchasing and outfitting your boat will become "freedom chips" for cruising.

CRUISING COSTS

Cruising costs less in the first year than it does thereafter. When you start off, fully equipped, and loaded with spares and food and your gear in perfect order, you only spend money on optional things such as entertainment, souvenirs, food and local wines.

A year later, the jib needs restitching, the bottom needs repainting, you've lost an anchor or a snatch block—and costs begin to mount. At the end of the second year, you need a new genoa or perhaps a radio; the sextant mirrors need resilvering, and possibly you've sailed out of the area covered by your on-board charts and navigation books, and must buy new ones. No longer can you go to your local second-hand shop for bargain replacements. Far from home you pay full prices.

Then there are "people" expenses: Someone on board requires some dental work, or some new clothes. These costs don't usually occur in the first year of cruising because, in general, people take care of such things before sailing.

Taking into consideration all of the above expenses, we have divided the monthly cruising costs for the boats we surveyed into four cost categories. 1) boats 24-33 feet; 2) boats 24-33 feet, cruising two years or longer; 3) boats 33-49 feet; 4) boats 33-49 feet, cruising two years or longer.

Fourteen surveys covered boats under 33 feet. During the first year of cruising their costs ranged from $100 to $350 per month, with an average of $240. Five of the 14 had cruised for over two years, and their costs ranged from $200 to $350 per month, with an average of $260. There was only one $100-per-month example in

TABLE 2

Average Monthly Cruising Costs
All People Surveyed

Boats were grouped by size, with boats over 25 feet being placed in the next higher category. Each number in a box represents one boat and reflects the number of years the respondent has been cruising as of the date the survey was taken. Since all surveys were filled out in 1974-1975-1976, these figures are accurate, and include the effects of the recent inflation. (Although we met many people aboard yachts 40 feet and over, we could not include them in our figures as they were either chartering or had not been cruising for a year.)

NOTE: Exceptional cases are indicated thus (*) and are explained on this page.

COST PER MONTH	LENGTH OF YACHT													
	24′	26′	28′	30′	32′	34′	36′	38′	40′	42′	44′	46′	48′	50′
ABOVE $650								3						
600							3	4						1
550														
500						3			1					
450								3	1					
400							3	2 3						
350			1	1		1			1					
300	7													
250		1		2										
200	1	3		1	1	9*			1					
150										3**				
100			1	5	1									

Fig. AI-2. Table 2: Average Monthly Cruising Costs—All Boats Surveyed.

EXCEPTIONAL CASES:

*This couple returned home after four years of cruising and spent $20,000 on a complete refit. If you add this cost to their next five years of cruising, their monthly cost would come to $500.

**The owner of this boat stated in his survey report, "This is a new boat, designed and built especially for ocean sailing, and practically no money has been spent on the boat so far, although maintenance costs will go up rapidly in the next couple of years because we need a proper haul-out, new sails and an engine overhaul."

the second category. Eighteen boats 33 feet and longer cruised the first year on an average of $425 per month. Eleven of these, the boats which cruised longer than a year, had an average of $550 per month.

People who had to take time out from cruising to earn money along the way learned to be careful with their expenditures, and thus had slightly lower monthly costs than people with independent incomes. People who worked along the way, and had boats under 33 feet, averaged $240 a month; those who had boats over 33 feet, averaged $450.

These figures are based on 1974-1976 expenses shown in surveys from all over the world, and they confirm our own experiences over the past eight years of cruising.

WHERE DOES THE MONEY GO?

Brian and Margaret Tilston, who plan to go cruising, looked at our figures and asked, "Where does the money really go? We've read about people who cruised around the world for practically nothing."

True, but times have changed. When Joshua Slocum sailed alone around the world (1895-98) he was the first; that's why an Australian yacht club gave him a new suit of sails. In those days, Slocum was a rarity and therefore a celebrity to be honored and cherished.

Today, there must be 2000-3000 boats cruising the oceans. Last year, during the 1974-1975 cruising season, nearly 500 yachts passed through the Panama Canal. Over 100 boats stopped at Horta in the Azores on their way across the Atlantic. Cruising yachtsmen are no longer salty heroes to be admired; they have become "rich yachtsmen," and in many favorite harbors, formerly free, they are charged for mooring. Mooring charges range from a modest 10 cents a night (Fowey, England) to over $5.00 a night (Antibes, France) for a boat our size. Water can cost up to 10 cents a gallon. Haulouts cost money, and you often need two a year. They cost from about $60 for boats up to 30 feet, to $150 for 40-footers.

Then there are gear replacements or additions. The survey asked people to list gear costing over $50.00 they had bought during the previous two years. Only two boats in their second year had made no major purchases. Sails were most often mentioned. Engine parts, even complete engines, came next. Anchors, warps, a new rudder, a windvane, awnings, a stereo, and a Seagull outboard were on the list. Two people had to buy new inflatables because theirs had been stolen. Generators and radios appeared on four lists.

What surprised us most was that 24 out of 32 respondents said food and liquor were their biggest cruising expenses! Finding cheap food in foreign ports is difficult—it takes time and money to track down bargains. Since you're unfamiliar with local foods you often reach for familiar but more expensive items. For example, rabbit is one-third the price of beef in Spain, yet we've never tried this economy. When you sail on, you need costly canned and prepared foods.

Finally, there's entertaining. Five boats come into a deserted bay within hours of each other, and a party develops. Everyone brings a favorite dish to a barbecue on the beach, which depletes stores of possible expensive items. One evening, we opened eight bottles of wine as an afternoon cup of tea grew into an evening-long party.

For people cruising on a pension or private income, $450 to $550 a month may seem little enough to pay for a wonderful way of life—and it's far less than most average American families spend ashore. But people who start cruising with a fixed number of dollars in the bank watch the money flowing out and none

TABLE 3

Monthly Cruising Costs For People Cruising Over 24 Months

COST PER MONTH	LENGTH OF YACHT													
	24′	26′	28′	30′	32′	34′	36′	38′	40′	42′	44′	46′	48′	50′
ABOVE $650								3						
600							3	4						
550														
500						3								
450								3						
400							3	2 3						
350														
300	7			10										
250				2										
200		3				9*								
150										3**				
100				5										

Fig. AI-3. Table 3: Monthly Cruising Cost For Boats Cruising Over 24 Months.

EXCEPTIONAL CASES:

*This boat was purchased "as-is-where-is" in Motril, Spain, where it had fallen from a ways car and been holed. It lay in seven feet of water for almost six months before the new owner purchased it. Although the purchase price was low, the owner spent two years repairing her before he could go cruising, and it now costs him $600 per month in expenses because, as he says, "I keep having to fix all sorts of unexpected things that were ruined while she lay under water."

**This backyard-built ferro-cement boat was built in New Zealand by a man who did every bit of the work himself, including all of the plastering of the hull, and the sailmaking. The boat has no electrical gear and uses oil for lighting. The engine is of low HP, was purchased second-hand and was rebuilt by the owner.

coming in. If they can plan a budget of $250 per month instead of $500, then $3000 represents one year of cruising instead of six months.

HOW TO CUT COSTS

The survey confirms that big boats cost more to purchase and to maintain. So if you are looking for a cruising boat, the most obvious way to save is to get something 33 feet or smaller.

Eliminate "complicated" gear and you'll save money. John Keating, who has cruised for three years on his 34-foot *Paradox,* wrote in his survey reply: "As we are both in our early sixties, I thought it would be prudent to [buy equipment costing] in excess of $14,000 to outfit the boat for our cruise. Now I realize that three-quarters of the equipment was unnecessary, and doesn't work. The only electronic items that do work are a portable radio we use for news and time signals, and a depth-sounder which tells me when we've run aground."

In cruising, it is a truism that if you spend good money to buy elaborate electronic gear, then you spend more money to try to keep it running. And it is so unnecessary. A lead line still works. A sextant, radio receiver, and chronometer are completely adequate for safe navigation. Oil lamps give good light and don't cost nearly as much to own and run as a generator and electric lights. Oars have propelled dinghies for years, saving the cost and complication of an outboard. Every piece of electronic or mechanical gear you don't buy saves you money twice: First, when you don't buy it; second, when you don't have to repair it!

Labor is the largest item on any bill for boat maintenance. Acquire as many skills as you can before you start cruising. For one thing, read all you can about sail repairs. With sails, it's truly a case of "a stitch in time saves nine." Don't be put off by the idea that sailmaking is only for professionals. A sail is a simple thing: If the stitching is maintained, chafe is avoided, and if a sail cover is used regularly your sails should remain in good condition for up to eight years.

Make legs for your boat, or lean it against a seawall in a place that has a sufficient range of tides, and you can scrub or paint it without paying for a haulout. "Do it yourself," should be your motto for all boat work. Anything you maintain yourself, saves dollars. Five people out of 32 surveyed acknowledged they were not mechanically inclined or handy, and their monthly expenditures for cruising were all above $450 per month!

Choosing an isolated area for your cruising grounds can cut expenses in half; large cities double your costs. The Gulf of Mexico, South America, Turkey, Chesapeake Bay, and Indonesia appear to be cheaper cruising areas: Local food is cheap, and there are few mooring fees. But in the Caribbean, you can pay 7 cents for a pound of ice, $4.00 for an overnight mooring, 25 cents for a lemon. England, Sweden, France and the Mediterranean are much the same. When you go to large cities or popular resorts such as Palma in the Balearics and have a cup of tea at a sidewalk café it's 50 cents. On the other hand, in the northwest corner of Spain, an area of beautiful rivers and islands, a large glass of wine in a local café costs 10 cents and you get a plate of olives with it.

You can save by dining out rarely or not all. Of the crews surveyed, 14 had dinner out less than once a month. Their costs were definitely lower than those of respondents who ate out more often. A native meal eaten at a café seems to average $2.50-$3.00 per person, worldwide. For two people, that's about $12.00 for two dinners out a month, which isn't much. And, the cook gets a night off, everyone has a chance to savor new cuisine, and there's an occasion for dressing up, if that's something you like.

One important way to save is by always anchoring off when you are in ports that charge mooring or docking fees. Your anchorage is private, clean and quiet. For the small "price" of having to row ashore in your dinghy, you can probably save enough money to pay for one month's cruising each year! But your dinghy must be easy to launch and row to make this practical. There are few places where you are required to tie to a quay or dock in order to enjoy the port.

The charts needed to cruise from Panama to Key West, Florida, cost $120. We inquired around, until we met a couple heading toward California and traded charts with them. A current *Light List* was all we had to buy. Later, when we got to Florida, we used that set of charts to trade for Atlantic Charts.

By looking for opportunities to swap, we have spent less than $200 on charts in seven years. People going "the other way" can also provide valuable information. For example, when we learned that canned food is hard to find in Italy and Turkey, we stocked up before leaving Spain.

One way most cruising people hope to save money is by fishing. Don't count on it. Only five people answered the fish-catching question on our survey with a definite, "Yes, we do catch fish." The rest said, "No" "Occasionally," or "We try." Fishing provides food variety when it is successful, but is not a dependable means of saving money.

Hal Roth pretty well summed up the ways of saving money in his survey response. He and his wife have cruised nine years on their 35-foot *Whisper,* and their costs were the lowest in the over-33-foot category. He wrote: "In general I think the key to low-cost cruising is to cut fixed expenses, go to remote places, and do your own work. Have a simple uncomplicated yacht with no high-maintenance items."

INSURANCE

What do you do about insurance? It's a big expense, if you carry it, and you will pay a hefty extra premium to cover your boat for an ocean crossing. Of the 32 boats we surveyed, 24 had no insurance at all. The other eight paid an average of $700 a year for "total loss" coverage. When you consider that few boats are ever a total loss, that's a lot of money spent for negligible protection. Most boat damage happens in collisions that cost under $1000 to repair. Insurance to cover such accidents costs about $1200 a year. So the average boat owner seems to say, "I'll take care of the boat, be careful, and cover my own losses in exchange for the extra months of free cruising I get each year."

HOW DO PEOPLE PAY FOR THEIR CRUISING?

Less than half of the people interviewed had private incomes. They paid their way from savings, pensions, retirement funds, a business income from home, or a house rental.

But 16 people managed long-distance cruises by working along the way. Two couples, including Hal Roth and his wife, pay all of their expenses by writing and lecturing about their cruising. We pay half of our expenses that way. One dentist cruises for nine months then substitutes for another dentist for three months. Two people earned their money by working on construction jobs in various countries. Most make money by doing yacht repairs, painting, sailmaking, engine work and rigging. The ability to do rigging work is a really marketable skill. Worldwide, there is usually work available for a person who can do rope-to-wire splices,

Liverpool splices and other specialized rigging jobs. A small, hand-operated sail-sewing machine that can zigzag stitch will more than pay its way if you carry some basic sailmaker's tools. Carpentry and rigging are our forte. All the tools that built *Seraffyn* are on board, plus an assortment of screws, nails and wood. The skills gained building *Seraffyn* gave Larry a trade that is valuable everywhere. We always keep *Seraffyn* in top shape because we think our boat's condition is our calling card—and it leads to getting repair jobs.

Also, if a potential delivery customer sees your boat in sparkling condition, he'll assume you will care for his boat the same way, and may give you the job. But the delivery business is a spotty way to make money, and only two boats in our survey earned significant amounts at it. There is simply too much competition from big firms and full-time professionals. The cruising sailor may get one or two jobs a year by being in the right place at the right time, but it's not dependable.

Not one respondent listed chartering as a main source of income. It just doesn't work: Either you charter or you cruise. To earn money at chartering you have to stay in one place for a long time and become known. If you try to day charter, you work so hard that sailing stops being fun. One respondent made $400 when a film company chartered his boat for a few days, but he said they did almost $400 damage during the filming. Charter work means you share your home with strangers, and for a few weeks of charter work (when you need extra space) you carry around an extra 10-12 feet of length all year long. This doesn't make economic sense.

With prior planning based on facts, not guesses, you can acquire and outfit your boat, and enjoy your cruise without being "overboated and underfinanced." With the proper-sized boat, most people can realize their cruising dreams. We've probably said this a dozen times already in this book, but we think it's worth repeating:

Go simple, go modest, go small, but go!

APPENDIX II

After Seven Years, I'd Choose Her Again

By Larry Pardey

I WAS LOUNGING ON THE PORT SETTEE, feet up, drinking a cup of coffee after a great lunch the other day. I looked around *Serraffyn,* our traveling home for the past seven years, and said to Lin, "We've got a hell of a boat here." We thought about this for a while and then began discussing just why *Serraffyn* has worked out so well for us.

First, we know the one vital factor that has allowed us to go—and keep going—is *Seraffyn's* small size. We only have to stop cruising for 12 weeks of the year—10 weeks to earn enough money to live on; two weeks to maintain *Seraffyn.* That leaves us 40 free weeks.

An average working person, who like myself can earn $10,000 to $12,000 a year working full time, probably should not own a boat much over 30 feet, particularly with the inflation of the past few years. (Buying power is down, yachts and gear prices are up.) A small boat is the answer.

Seraffyn's small size and low maintenance costs allow us to be our own insurance company. What we do is to keep an amount equal to about 50 percent of our boat's cost in quickly convertible form, so that if we get sick or our mast breaks we don't have all of our funds tied up in the boat. *(See Appendix I for the reasons why few cruisers carry full insurance.)* With this cash reserve earning interest, we have financial security and thereby enjoy cruising more.

Seraffyn's small size makes for other benefits. When we haul her, scrub and paint the bottom, paint the topsides, check and grease the through-hull fittings and rudder fittings (and we can do it all in three days) we're usually tired—and we're awfully glad *Serafyn* isn't one inch longer.

Seraffyn is just large enough to accommodate two keen sailing friends for a few days. We've found that the farther we get from our home port, the less likely it is that friends will join us for a visit, and it doesn't make sense to lug a larger boat around the world just to provide comfortable accommodations for a rare guest.

Seraffyn has drawn interested spectators wherever we cruise. Because she is small, we can keep her shipshape and Bristol fashion. Local people introduce themselves and ask about our little floating turtle shell; the same people ignore larger yachts. I think it is because a modest-size vessel fits the dream of many average people. A large yacht seems financially out of reach.

We have noticed that larger yachts rarely up-anchor and go for a daysail. The size of their gear and the work involved are just too much. But with little *Seraffyn* we can take the interested people we meet out for an afternoon sail. Her small size and handiness allow us to be sailing in 10 minutes, and we don't have to depend on extra crew to do it.

Seraffyn is easy to sail. In fact, Lin can sail her alone. It's not just our boat's size that makes this possible, but also the rig designed for her by Lyle Hess. The marconi-cutter sail plan he drew has the intermediate shrouds running to a chainplate two feet abaft the mast. This system has no disadvantages that I know of and eliminates one of the nuisances of the cutter rig—running backstays.

Since we have two headsails, either of us can easily shorten sail by dropping the staysail on deck. If the wind increases, we reef the mainsail. The next sail reduction is usually done in Force 5 to windward or Force 6 off the wind, when we take the working jib off the bowsprit and reset the staysail. It's relatively easy to take the sail off the bowsprit safely in these conditions. We haul the jib down and secure it with the downhaul. Then we sit on the bowsprit and unhank the jib with our feet braced in the jib net, hands on the lifelines. At this point *Seraffyn* has an all-inboard rig, and we don't have to go out on the bowsprit again until the wind lightens. With three reefs in our mainsail and one in the staysail, we still have more balanced inboard sail reductions left for heavier winds. *(See dust jacket photo)*

Lyle gave *Seraffyn* a large working rig so we wouldn't need large overlapping jibs, which are hard to tack alone and require big, expensive winches. The high-cut lapper he drew has an area of 260 square feet and gives us good visibility while we beat to windward. With the main and lapper set, we get very good performance in winds from five to 15 knots. For lighter winds we have a 469-square-foot drifter and an even larger 1000-foot spinnaker. These light-weather sails give added fun when we are invited to sail in local cruiser-class races. *Seraffyn* surprises everyone with her light-weather performance.

We have come to love *Seraffyn's* shapely hull and fine bow, with her maximum beam well aft. Her hull shape allows her to go to windward in spite of her nine-foot beam. She has beat to windward in winds as strong as Force 9 and Force 10, well-reefed-down. Her exceptional beam produces an easy motion downwind. Her long keel and modest forefoot, combined with a large rudder, give her good directional stability. The forefoot is deep enough to help *Seraffyn* heave to in all conditions, and the large rudder allows her to come about or gybe quickly, even in the lightest winds and closest quarters.

The self-steering vane is the greatest single advancement in cruising yachts since outside ballast. *Seraffyn's* outboard rudder made possible a simple, inexpensive vane, with a trim-tab attached to the trailing edge of the rudder. The boomkin provides a natural support for the dacron-covered stainless steel-tube frame of the windvane. But most important for good performance from a windvane is having a well-balanced boat that will almost sail herself on most points of sailing. *Seraffyn* gives our vane no trouble at all until she is pushed beyond six knots. Then she starts to wander 10° or 15° to either side of her course. This is easily corrected by shortening sail. Our windvane, Helmer, will steer in all conditions from one or two knots of apparent wind, to Force 10 downwind under bare poles.

Seraffyn's outboard rudder not only made fitting a windvane simpler, but makes rudder removal easy for repairs, or for gudgeon and pintle inspection. That job on a yacht with an inboard rudder becomes a major chore, because the rudder shaft goes up into the hull, and you have to haul out on a travel lift, or dig a hole between the tracks of the ways car to remove the rudder shaft from the boat. I wouldn't consider a cruising boat with an inboard rudder!

The shipyard operators we've dealt with in Mexico, Costa Rica, Denmark and Spain have been pleased to haul *Seraffyn* because she has a long keel. They don't like fin-keel boats. We also carry a set of plans to provide the measurements the yard foreman needs to fit a cradle properly. Few countries we've visited outside the U.S. have travel lifts.

Seraffyn is perfectly safe just leaning against a seawall, and in one tide I can scrub and paint her alone. As we mentioned before, we have hauled her on a hard sand beach and her 12-inch wide keel keeps her from sinking. If we ever accidentally run aground on a falling tide, we plan to saw our spinnaker pole into supports and fit them under our channels. Naturally, I hope we never have to do that, but it pays to have a plan worked out in advance.

Seraffyn's cargo-carrying capacity is considerable. Lyle Hess allowed for one-and-a-half tons of cruising gear. This has given us the ability to carry 50 fathoms of 5/16″ chain, three anchors, several warps, 45 gallons of water, three months' supply of canned food, all the tools I built the boat with, and our personal belongings. After seven years of living aboard, *Seraffyn* is still right on her designed waterline. It's surprising how few cruising boats are designed to carry all of the gear required.

Increased demand has lowered the cost of high test chain so we now would consider carrying ¼-inch high test instead of 5/16 BBB. That would save about 130 pounds for other stores.

Seraffyn is also designed to carry a ''hard'' sailing dinghy on her cabin top. On a small cruiser that's the best place for a tender. It keeps the weight amidships and is least in the way. A hard dinghy that can also be sailed is an important piece of cruising gear. Ours is a Montgomery pram 6′8″ long, made of fiberglass, simple to repair, lightweight (55 pounds), and easy to launch or stow. Only a ''hard'' dinghy can take the rough usage of long-distance cruising: Kedging out anchors and chain, being hauled up on rugged beaches, and landing against barnacle-encrusted piers. For exploring a large shallow bay with a picnic lunch, nothing is more enjoyable than a sailing tender.

Seraffyn has eight-inch-high bulwarks that not only keep Lin and miscellaneous items from sliding overboard, but with their one-inch-high scuppers, running almost full-length along the deck, they make possible a fully adjustable jib sheet lead. We use a swivel snatch block attached to a flat nylon strap, which can be looped in any location, through the scupper and around the bulwark. *Seraffyn's* 24-inch-wide side decks are possible because of her beam. They make sailing easier because we can stride forward to the mast quickly.

Yes, during the past seven years we have learned that *Seraffyn's* size and basic design concepts make her fun to cruise, fun to sail, weatherly, practical and truly seaworthy. The credit belongs to Lyle C. Hess and the 4000-year-long evolutionary process that developed the English working cutters, the little ships *Seraffyn* was modeled after.

APPENDIX III

It's the Details That Make Life Easier

By Larry Pardey

THE HARD AND FAST RULE we stuck to while building *Serraffyn* was: KEEP IT SIMPLE! Of the boats I had sailed before, the simple ones, the ones with the least machinery and electrical equipment, were the most fun and the easiest to maintain. The complicated boats almost always spoiled my day—forcing me into the bilge to repair a leaking fuel line, or making me sail at night without navigation lights because of a short circuit.

By the time I started *Seraffyn* I knew I wanted the method of construction that would be repairable any place in the world, so I chose traditional wood-and-bronze because you can usually find these materials in the most remote places. I knew it would be difficult or impossible to find someone in the Tuamotus with the technical know-how or the materials to weld an aluminum spar, rebuild a stainless steel spreader fitting, or patch a glass hull.

The first step in keeping *Seraffyn* simple was to eliminate an engine. Once under way, we found we didn't need an engine because of her excellent light-weather performance, which is further improved by having neither propeller drag nor the extra weight of machinery and tanks. In seven years, including one spent in the Mediterranean, we have carefully logged our average speed, anchor-up to anchor-down, and it works out at 3.4 knots or 81.6 miles a day. This includes calms, working in and out of harbors, and going to windward. I use a 14-foot ash sweep for sculling in tight quarters, and once we get *Seraffyn* moving we switch the single sweep to the port side. Steering with the tiller between my legs I can move her at about three-quarters of a knot on a calm day. This "Ash Wind" requires no maintenance and can be replaced for about 10 dollars.

As we rigged *Seraffyn* I always asked myself, "Can Lin, the 4'10", 100-pound Mighty Mouse, handle this job?" I simplified everything to meet that requirement. So we have extra-large, non-geared, sheet and halyard winches, a downhaul on the jib, jiffy reefing, and an easy-to-use anchor winch that brings the 25-pound CQR anchor up to the plastic covered bobstay where it hooks on for easy stowing. (A bowsprit is worth having, just to make handling ground tackle simpler.) Lin has sailed *Seraffyn* single-handed from Plymouth to Falmouth, and in and around the Falmouth estuary, gaining much confidence in her ability to take care of all three of us if I were ever sick or injured.

All of our navigation is done with a lead line, taffrail log, compass, sextant, and oil navigation lamps. None of this gear has ever failed to work when we really needed it. If the oil lamps do go out, it is just a matter of draining water out of the oil reservoir or trimming the wicks to get them working again. The only piece of electrical gear we really rely on at all is our Zenith transoceanic radio receiver (and that runs on flashlight "D" batteries). We use it for time checks, and for weather reports. This radio has been completely reliable for seven years, which is unusual as most electrical items have a poor track record at sea.

Most of the small pieces of exterior trim on *Seraffyn* —her decks, spinnaker pole, and sweep—are bare teak or ash, and require no paint or varnish; this reduces maintenance time.

The layout below is ideal for living in mild and tropical climates. If we find ourselves in an area with a real winter, we usually rent a small place for much less than it would cost us to own a boat large enough for winter living. And living on boats, even 35 to 40 feet long, isn't much fun in freezing weather. We have only had to move off the boat twice in seven years to avoid cold weather.

Seraffyn has two "honeymoon" bunks. The first is our double bunk forward, with storage areas under it for clothes and canned goods. The original *Renegade* layout shows a head in the fore peak with sail storage and bins for spare gear. Since we planned to live aboard, we decided we would spend more time in bed than·on the head, and chose the bucket-and-chuck-it method, and we stored our sails, bosun's stores, spare paint and varnish, rigging spares, wet weather gear, sea-anchor and two cases of paper towels under the cockpit where an engine would have been. These changes in design gained us a private stateroom forward, and further simplified the boat by eliminating a mechanical head and its through-hull fittings. Our bunk on *Seraffyn* was 3'6" wide.

The double bunk is wonderful in port, especially at anchor. When you are lying in the bunk, you can hear any noise made by the ground tackle, and know immediately if there's anything wrong. You can hear the anchor chain as it grumbles along the bottom when the wind shifts. If your anchor drags, it usually telegraphs an intermittent *thump, thump, thump* noise up to the forepeak—and you have an automatic anchor alarm. But for this alarm to work, you must use chain, not nylon, as rope will not transmit noise. If you are in the forward bunk and a sea starts to build up, you will soon feel the increased pitching—movement that is usually enough to wake the most determined sleeper. On the other hand, the double bunk forward is a poor place to sleep when you are sailing to windward.

Our second "honeymoon bunk" is the cockpit, which is designed for sleeping together under a tropical sky, taking advantage of cooling breezes. This is so enjoyable that it is well worth the trouble of taking the two quarter-berth cushions up into the cockpit to make a 6'2" x 4' wall-to-wall mattress. Our tiller fits into a mortice in the rudder head so we can remove it to clear the cockpit. As protection against dew, we put up our cockpit cover.

Our two quarter berths with their lee cloths are used at sea. The foot of both berths is used in port for stowing jackets, cameras, and other junk.

Our propane stove has three burners and an oven large enough for a 20-pound turkey. It has a grill-broiler which will handle three large porterhouse steaks. Lin and I agree that the two most important features on a live-aboard interior are a large easy-to-use stove (we use Propane) and a large double bunk: You spend most of your time below decks either sleeping or eating. A close third in importance is a self-draining sink next to the stove: At sea you can grab a pot that is boiling over and pop it into the sink quickly and safely.

On deck between the mast and cabin is a self-draining, bottomless deck box which houses the propane tank and a 10-gallon gravity-feed water tank. This allows the water to flow down to a simple swing valve over the galley sink—with no pumps or machinery to go wrong. Just below the waterline is a seacock for salt water that leads to a convenient tap near the galley sink so Lin can easily get salt water for her favorite chore, washing dishes. She also uses salt water for boiling potatoes and other vegetables, to conserve fresh water on long passages.

In a small live-aboard boat like *Seraffyn* every bit of storage space is important, and top opening bins are the most efficient and the simplest to build. You can load them right to the top and see the contents easily, and cans don't fall out in a seaway. We don't have any drawers aboard: they just take up too much space.

Our top-loading icebox is a well-insulated bin with a drain. It works fine when ice is available and 85 pounds lasts about nine days. Even when we don't have ice it is still useful as a ''cool'' box that keeps perishable foods fresh and protects them from insects.

All lighting below is by gimbaled Perko oil lamps with extra-large smoke bells to protect the overhead when we're going to windward. With the wicks properly trimmed and a mirror reflector behind each one, they give a fine light for reading. To make filling the oil lamps easier at sea, we installed a gravity-feed eight-gallon tank forward of the chain locker, with a copper tube leading aft to a petcock in the main cabin. This is absolutely necessary with an oil lamp system; filling lamps in a rough sea with a can and funnel will exasperate even the most patient sailor.

Ventilation is the life blood of a wooden boat and vital for the comfort of the crew. Air flow on *Seraffyn* is provided by a cowl vent forward, a hatch over the double bunk, a four-way-opening hatch over the galley with glass for light, four 4″ x 7″ opening ports in the cabin sides, and sliding doors at the foot of each quarter berth which allow air to flow through the bunks and below the cockpit.

The one piece of gear we have on board that has consistently given us trouble, but also a lot of pleasure, is our dry-cell battery-operated stereo cassette player.

Which just shows what happens when we break our own rule:

Keep it simple!

APPENDIX IV

Seraffyn of Victoria

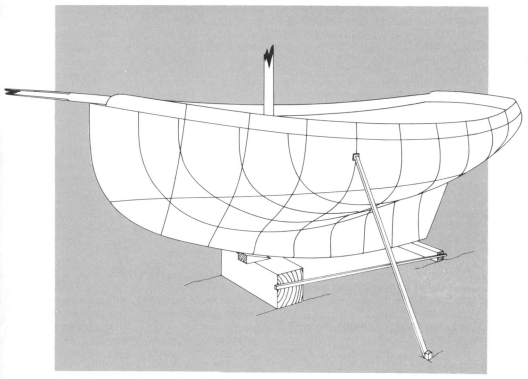

Fig. AIV-1. Isometric drawing of *Seraffyn*.

SPECIFICATIONS

Length Overall ....24'4"
Length Waterline ....22'2"
Beam ....8'11"
Draft...4'8"
Displacement ....10,686 lbs
Ballast Keel (lead) ....2720 lbs
Sail Area: Mainsail ....200 sq ft
           Staysail ....105 sq ft
           Jib ....156 sq ft
           Lapper ....260 sq ft
           Drifter ....469 sq ft
           Spinnaker ....1050 sq ft
Prismatic Coefficient 535
Displacement/Length Ratio..296
Pounds/Inch Immersion ....630 lbs.
Sail Area/Displacement Ratio..15.29

SAILS					
	MATERIAL	LUFF	FOOT	LEACH	AREA
MAIN	7 OZ. DAC.	30'-0"	13'-0"	31'9"	200ᵘ'
JIB	7 OZ. DAC.	33'-0"	16'0"	22'-6"	156ᵘ'
STAYS'L	1 OZ DAC.	22'3"	10'-4"	20-3'	105ᵘ'
GENOA 150%	6 OZ. DAC.	33'-0	25'-6	31'-6"	396ᵘ'
STORM TRYS'L	8 OZ DAC.	12'-0"	10'9"	18'-0"	63ᵘ'

Fig. AIV-2. Sail Plan, *Seraffyn.*

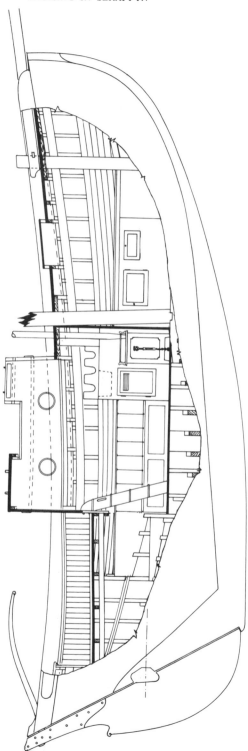

Fig. AIV-3. Inboard Profile, *Seraffyn.*

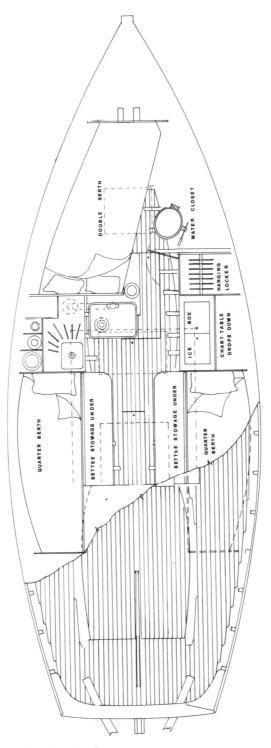

Fig. AIV-4. Accommodation Plan, *Seraffyn*.

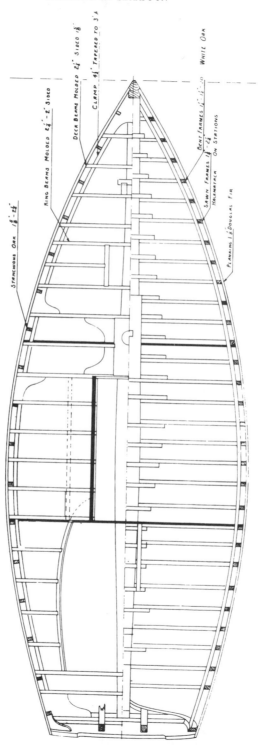

Fig. AIV-5. Construction Drawing, Deck, *Seraffyn*.

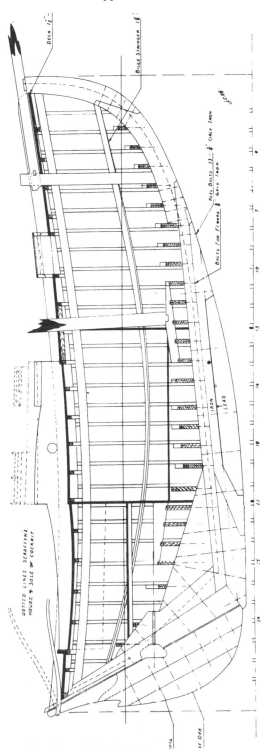

Fig. AIV-6. Construction Drawing, Profile, *Seraffyn.*

LYLE C. HESS
Designer of *Seraffyn of Victoria*

Address all inquiries about *Seraffyn's* plans to:
Lyle C. Hess
1907 West Woodcrest Ave.
Fullerton, CA 92633